VOLUNTARY MATTERS

*Management & Good Practice
in the Voluntary Sector*

Edited by

Paul Palmer & Elizabeth Hoe

with a foreword by Jon Snow

Voluntary Matters
Management & Good Practice in the Voluntary Sector

Copyright ©1997 The Media Trust and The Directory of Social Change

Published by The Directory of Social Change for The Media Trust
The Directory of Social Change is Registered Charity no. 800517
The Media Trust is Registered Charity no. 1042733

Printed & bound by Page Bros., Norwich
Cover design by Kate Bass
Designed and typeset by Linda Parker

British Library Cataloguing-in-Publication Data
A catalogue record for this book is available fron the British Library.

ISBN 1 900360 17 9

Further copies of this book and a full publications list are available from The Directory of Social Change at the address below.

The Directory of Social Change,
24 Stephenson Way, London NW1 2DP
Tel: 0171 209 5151 Fax: 0171 209 5049
e-mail: info@d-s-c.demon.co.uk

Other Directory of Social Change departments:
Courses and conferences tel: 0171 209 4949
Charityfair tel: 0171 209 1015
Charity Centre tel: 0171 209 0902
Research tel: 0171 209 4422

Directory of Social Change Northern Office:
Federation House, Hope Street, Liverpool L1 9BW
Courses and conferences tel: 0151 708 0117
Research tel: 0151 708 0136

The Media Trust, 3-6 Alfred Place, London WC1E 7EB
Tel: 0171 637 4747 Fax: 0171 637 5757
e-mail: mediatrust@theframe.com

Voluntary Matters is an initiative by The Media Trust in association with South Bank University and the Directory of Social Change, with major funding from Camelot Group plc. Also supported by C&A, Levi Strauss & Co. Europe, General Electric Company plc. and the Department of National Heritage.

CONTENTS

CONTENTS

FOREWORD

Charities and voluntary organisations play an increasingly important role in our society. *Voluntary Matters* provides a new resource for anyone involved in running these essential organisations.

As a trustee of The Media Trust, the charity that produces *Voluntary Matters* for BBC2's *The Learning Zone*, I think this book makes an excellent companion to the television series for people who want to investigate management topics in more detail. Fundraising, law, marketing and accounting are all areas we need to understand well for our voluntary organisations to perform better.

Incredibly, almost half the population in the UK plays some sort of a role in a charity or voluntary organisation. Most of us learn what we do by getting involved in an organisation and committing time and energy and personal skills. Trustees, staff and volunteers can now go one step further by using *Voluntary Matters* to get a broader understanding of good practice in the voluntary sector.

I commend this well-researched book to you, as an excellent resource, especially when used in conjunction with the *Voluntary Matters* video.

Jon Snow

INTRODUCTION

The aim of this chapter is to introduce the reader to the voluntary sector, explain its significance in terms of size and policy and stress the vital importance of effective management to voluntary organisations. The chapter will also explain how this book is constructed and how to use it to gain the maximum benefit from the work of its expert contributors.

Statistics and Policy

Philanthropic activity is almost as old as civilisation. There is evidence of charitable activity from the earliest written records across all societies. But charities have always changed with the times. In Great Britain the changing nature of social policy in the 1980s and 1990s has meant that many voluntary groups have had to negotiate a new role in relation to the state. The recent Commission on the Future of the Voluntary Sector raised the key issue of state funding and its impact on the independence of the voluntary sector from government action and priorities.

In 1996 the Office for National Statistics published a profile of the United Kingdom Charitable Sector. It found 178,000 charitable organisations, of which 120,000 were active. This represents an increase of 25% on the results of a similar survey in 1991 which found only 97,500 charities. According to the Charity Commission this growth rate has shown no visible signs of slowing down. In addition to these registered organisations, there are also another estimated 400,000 voluntary organisations.

This phenomenal growth has been linked to changes in the delivery of welfare services. Previously many services were part of statutory provision by local and health authorities. Now such services are provided by voluntary organisations under statutorily funded contracts. This has led to the creation of new organisations and the registration of existing voluntary organisations as charities, a move which enables them to take advantage of tax reliefs and to receive government finance. Government funding of the charitable sector currently stands at nearly one third of its total income of £11,776 million.

As a result of the market reforms of the 1980s, the voluntary sector has moved into a new environment. Voluntary organisations now find themselves competing for economic resources, primarily against other voluntary organisations but also public and private sector organisations.

Where does voluntary sector funding come from? There are four main sources:
- government – central, local and agencies, through contracts and grants;
- the public – through donations and trading activities;
- the corporate sector – through donations, sponsorship or free/ subsidised services;
- the internal charitable sector itself – from investments and grants from charitable trusts.

In round terms, one pound of charitable income will be derived as follows: 40p from the general public; 31p from the Government; 24p from charities' own resources (primarily investments); 5p from the corporate sector.

Another reason for the growth of the voluntary sector has been the number of new organisations formed in response to concerns which have not been resolved by official action. Voluntary action can be found at local and international levels on education, health and environmental matters. A third of all registered charities consider they have an international scope to their activities. Many of these organisations will fail, others will continue and remain small, a few will become major ventures with millions of pounds of income.

All these organisations are competing for limited resources in finance and personnel. Whether they are 'big battalion' organisations, among the 10% who have 90% of the sector's income, or relative minnows, the concept of competition for resources – financial, physical or human – now applies to them all. This makes it all the more important to handle these resources efficiently once they are obtained.

Voluntary organisation activity now permeates all aspects of our lives. There have been grandiose claims that it is the 'democratic glue' of our society, suggesting that one characteristic of a democratic society is the size and importance of its voluntary sector. At the most practical level, there is the contribution of those who give up their time willingly and freely to some form of voluntary activity – an estimated 23 million people. With assets of £40 billion pounds and annual spending of nearly £11 billion, the voluntary sector now forms a very sizeable part of the UK economy. For comparative purposes agriculture, hunting, forestry and fishing together have a similar income at £11.5 billion, while mining and quarrying is slightly larger at £13.5 billion.

Understanding the environment in which a voluntary organisation operates is vital for the raising of funds. It is necessary to understand government funding priorities and how to win support from the general public (such as the dramatic way support for overseas aid organisations was boosted by the massive publicity for 'Band Aid'). There have also been changes in regulation and greater scrutiny of charitable affairs. Charities are firmly within the 'public domain', enjoying as they do some £1,000 million in tax reliefs. Efficiency, whether in the administration or delivery of services, is a legitimate public concern. Charities must be both effective and equitable in their affairs if they are to undertake the difficult role which is emerging for them in the next phase of their history.

The Importance of Effective Management

The 750,000 voluntary charity trustees, supported by 620,000 paid employees, therefore have considerable responsibilities. They operate in an important and sizeable sector of the economy which has its own distinct managerial practices. You would not expect to run a farm without training and knowledge of agriculture as well as the law and environment it which it operates. Similarly, running a charitable organisation requires an appreciation of its distinct legal and cultural environment. Charity law and accounting have specialist practices and obligations that do not apply in commercial organisations. The concept of trust and restricted funds are paramount. They mean that managers do not have the same freedom of operational movement as they would in a commercial organisation.

The management of volunteers is very different from that of paid staff and issues of accountability and governance in voluntary organisations have features that commercial practices would not recognise. The recent pronouncement by Shell that they needed a greater understanding of equity and accountability issues was a clear indication that some aspects of voluntary sector best practice could also be adopted by commercial organisations.

The economic environment in which charitable organisations operate is also distinct from the commercial world. The major income source of the voluntary sector is support from the general public. Yet this income source has been in decline since the late 1980s. Initially this fall was blamed on the recession. However, the long expected increase in voluntary sector income has still to emerge. The dramatic increase expected in charity donations deriving from more tax-efficient giving has also not happened. While individual schemes and benefits have been important, overall the impact of lower taxation has not seen a massive shift to increased personal giving. Perhaps the most dramatic example of this failure has been the corporate sector, which contributes a mere 4% of direct charitable donations, despite record profitability levels in recent years.

For charity managers these wider environmental considerations have important consequences. For charities needing to raise funds it means they will have to work harder and be more innovative in the raising of funds. Charities need to market themselves to ensure the public understands both the important work they do and why they need their support. All voluntary organisations need to demonstrate that having raised funding, they are also capable of administering it efficiently and effectively. Cost-effective administration and effective financial management is as important as raising the funds. Charitable organisations need to be commercially orientated, in the sense of recognising the importance of strategic planning and efficient cost-effective management. But they also need to be aware of their own unique environmental and cultural characteristics which mean that not all 'business management practices' are appropriate.

Charitable organisations must therefore avoid linking to inappropriate and perhaps dated management models, as a recent comment by Professor Nicholas Deakin on management consultants illustrates:

"It seems to me very often that what is on offer... is a model (to take an example), of leadership which is already looking rather dated – the kind of up-front, gung-ho, macho leadership so much the fashion in the 1980s. Elsewhere, people are coming to believe it may be time to be putting away the mobile phones and red braces and talking about a different style of leadership. None the less, the earlier style is still very much in the market. It suggests that some of the larger organisations in the voluntary sector may still be downsizing and out-sourcing in the late 1990s when everyone else is trying to be a good corporate citizen."

This book considers and promotes best practice for managing volunteers, for user involvement and governance. It takes as its philosophy that those with, or aspiring to, a managerial role in the voluntary sector must not remain ignorant of best management practices. Good voluntary organisation management combines the efficiency aspects of business practice with the equity characteristics of the voluntary sector. This book (accompanying the BBC 2 The Learning Zone television series *Voluntary Matters*) has been written to demonstrate this approach.

How to Use This Book

It is not expected that the reader will pick up the text and read it from cover to cover, although this is possible due to the consistency of format. Every chapter is capable of being approached as a separate topic. In this respect, the text offers a unique learning package for those involved or wishing to be involved in the sector, such as paid employees, volunteers, and especially trustees.

The book adopts a dual approach by encompassing theoretical knowledge within a framework of practical application, in the form of examples, case studies, checklist, quizzes and self assessment exercises. Although all twelve chapters in the book exist as individual and separate topics, they follow a consistent format that is designed to be 'user friendly' in presentation, with the text broken up by illustrations, diagrams and checklists. The focus of the material presented is on practical benefits, with the emphasis on good practice and improving the management of an organisation.

For those readers encountering a topic in which they lack expertise, the material will provide a comprehensive introduction. For those who are more experienced in a particular field, the material will illustrate challenging issues of management best practice in the context of current legislation and social policy.

References

Deakin, N.(1996). Future prospects for voluntary action. RSA Journal, August/September pp 62-72.

Meeting the Challenge of Change: voluntary action into the 21st century. The Report of the Commission on the Future of the Voluntary Sector'. NCVO Publications.

Vital Statistics. The Voluntary Sector Statistical Almanac. NCVO Publications.

'Shell confesses to misjudging public opinion'. Daily Telegraph. 12.10.96.

About the Editors

Series Editor – Dr. Paul Palmer

Dr. Paul Palmer (F.I.I.A, F.C.I.S) is the Director of MSc Charity Finance course and Head of the Centre for Charity and Trust Research at South Bank University, London. Prior to his University appointment in 1989 he worked in the Charity Sector for 10 years. He is co-author of Rethinking Charity Trusteeship with Dr. Jenny Harrow.

Assistant Editor – Elizabeth Hoe

Elizabeth Hoe (LLB, M.A) is Flemings Research Assistant at the Centre for Charity and Trust Research at South Bank University. Her research work has included surveys for NGO Finance on Audit Fees and Charity Shops.

Further Training

There are a number of very good short courses on aspects of voluntary sector management. For example the Directory of Social Change's programme of courses and conferences. In addition, longer post-graduate courses specialising in charity studies are provided by several universities, such as South Bank, LSE and the Open University. A full list of training providers is published by The National Council for Voluntary Organisations (NCVO).

Professional organisations such as the Institute of Chartered Secretaries and Administrators (ICSA) and the Institute of Fund Raising Managers (ICFM) are offering vocational qualifications for both their members and the public at large. Details are available from these professional bodies. Specialist organisations have also developed to support best practices in the sector and they also offer training/meetings. These include the Association of Chief Executives of National Voluntary Organisations (ACENVO) and the Charity Finance Directors Group (CFDG). Useful addresses are listed by chapter at the end of the book.

FUNDRAISING : 1

Antony Baxter

1. Introduction

Aims and Objectives

Strumming a few chords on a guitar is a million miles from the
world of a professional musician. And so it is with fundraising. A
volunteer shaking a tin bears little relationship to the complex world
of professional fundraising. In this chapter we hope to give a taste
of every instrument in the fundraiser's orchestra, so listen, practice,
then perform. By the end of the chapter the student should:

- understand the four basic stages of the fundraising cycle
- appreciate the need for research and planning
- understand the differences between long term revenue and short
  term capital fundraising
- understand the principles of big gift fundraising
- appreciate the need for a powerful case
- value affluent and influential leadership
- be able to keep meticulous records
- understand the need for review and evaluation.

The reader will also have a working understanding of the strategic
planning process, the identification of mission and objectives,
internal and external research, identification of key areas,
development of strategic plans and review and evaluation.

This chapter cannot offer a comprehensive training
programme, but provides an overview which will assist those
entering the profession, those wishing to broaden their sphere of
knowledge or those managing a fundraising function as part of
their job. Fundraising is a continuous process of experimentation
– some ideas succeed, some will fail. Minimise failures by studying
the work of the many experts who have gone before.

The Art of Fundraising

Fundraising is one of the world's oldest professions. Most major
churches, hospitals and institutions were built with the aid of public
donations and the basic principles of raising money have not
changed in centuries. But there are certain points to bear in mind:

- people give to people, so a personal approach is always best
- if you want money you have to ask for it

• the art of fundraising is knowing who, when, where and how to ask

The best fundraisers will raise the *maximum* amounts from the *smallest* number of people in the *shortest* time at the least expense.

The Purpose

Fundraising is about more than money.

"Fundraising is a function of idealism... the activity which makes caring service possible". Redmond Mullin

"Fundraising forms a compact between the institution and the community, when a donor makes a gift they become shareholders in our institution, we become partners with a common interest in assuring the future of the organisation". Stephen Ummel, President Lutheran General

Why do People Give?

Both parties in any transaction should receive a benefit. The recipient of a donation receives cash, but what about the donor? The donor's benefits can range from tangible recognition such as a plaque on a park bench, to intangibles such as "sense of belonging, friendship or the feel good factor". Understand your donors' motivation and you will succeed. As with any form of marketing the secret is: *"Identifying or creating a mutual need then fulfilling it"*.

2. The Critical Factors

Four key factors will make the difference between success and failure:
• meticulous planning and research
• clear objectives
• a powerful case for funding
• strong leadership

The Fundraising Cycle

In his 1994 book, Redmund Mullin argues that *"The Fundraising Cycle is a discipline applicable to any fundraising programme"*.

Articulate

Why are your needs urgent, why do you deserve support? A clear, powerful, urgent and unambiguous cause is essential to motivate the donor. Remember however that whilst the public are influenced by an emotive cry for help – the business community expect a carefully argued case for funding.

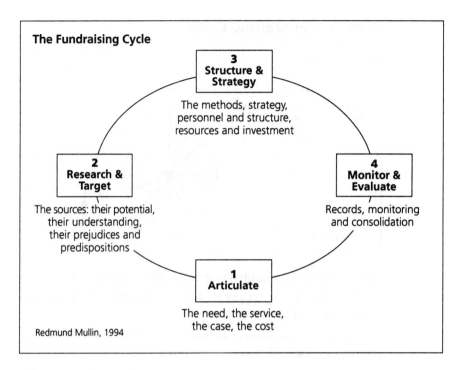

The Fundraising Cycle

3 Structure & Strategy
The methods, strategy, personnel and structure, resources and investment

2 Research & Target
The sources: their potential, their understanding, their prejudices and predispositions

4 Monitor & Evaluate
Records, monitoring and consolidation

1 Articulate
The need, the service, the case, the cost

Redmund Mullin, 1994

Research and Target

The Americans say "win the campaign on paper" and much more will be said in this chapter about the need for proper preparation. Remember the old adage that you can't sell freezers to Eskimos, or a Rolls Royce to a tramp. Don't waste your efforts on those unlikely to respond. Don't ask for inappropriate sums of money and do find out as much as you can about your prospects so that you can tailor approaches to the greatest effect.

Structure and Strategy

There is nothing magical about planning a strategy. Think of it as a journey – what questions will you ask before you set off?

Why do I want to go?	- the purpose
Where do I want to go?	- the objectives
When do I want to go?	- the timescale
How am I going to get there?	- the strategies

Choosing a train at random can be interesting but it won't get you to a particular place by a particular time. Decide where you want to go before you set off.

Monitor and Evaluate

Learn from your mistakes, refine, adapt and get it right next time round.

Another Fundraising Cycle

If all this seems a bit complicated, consider Antony Baxter's Penny Farthing.

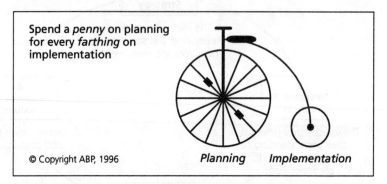

Spend a *penny* on planning for every *farthing* on implementation

© Copyright ABP, 1996   *Planning*   *Implementation*

A charity only has a limited amount of time, money and energy – use this wisely. The quality of response will be in direct relationship to the quality of planning.

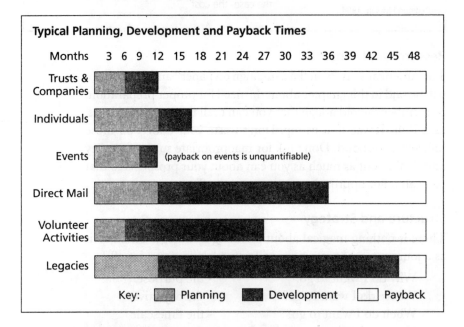

Typical Planning, Development and Payback Times

Months	3 6 9 12 15 18 21 24 27 30 33 36 39 42 45 48
Trusts & Companies	
Individuals	
Events	(payback on events is unquantifiable)
Direct Mail	
Volunteer Activities	
Legacies	

Key: ▨ Planning   ■ Development   □ Payback

Objectives

An objective is simply a statement of where you want to be and by when. A good objective is specific, achievable, worthwhile, timed and measurable.

Examples of Good and Bad Objectives

Good: To increase gross income from £1m to £1.2m by 31 March 1999, whilst maintaining costs at less than 15% and

operating within agreed moral and ethical guidelines.
(This objective shows worthwhile, achievable and measurable increase, with the constraints of the moral and ethical policy. Maximum expenditure is clearly stated).

Bad: To improve publicity so that we achieve a substantial increase in income
(To improve what publicity? How? How much is substantial and when will it be achieved?)

A Case for Funding

A clear, powerful, urgent and unambiguous cause with which the donor can identify is fundamental to the success of any appeal. Fundraising is not dissimilar to asking for a loan — if you were a bank manager which customer would you give money to:

Mr Livinhope: "I seem to keep losing my job, perhaps it's got something to do with my odious personality and lack of qualifications – I want to borrow £25,000 to buy a Mercedes sports car for promoting my new Trepanning for Pleasure and Profit business."

Mr Thoughtitout: "I have been marketing director for 5 years and have a track record of property acquisition and management. I have spent a year researching this opportunity and provide a mass of evidence, a business plan with endorsements from the council and 5 local businesses. I have backers who will provide £50,000, I will put in £25,000 of my own money and I want to borrow £25,000 to be repaid as follows…"

Leadership

Here we must distinguish between a short term capital appeal and longer term revenue fundraising. The former depends almost entirely on the stature and asking power of the Chair and Committee and their willingness to become involved. A long term revenue appeal uses paid or volunteer fundraisers who are skilled in fundraising techniques.

Quiz

Questions
1. Name four key factors which make the difference between success and failure
2. Name the 4 stages of the Redmund Mullin Fundraising Cycle

3. Where is the best place to spend a penny?

4. Name the 5 attributes of a good objective

Answers

1. *Planning and Research; Objectives; Case for Funding; Leadership*

2. *Articulate; Research and Target; Structure and Strategy; Monitor and Evaluate*

3. *On planning*

4. *Specific; Achievable; Worthwhile; Timed; Measurable*

....

3. Assembling Your Strategy

Let's go back to basics — what is the purpose of fundraising? To raise income? To raise profile? To recruit supporters? To build something? Be careful — these are 'means' not 'ends'. Ask *why* rather than *what* and the answer is more likely to be: to raise money to help the organisation achieve its primary purpose.

Everything you do must relate back to this primary purpose. Every fundraising plan should start with a reiteration of the organisation's purpose and the role of fundraising in helping to achieve it. Your strategy should be constructed in the following sections:

1. organisation's purpose and mission
2. fundraising objectives
3. case for funding and leadership
4. analysis of your organisation
5. analysis of the market place
6. key areas for development
7. strategic plans
8. monitor and review process

Self Analysis

By now you should have established your purpose, objectives, case and leadership — so it's time to contemplate your navel. How does your organisation really work? Who is responsible for what? What are your main sources of funds and how are they spent? What is your history of fundraising? A compelling and visual way of presenting this analysis is to produce cost/income charts for each of your activities. You can then split them into three groups:

1. very profitable
2. marginal – needs careful appraisal
3. unprofitable – abandon

Given the right circumstance, any of the following can be profitable. These charts are for illustration purposes only.

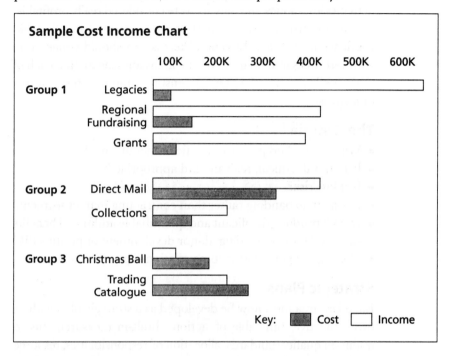

Sample Cost Income Chart

		100K	200K	300K	400K	500K	600K

Group 1 — Legacies, Regional Fundraising, Grants

Group 2 — Direct Mail, Collections

Group 3 — Christmas Ball, Trading Catalogue

Key: ■ Cost □ Income

Market Analysis

It's a big wide world and you are shopping for opportunities. Read magazines such as *Professional Fundraising, Third Sector* and *Charity.* Buy the Directory of Social Change publications and study *Dimensions of the Voluntary Sector.* The Internet or World Wide Web have been highly publicised as a tool for the fundraiser of the future. Amnesty International and a variety of international charities have Internet sites which are becoming increasingly profitable and The Net is a rich source of information and research, particularly for those charities looking for American generated information. UK generated information of use to charities is still in its infancy. Complete a formal S.W.O.T. analysis which lists your Strengths, Weaknesses, Opportunities and Threats — remember opportunity can be something new, or simply improving something you already do.

Key Areas for Development

This is what you've been working towards. You now have to decide where to concentrate your efforts to achieve the fastest progress towards objectives. A large and famous institution was involved in over 100 different fundraising and trading activities. Research showed that one activity earned £235,000 but cost £225,000, another activity earned the same but cost only £31,000, many activities lost money and only six were considered really profitable. By ruthless pruning, an £80,000 loss was turned into a £200,000 profit within 2 years. In general terms you should concentrate your resources into no more than 6 areas and ensure that each of these fulfils a series of criteria to ensure rapid progress towards objectives.

The Criteria

- Will the method produce significant net income?
- Is it moral, ethical, relevant and appropriate?
- Is it low risk?
- Is it in an expanding rather than contracting market segment?
- Does it produce significant and quantifiable additional benefits such as database building, donor development or positive PR?
- Has it got a good cost income relationship?

Strategic Plans

Each key area must now be developed as a strategic plan with its own objective, timetable of actions, built-in measurements to maintain quality standards, allocation of responsibilities, resource implications and financial projections. These are your action plans.

Monitoring and Review

"Evaluation is only worthwhile if measured against objectives." The monitoring and reviewing process is one of the most important discriminators between success and failure. Keep meticulous records, learn from your failures and improve on your successes. The world does not stand still and you must constantly refer to and adapt your strategy to keep it vibrant. So get on your bike and raise some money – good luck!

Quiz

Questions

1. Name one fundraising "means"
2. Name one fundraising "end"
3. What are the stages in a strategy?
4. What is a S.W.O.T.?
5. What criteria should a key area fulfil?

Answers

1. To raise money

2. To help the organisation to achieve its primary purpose

3. *Organisation's purpose and mission*
   Fundraising objectives
   Case for funding and leadership
   Analysis of your organisation
   Analysis of the market place
   Key areas for development
   Strategic plans
   Monitor and review
4. *Strengths, Weaknesses, Opportunities and Threats analysis*
5. *Produces significant net income*
   Is moral, ethical, relevant and appropriate
   Is low risk
   Is in an expanding market segment
   Produces quantifiable and significant additional benefits i.e. database building, positive PR, donor development

4. Capital/Big Gift Campaigns

Leadership

In most cases 'people give to people' first and 'to good causes' second. In major gift fundraising, finding the 'right person' to facilitate introductions and 'do the asking' is a crucial factor in success. The most successful appeals have been supported by trustees and committees comprising people of influence and affluence who are able to provide a wide network of useful contacts.

Committee members should be asked to:
- act as ambassadors for the cause
- assist with the identification of personal contacts in target organisations
- act as 'door openers' in planned and targeted approaches
- host prospective donors at visits, presentations and events designed to show the organisation's work and specific needs.

All of this work should be directed and supported by experienced fundraising staff who will undertake research, provide administrative back up, compile written submissions, advise on methods of giving, consider legal and statutory matters and plan the timing of fundraising approaches. In capital appeals it is not usual for paid or consultant staff to 'do the asking'. Fundraising committee members must also be prepared to bring a personal gift (however small) to the appeal to demonstrate their own commitment and to give credibility when approaching prospective donors, or acting as a 'door opener' for an approach by someone else.

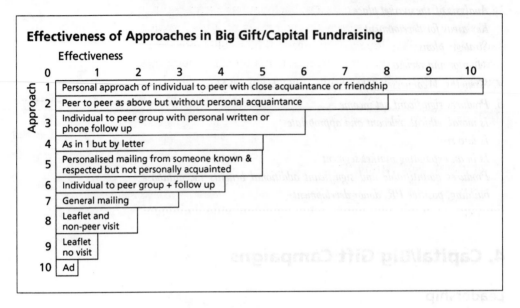

Effectiveness of Approaches in Big Gift/Capital Fundraising

Effectiveness

Approach		Effectiveness (0-10)
1	Personal approach of individual to peer with close acquaintance or friendship	
2	Peer to peer as above but without personal acquaintance	
3	Individual to peer group with personal written or phone follow up	
4	As in 1 but by letter	
5	Personalised mailing from someone known & respected but not personally acquainted	
6	Individual to peer group + follow up	
7	General mailing	
8	Leaflet and non-peer visit	
9	Leaflet no visit	
10	Ad	

Process/Phasing

The classic three phase approach was used by Great Ormond Street Hospital and by most other successful capital appeals in the last ten years.

During this phase the foundations are laid. Expect to spend at least a year on planning – Great Ormond Street spent four!

By the end of the phase you should have:
1. a Chairperson
2. an Appeals Committee
3. an Appeals Executive (director, consultant or project manager)
4. a strategy
5. a database of targeted trusts, companies and wealthy individuals
6. identified high level contacts prepared to make personal approaches
7. support systems for recording and monitoring
8. a powerful and motivating case statement
9. a 'shopping list' of projects for funding

The Private Phase

During this phase, targeted and personal approaches are made to trusts, companies, statutory bodies and wealthy individuals. It is common practice to raise as much as half of the target from private approaches before the launch of the final phase.

The Public Phase

Some consider this phase to be a public relations exercise. But it is unwise to concentrate purely on the raising of a fixed capital sum and ignore the longer term needs. The public appeal can provide the funds needed for longer term maintenance but prime sources of 'un-earmarked income' such as legacies can take three or four years to develop so must be planned at the same time as the shorter term capital appeal.

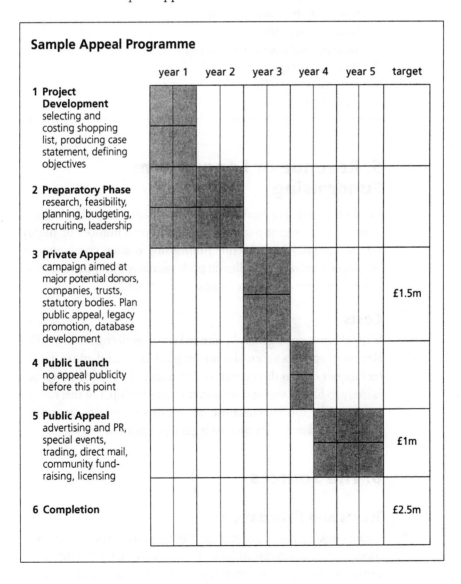

Sample Appeal Programme

	year 1	year 2	year 3	year 4	year 5	target
1 Project Development selecting and costing shopping list, producing case statement, defining objectives	■					
2 Preparatory Phase research, feasibility, planning, budgeting, recruiting, leadership	■	■				
3 Private Appeal campaign aimed at major potential donors, companies, trusts, statutory bodies. Plan public appeal, legacy promotion, database development			■			£1.5m
4 Public Launch no appeal publicity before this point				■		
5 Public Appeal advertising and PR, special events, trading, direct mail, community fund-raising, licensing					■	£1m
6 Completion						£2.5m

Quiz

Questions

1. What should committee members do?
2. What is the most effective type of approach?
3. What are the three phases of a capital appeal?
4. How much of your target should you raise in the private phase?

Answers

1. *Act as ambassadors*
   Identify personal contacts
   Act as door openers
   Host prospective donors on visits
   Bring a personal gift
   Make personal requests for donations
2. *Personal peer to peer*
3. *Planning, Private, Public*
4. *Up to 50%*

5. Revenue or Longer Term Fundraising

Whilst the capital appeal is dependent on affluent and influential leadership, peer group solicitation and a small number of highly targeted approaches (revenue fundraising is often conducted by employed fundraisers), relies on professional techniques and seeks larger numbers of smaller 'un-earmarked' gifts.

Costs

Capital fundraisers generally aim to keep overall costs below 10%. Revenue appeals often use more paid staff and more costly techniques such as direct mail and trading. A long term campaign is likely to have a worse cost/income relationship, but this can be improved by the judicious use of volunteers and concentration on high yield activities such as legacy promotion.

6. The Sources

Trusts and Foundations

Grant-making trusts are one of the most important sources of income, both in capital and revenue fundraising. Charitable trusts are bodies set up to give money away for charitable purposes, but do not normally undertake charitable work themselves. Over £1 billion in grants is distributed each year by over 3,000 grant giving trusts in the UK, with the largest 27 distributing around £0.5 billion. In 1993/4 the top 500 distributed a total of £705.1 million in grants and received £846.7million in income.

Broadly speaking, trusts can be categorised as follows:

Charitable or non-charitable: The majority only give grants for charitable purposes but a few such as The Joseph Rowntree Foundation, which focuses on social services and social policy, can make non-charitable grants.

Local or national: Whilst most larger trusts have a national remit, many still prefer to concentrate their activities in defined geographic locations.

General or defined purpose: A large general trust such as the Tudor Trust can support a wide range of welfare, training, employment, arts and education activities, whilst others are set up to concentrate on narrowly defined areas such as research into a rare disease.

Family, company or independent: Many trusts are limited to a particular family or company whilst others are associated with city livery companies. Most of these operate in clearly defined areas.

Do Your Homework

Trust fundraising is one area where you will have no difficulty in getting information. A mass of research has been produced by the Directory of Social Change, Charities Aid Foundation (CAF) and others. This will help you target your approaches to the greatest effect.

Some important facts and figures

1. *Dimensions of the Voluntary Sector* lists the three areas which trusts are most likely to fund as being education and research, health and social services. 67% of all grants given are made in these areas.
2. A CAF survey showed that 79% of trusts prefer to give grants at local levels.
3. CAF also found that the top quarter of trusts and foundations

gave 82.1% of total grants. The second quarter gave 10.3% of grants, leaving the lower half of trusts and foundations responsible for less than 10% of all grants.

Get Ready

Before making any approach to a trust, ensure that your purpose, objectives and case for funding are clear, relevant and convincing. Be specific: the Directory of Social Change suggests that the main ways of annoying a trust and encouraging rejection are:

- asking a trust to contribute towards a general public appeal
- asking for general donations rather than seeking support for a particular project.

Their *Raising Money From Trusts* suggests that in order to fund core costs which are never particularly attractive to a donor, charities should:

- divide their work up into differently priced 'packages'
- find trusts who are interested in these aspects of their work
- allocate a proportion of admin and overheads to each package.

Take aim

A scatter-gun approach occasionally hits a target, but you more often shoot yourself in the foot. Many trusts will not consider a second application for a year following a rejection and an ill considered mailing may damage future prospects. Your first port of call will almost certainly be a Directory of Social Change publication or the CAF Directory although you should not forget those who have given in the past. They may be your warmest supporters.

Think Hard

Even after you have carefully selected trusts where there appears to be a close match or a strong geographic affinity, you may be left with a long list. Examine their guidelines and look for exclusions. A trust set up to help the poor children of the City of London might refer to the City's square mile. An approach from a worthy organisation in Vauxhall would receive an automatic rejection. The Directory of Social Change cites examples of: London based charities applying to Cadbury Trusts which only fund in the West Midlands; an old people's charity applying to the Prince's Trust which only supports youth; and requests for £15,000 to trusts with total incomes of less than £1,000.

Think Again

Go for the big ones first. Remember that the largest 25% of trusts distribute a massive 82% of all grants.

The large trusts are mostly very businesslike and will appraise all applications in a formal way. Your case and presentation must be strong, well presented and fully supported – so it is not as easy as it sounds.

Then Fire

By now you should have a powerful case and a list of targeted trusts. Look at it from the trust's point of view – they have thousands of requests for funds and they will almost certainly reject those that:

- are badly presented or incomplete
- do not arrive in the requested format
- do not match the trust's funding objectives
- request an inappropriate or unrealistic amount of money
- arrive immediately after a trustee meeting when all the funds have been spent.

The letter

Your letter should be concise (maximum two pages), factual and unemotional. It should be personally addressed to the correspondent of the target trust. The letter should be signed by the Chair, Chief Executive or other appropriate senior representative of your charity and the trust's guidelines for application (published or unpublished) should be followed scrupulously. Include the following:

- background – when and why your charity was set up
- the need which your charity is addressing
- how your charity is meeting the need – achievements and future plans
- what it will cost – itemised requirements, evidence that the project is viable, details of how it will operate and who will benefit
- conclusion – a brief résumé of the needs and benefits of the project and a specific request for support.

Supporting materials should normally be no more than two or three pages. Include annual report and accounts where requested.

Building the Relationship

Say 'thank you' and listen. You may not like what you hear but with sensitivity, problems can be turned into opportunities.

Company Donations and Sponsorship

Gone are the days of cocktail parties and smoke-filled rooms. Most companies have a staff committee often regionalised which allocates charitable donations.

Who to approach? The Chairperson is of course at the top and retains much influence, but their 'discretionary charity budget' is likely to be much smaller than it was in the 80's. Other influential people in companies include: the Marketing Director – the key decision maker in terms of licensing and sponsorships (where the company receives benefit in return for support). Public Relation's remit is to positively promote the company — perhaps by charitable associations. The Corporate Affairs department is responsible for external relations with groups who could influence the company's performance. The Personnel Department is responsible for payroll giving, employee fundraising, secondment and many community activities. Sales Promotion and Marketing Agencies are often charged with seeking out and developing appropriate and beneficial charity relationships for companies.

NB: almost all of the above sources will be looking for some benefit in return for their donation. So once again, you must start with careful and detailed research.

What does the donor company wish to achieve?

Sales boost – improved image – new customers – access to famous people – community involvement? Look at the company's objectives and charitable guidelines before any approach is made.

What market is the company in?

Not an easy question. Haägen Dazs would appear to sell ice cream but are in reality selling entertainment. British Airways sell communications and so are under threat from telecommunications companies.

Develop a targeted proposition

Many charities believe they can help raise awareness or build the company's image. This is wrong. Most national companies have an awareness level of 80% or more and a flood of goodwill will not follow from having their name mentioned in a newsletter. So:
• research companies, brand strategies, image, market position and objectives
• match a request or proposition to suit individual companies
• identify benefits to the company and sell hard
• prepare a careful and thoroughly professional presentation.

In practice the process will involve identifying companies or institutions which have an interest in giving support in your area of operation. They will have the capacity to give a significant donation, a history of funding similar projects and some kind of geographic, personal or previous business link with your organisation. A strong, convincing and targeted case must be developed, which fulfils both the objectives of the company and the charity.

Councils, development corporations and business advisory centres will be happy to provide lists of companies within a geographic area. Many of these will be local offices of national or regional companies and further information can be obtained from head office. Annual and interim reports and accounts will describe the company and its activities, and often give the names of directors and management. These should be validated by telephone before making any direct approach. Lists of directors of targeted companies can be circulated amongst the senior supporters and management of the charity in order to identify direct contacts who may be used for 'door opening'.

It is more difficult to find out who is in charge of the charitable donations committee, since this is often a staff appointment which rotates on a regular basis. The public affairs or press department are usually most knowledgeable and helpful and make a good first point of contact.

Individual Donations

The vast majority (91%) of respondents to the Individual Giving & Volunteering Survey (IGS) felt that government has a basic duty to look after those who are unable to take care of themselves. 87% felt that the Government relies too heavily on the voluntary sector and should itself be giving more help.

The survey also highlighted the following results:
- 79% liked to support charities where they could see how their money is being put to use
- 66% found it more rewarding to support local charities.

Individual Giving Patterns

Those most likely to donate were aged between 25 and 34 and gave an average of £11.31. Women were more likely to donate to charity than men. Those who stated that religion was of great value in their lives had a greater tendency to give and gave the highest average donation of £23.75.

Methods of Individual Giving

Results of the IGS survey show that the most popular method of giving was through door-to-door collections. 37% of respondents donated using this method although it only generated 6% of income received. 14% of respondents purchased through charity shops. This method produced the most income, accounting for 11% of total donations.

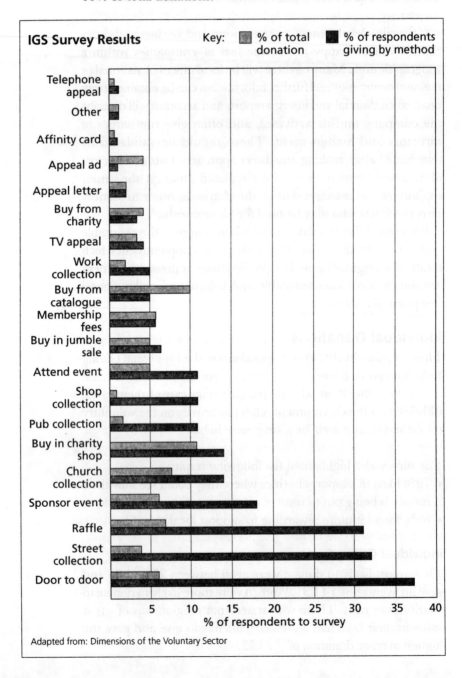

IGS Survey Results   Key: ▨ % of total donation   ■ % of respondents giving by method

Categories (top to bottom): Telephone appeal, Other, Affinity card, Appeal ad, Appeal letter, Buy from charity, TV appeal, Work collection, Buy from catalogue, Membership fees, Buy in jumble sale, Attend event, Shop collection, Pub collection, Buy in charity shop, Church collection, Sponsor event, Raffle, Street collection, Door to door

x-axis: % of respondents to survey (5, 10, 15, 20, 25, 30, 35, 40)

Adapted from: Dimensions of the Voluntary Sector

Public Fundraising

UK capital appeals have traditionally concentrated on grants, major donors, corporate gifts and statutory funding. The public appeal is often dismissed as a PR exercise to provide icing on the cake – always time consuming, sometimes risky and occasionally irrelevant. The British are notorious for taking the short term view. Americans, on the other hand, believe that the primary purpose of a public appeal is to build long term relationships with the community. Certainly the income is important and keeps many charities alive, but economic survival is not the primary motivator for most institutional fundraising.

American institutions are not just service providers but also sources of pride. Philanthropy is seen as the main way of building trust and forging long term relationships. It is an ongoing mechanism to form a compact between the organisation and the community. By asking for funds, the organisation is saying "We understand the needs of the community and with your help we will achieve them". The donor becomes a 'stakeholder' whose heightened loyalty and ability to focus on overall issues creates an invaluable long term asset.

In the beleaguered field of American healthcare, costs of equipment and procedures escalate whilst public opinion of management declines. Stephen Ummell, the respected Chief Executive of Lutheran General Hospital calls fundraising a "great integrator" which forces the leadership to make decisions with the community uppermost in mind, forces longer term strategic thinking and becomes an integral part of achieving the organisation's mission.

Legacies

Whilst trust, company and individual donations often get an appeal underway, legacies dominate many charities' longer term income. The top 500 charities in the UK received £571.6 million in legacies in 1995, almost 1/3 of all voluntary donations. Research by legacy experts Smee & Ford shows that in 1995 25,236 people made charitable wills, of which 49% were changed or written within three years of death. The average number of charitable bequests per will was 2.8.

Charitable Bequests by Sector

Cause	legacy nos.	% of total
Health & care	16810.00	23.5%
Animal welfare	10890.00	15.2%

Physically disabled	6846.00	9.6%
Cancer research	5739.00	8.0%
Medical research	5646.00	7.9%
Services/marine	4534.00	6.4%
Religious	4488.00	6.3%
Child welfare	4380.00	6.1%
Aged welfare	2562.00	3.6%
Overseas aid	2370.00	3.3%
Environment/conservation	2305.00	3.2%
Education	1222.00	1.7%
Mentally disabled	919.00	1.3%
Arts	533.00	0.7%
Unclassified	2305.00	3.2%

Smee & Ford, 1996

Ages at Death of Charitable Will Makers:

22.8%	70-79 years at death
43.5%	80-89 years at death
66.3%	between 70 and 89 years at death

The main types of charitable bequest are:
Pecuniary – where a fixed sum of cash is left to the charity, and
Residuary – where the residue of the estate is left to the charity.

Pecuniary bequests are easier to promote and convert into funds, however the value starts to diminish as soon as the will is made. Inflation can dramatically erode the original gift. In 1994, the average pecuniary bequest to charity was £3,230. In contrast, residuary bequests were worth on average £20,040 in the same year, and for this reason, have been vigorously promoted by charities. As a result the percentage of residuary bequests has risen to 48% of all charitable wills.

And the possible decline of legacy giving

Legacies are important to many charities – but there are storm clouds on the horizon. Greater life expectancy and the need to provide for old age means that bequests take longer to come and are worth less. Any decline in property values makes residuary legacies smaller and often difficult to convert into cash. There is more competition for legacy income, with most large charities having sophisticated legacy marketing campaigns.

It's not quite nice!

Some fundraisers are still uneasy about legacy promotion because it is morbid and involves death. This is not a view held by potential donors, the majority of whom are happy or even eager to discuss this topic. Another argument is that legacy promotion is long term and unpredictable. Not so: there is clear evidence to suggest that positive promotion affects legacy income in around 4 years but don't forget: 23% of all last wills are made in the year before death.

Legacy Case Study – Arthritis Care

Presented by Peter Maple, ICFM Conference 1995

Between 1983 and 1993 income from legacies quadrupled, but the number of bequests stayed about the same. In the same period, average residuary legacies fell from around £30,000 to £20,000 and have subsequently fallen to below £10,000. Whilst local branches felt that most legacies came from grateful members, only 20% could be proved to come from members or immediate families, suggesting that direct contact does not necessarily predispose a bequest. Research suggested that solicitors rarely influence the choice of beneficiaries in a will. The majority of legacies were shared with four or more other charities, with a clear preference being demonstrated for either care or research.

A.I.D.A.

The response to advertising suggested that the first two parts of A.I.D.A – Attention and Interest had been achieved but the campaign had failed to complete with Desire and Action. Arthritis Care wrote to 1,500 respondents asking whether they would be prepared to receive a phone call. Amazingly, less than 10% opted out, within five days 20% of those telephoned had pledged a bequest and 10% actually returned a pledge card. In the whole campaign only three people complained (two of whom turned out to be Branch Committee Members).

Legacy Case Study – Great Ormond Street Children's Hospital

Following the publicity generated during the Wishing Well Appeal in 1987/8, Great Ormond Street Hospital experienced a big increase in unsolicited legacies. By 1992 the increase was levelling off and there were concerns that the trend would reverse. Research showed that the market was flooded with packs from other charities so an original scheme was devised to target affluent over 55s, in 13 selected areas, commencing with Bournemouth.

Local solicitors were asked to draw up wills free of charge in return for beneficial publicity and leads for future business, including being named as executor in the will concerned. The local newspapers were pleased to assist by running a week-long reader offer featuring: stories of local children who had been treated at GOSH; stories on the importance of making a will; descriptions of the problems of intestacy; and the way an organisation such as GOSH could benefit from a bequest.

Tokens were printed and the reader asked to exchange three of these for their free will. Although encouraged to make a bequest to Great Ormond Street, the free will was not conditional upon this. Prospects were further motivated to make a pledge by a free inscribed copy of James Barrie's book Peter Pan and inclusion in a 'book of remembrance' at the Hospital. Solicitors reported that this was a strong motivating factor. At a subsequent award ceremony, the agency and Director of Marketing reported an astounding £1.4m worth of pledges at a cost of £5,644 plus at least £890 in spontaneous donations.

Source: Codicil, Professional Fundraising and GOSH

The Lottery

Much has been written about the right and wrongs of running a lottery, its effect on society and the voluntary sector in particular. Undoubtedly there have been both winners and losers. This is a debate which we do not intend to join. At the end of the first year there were calls to reorganise the distribution process and certain modifications have already been made, with more in the pipeline. With much of the lottery process under review, it would be foolhardy to do much more than point you towards up to date sources of information.

Lottery grants are distributed by five different bodies:

1. The Arts Council

Through the Arts Councils of England, Scotland, Wales and Northern Ireland the Arts Council had distributed over £250m by the end of 1995. It funded capital projects such as the construction and renovation of arts buildings and facilities and the purchase of new equipment.

2. The National Lottery Charities Board

The NLCB was set up to help meet the needs of those most disadvantaged in society and to improve the quality of life in the community. The board deals with applications on a sector by sector basis in three 'rounds' each year. In 1997 the first two rounds were:

- New Opportunities and Choices
- Voluntary Sector Development

Future programmes will include:

Improving People's Living Environment: through improvement and maintenance of the physical and social fabric of communities (including accommodation for people in need and creating a better living environment especially in isolated areas).

Community Involvement: through increasing everyone's sense of belonging, encouraging involvement and volunteering in their communities and encouraging involvement of those people who are marginalised in society in rural and urban areas.

Small Grants (initial pilot scheme in Wales only) Grants from £500 to £5,000: open to groups with annual incomes of less than £1,000.

Overseas Grants: UK based charities working overseas.

The NLCB welcomes applications from all parts of the UK, particularly small and locally based groups. Generally speaking it will only fund organisations "independently established for charitable, benevolent or philanthropic purposes" and will not make grants to NHS trusts or grant maintained, private or LEA schools. Demand always outstrips supply and applications must be well focused to succeed.

The NLCB gets 5.6 pence for every £1 spent on the lottery and awards through five committees which cover England, Wales, Scotland, Northern Ireland and UK as a whole. England is divided into nine regions with an advisory panel and a regional manager. Information may be obtained from the NLCB head office, St Vincent House, 30 Orange Street, London WC2H 7HH, Tel: 0171-747 5299. Application packs may be obtained from 0345-919191 (Welsh language 0345-273273). The grant making in England is decentralised to nine regional offices each with its own advisory panel, staff and budget for each round.

3. The Heritage Fund

The Heritage Fund is operated by the National Lottery Memorial Fund. This fund has so far distributed the smallest proportion of income available within its five selected fields. These are museums and galleries, land, buildings, manuscripts and archives and industrial, transport and maritime heritage.

4. The Millennium Commission

The Commission will cease to exist on 31 December 2000 but before then will give away an estimated £1.6 billion to reward projects which mark the passing of the old millennium and look forward to the new one.

5. The Sports Fund

The lottery sports funds are distributed by the Sports Councils in England, Wales, Scotland and Northern Ireland. Grants for sport have been in serious decline for several years with a major fall in local authority expenditure. Many lottery applications have come from local authorities. Sports lottery funding concentrates on participation and excellence and in 1995, 90% of the money was given for participation.

Application Procedures

Each of the boards has different application procedures and criteria. Since these change from day to day, it is impossible to give more than the broadest guidelines on how to achieve success. In general terms, follow the guidelines scrupulously, get applications in early, be realistic in your request and provide strong supporting evidence. Don't ask for more than you need and triple check all your figures (there were reported to be a large proportion of applications containing basic addition errors in the first round).

For further information refer to the Directory of Social Change's *National Lottery Yearbook* which contains detailed information on application procedures and criteria, or the ICFM Update Special, *The Fundraiser's Guide to the National Lottery*.

Trading Companies, Shops, Mail Order, Licensing, The Law

Trading almost always involves an element of risk. For this reason a 'rule of thumb' risk assessment has been included for each of the following sections. Use this as a guideline only and remember that everyone involved with a charity has a duty of prudence, so never gamble with charitable funds.

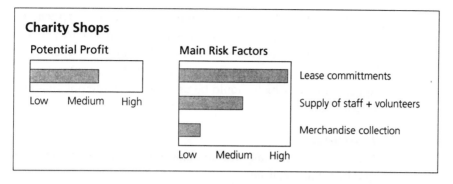

Footfall is a key word. Most people will not travel to a charity shop – often they won't even cross the road. If nobody passes the site, don't open the shop. The biggest risk factor is getting trapped in a long lease where footfall has declined. Town centre movements and falling property values have caused major problems for charities who signed long leases in the boom years of the 1980's.

A report by Mintel, *Survival of the High Street*, is gloomy about the future of the high street which it believes to be a "symbol of a bygone era" to a whole generation of younger customers. Out of town complexes already account for a quarter of all retail sales and this will rise to a third by the end of the century.

As traditional retailers move out of the high street, charity shops move in and saturation has become a concern. The charities responding to the *NGO Finance* survey felt that this would affect the small players first with the professional operators having the skill and resource to differentiate themselves. Other threats are seen as a minimum wage and loss of council tax concessions. A more general threat is theft, which is believed to be widespread and damaging to morale and profitability.

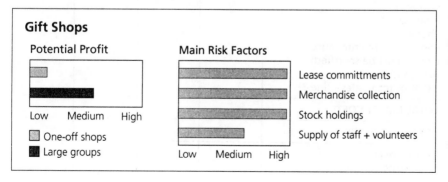

Economy of scale has helped The National Trust become a leader in this risky but potentially profitable field of gift shops. Buyers, merchandisers, display teams, shop designers, analysts and distribution networks need to be as professional as those in Marks and Spencer or W H Smiths. No one will buy an overpriced or unattractive item just because it is stamped with a charity name. Many have tried and failed to successfully run a charity shop.

The following example is a greatly simplified version of an appraisal form which should be used before contemplating any charity shop.

Remember
Estimate your footfall and potential sales, take away your cost and be totally realistic

Never
Work out your costs then aim for enough sales to cover them

And
Get professional advice before it is too late!

Charity Shop Appraisal					
(a)	(b) Sales	(c) Year 1	(d) %	(e) Year 2	(f) %
1	Sales of donated goods				
2	Sales of new goods				
3	TOTAL SALES (cash in till less VAT)				
4	Cost of merchandise				
5	TOTAL GROSS PROFIT (3–4)				
	Direct Costs				
6	Rent				
7	Salaries and wages				
8	Cost of repairing / cleaning / collecting goods				
9	Service charge (where applicable)				
10	Rates				
11	Insurance				
12	Heat / Light				
13	Phone				
14	Repairs and maintenance				
15	Other (must be specified)				
16	Add contingency (5% of total sales – line 3)				
17	TOTAL DIRECT COSTS				
18	NET PROFIT (5-17)				
	Set Up Costs				
19	Legal costs				
20	Survey cost				
21	Decorating/building work				
22	Premium (where applicable)				
23	Fixtures and fittings				
24	TOTAL SET UP COST				

With a shop, the key factor is footfall. With mail-order the equivalent is your list. Targeted lists are expensive to acquire so don't expect pay-back for two or three years. Keep a close watch on stock levels. Whilst it is embarrassing to run out of Christmas cards at the beginning of December, this is better than being left with stock which wipes out your profit in January. Don't over-estimate response rates. Remember that a 10% response is also a 90% failure.

An alternative is to allow a company to trade on your behalf. The disadvantage is that you will never make big profits, you will lose control over presentation and selection of merchandise and could end up looking like everyone else.

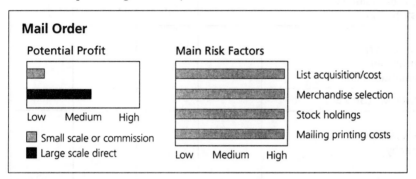

Licensing

Commercial licensing, sponsorships and joint ventures involve a trade whereby the charity allows the use of its name or logo in return for payment of cash or donations. This kind of activity should normally be conducted by a trading subsidiary and not the charity itself.

Do not attempt these types of activity unless you have professional staff who understand the complexities of commercial negotiating and contracting. In the right circumstances, however, licensing can be very profitable – organisations such as Great Ormond Street Hospital and WWF make substantial income without the associated stock and distribution risk of other forms of trading.

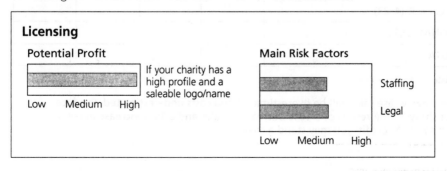

Mail Order Appraisal List	Prev. Year	Last Year	This Year	Next Year
List				
Number of traders				
% response				
Average order val;ue £s				
Number of donors/supporters				
% response				
Average order value £s				
Number of repeat mailings				
% response				
Average order value £s				
Other_____(specify)				
% response				
Average order value £s				
Total distribution				
Sales				
1 sales (net of VAT)				
2 gross profit (GP)				
3 sales commissions (SC)				
4 TOTAL INCOME (GP + SC)				
Expenditure				
5 artwork & design				
6 photography				
7 copy				
8 typeset				
9 repro				
10 print				
11 tape/discs				
12 labels				
13 post office mail sort				
14 brochure enclosing				
15 brochure post				
16 product store				
17 product fulfil				
18 credit card charges				
19 back order/substitution charges				
20 fees (specify)				
21 other (specify)				
22 contingency (4% of total income)				
23 TOTAL COSTS				
Net Contribution/Profit				
24 N.C. / N.P. (4–23)				
25 DONATIONS				
26 TOTAL				

© Antony Baxter Partnership 1996

NB. In almost every case sales will be overestimated and costs underestimated. Produce alternatives showing the results of a 10% decrease in sales and a 10% increase in costs – if you still show a net profit, you may stand a chance!

Charity Trading Law

It is essential to obtain proper legal advice before contemplating any trading activity. The law is complex and continually changing, as are the taxation and VAT regulations. In broad terms, charities are not permitted to trade. This is why many form separate companies to trade on their behalf then pass the profits back to the charity by way of a covenant. There are, at the time of writing, a number of exceptions listed below.

1. Under charity law a charity may trade if the trading is integral to its main objects as a charity. e.g. a school charging fees is trading, but also simultaneously carrying out its main object of providing education.

2. Under tax law a charity is also permitted to trade in furtherance of its main objects or if the work in connection with the trade is carried out mainly by the beneficiaries of the charity. One-off events such as jumble sales and coffee mornings are usually permitted provided that all of the following conditions are met:

   a) the activity is not carried out regularly by the charity

   b) the activity is not in competition with other traders

   c) the public knows that the proceeds are going to charity

   d) the profits are applied for charitable purposes.

   The above are only concessions however and may be withdrawn. In case of doubt always take professional advice.

Special Events

Special events can be time consuming, difficult and risky — but trustees and volunteers love a good party, so beware. Before considering any event ask yourself the following questions:

• are you doing it simply to make money?

• are you doing it because every other charity is doing it – "so it must be a good idea"?

• are you doing it to 'use up' a venue, celebrity or Royal?

If you answer "yes" to any of the above, you are probably heading for trouble.

So why bother? Because a properly planned event will involve and motivate your volunteers and attract new support — and as a by-product may generate indirect income. Special events are times of intense activity when you can make introductions, build relationships and focus attention on your programmes — Americans call it 'working the room'.

Special Events Case Study – Great Ormond Street Children's Hospital

Four years after the successful Wishing Well Appeal at Great Ormond Street Hospital the building was ready for commissioning. Hundreds of individuals and organisations who had raised money were invited to name areas of the new building. For almost a year, groups of donors were invited two or three times a week for a presentation, a tour of the new hospital, the naming of their area then an informal buffet supper. Staff acted as 'minders' to named individuals and the donors' enthusiasm and wish for continuing involvement was amazing to witness. The cost of these evenings was repaid hundreds of times over in further donations, long term commitments and legacy pledges.

Has it worked?

As with all fundraising and promotional activity it is essential to evaluate success. Vague assurances about "raising awareness, or profile" often translates as "it was hard work and lost us money!" Never forget Murphy's law. Everything that can go wrong, will go wrong: always plan for contingencies. Assume that everything will cost twice as much and take twice as long as you expect.

Volunteers

Volunteers often need a great deal of staff support and sometimes seem more trouble than they are worth. If you fall into this trap, however, you are ignoring one of the primary purposes of conducting an event in the first place – to involve your volunteers and attract new support.

Direct Marketing

First there was the corner shop providing a personal service to the local community. Next came the global market, television and mass mailings. Direct marketing can be a way of attracting/contacting hundreds or thousands of customers. The following are the key elements of this technique – get them right and you'll be well on your way:

The list

A letter from your local club, a family member or friend is unsolicited but usually welcomed — mail only becomes junk when the targeting process has failed.

The proposition

Successful marketing is *identifying* then *satisfying* a mutual need. Your need is for money, but you will not succeed unless you *identify* then *satisfy* the donor's need.

Promote benefits not features

Consider the following:

1. buy our product because it is well designed and cheap
2. buy our product because it will make your life easier, it will make you happy and it will save you money.

The second is client centred, understands their needs and offers solutions — it is much more powerful.

The presentation

Finally there is design, copy, print and presentation. Of course this will make a difference but only if you have got the proposition and the list right. Professional techniques abound. John Fraser Robinson, Ken Burnett and Christian Brann have all produced fascinating and useful work on the subject.

Direct marketing can be very useful for developing long term relationships and building donor loyalty but it is never cheap. Take professional advice and don't expect an instant payback.

Overseas Fundraising, US and Japan

Fundraising from America is possible but complex and will need to be done through a third party agency or by setting up your own American charity (known as a 501(c)3). Tax deductibility is an important issue since Americans can claim all charitable donations as an expense. Expatriate Americans living in the UK are still liable for US taxes and can therefore deduct donations made to a 501(c)3 in the US. Many UK-based expatriates will be happy to help: some may see support of a charity as providing links with royalty (an important motivator), a link into the local community and an opportunity to network with other expatriates.

Groups with access to expatriates include:

- British and American Chambers of Commerce
- American Embassy
- American Junior League
- *The American* newspaper

Japan

Japan now believes that it must become part of the world and share its solutions (and problems). Tax laws have been changed to promote philanthropy and Japan sees itself as an instrument of change.

There are many obstacles to forming a relationship with Japan although the effort can be worthwhile. Culture, language and distance mean that it may take a very long time to develop a relationship. To succeed a charity must use contacts, introductions and intermediaries, provide cultural exchange, give status, access to debate on community issues and have an edge over competitors.

Ceremony and etiquette are very important and the Japanese are far too polite to react to a breach. A whole relationship can founder however because of an unintentional slight. Learn a few words and use them — you will cause amusement but it will be appreciated.

Overseas Fundraising Case Study – Great Ormond Street Children's Hospital

Great Ormond Street Hospital raised money from passengers on the Tokyo/London route of Virgin Airlines and shared part of the proceeds with Tokyo Children's Hospital. The Japanese were enthusiastic about developing joint fundraising initiatives and medical exchange visits with Great Ormond Street. So the Peter Pan Children's Fund was created. Its aim was to exploit Great Ormond Street's rights to James Barrie (the author of Peter Pan) in partnership with Japanese hospitals and Japanese industry. It is now producing substantial income for both Great Ormond Street and Japanese children's hospitals.

Public Relations

The Institute of Public Relations defines public relations practice as "the planned and sustained effort to establish and maintain goodwill and mutual understanding between an organisation and its public".

Note the words *planned, sustained* and *practice.* Public relations must be managed and fundraising mechanisms need to be established to convert interest into action.

Plan then implement! There is no substitute for careful research and planning.

Set your objectives

Define your audience. PR is expensive – target your efforts where they will achieve the maximum results. Choose your weapons carefully. The choice of media and techniques will depend on the audience you target, and the PR budget. PR is not free advertising – it takes time and money to develop but a well-placed news story or feature article can have a higher value than paid advertising since it is perceived by the public as non-commercial.

Factors which make a story newsworthy:
- unusual behaviour
- conflict
- emotion
- pain
- scandal
- glamour
- uniqueness
- hardship and danger
- horror

"News is what someone, somewhere wants to suppress – everything else is advertising". Anon

7. Donor Development

A committed donor is your most important resource – but the cost of recruiting new donors is very high. If you send a letter to names from a telephone directory, maybe one in a thousand will reply. The same letter to your most committed donors might get a 50 or 60% response.

The McGraw Hill Loyalty Ladder

This marketing theory applies equally well to fundraising. It suggests that every organisation has five levels of customer or donor as follows.

The McGraw Hill Loyalty Ladder	
Advocates	**Advocates:** people who are so supportive they not only give, but also promote the cause on your behalf
Clients	**Clients:** long standing donors or purchasers who give in a variety of different ways
Customers	**Customers:** customers or donors (first time)
Prospects	**Prospects:** have expressed interest or requested information but not yet given
Suspects	**Suspects:** are members of a targeted group, e.g. they support a similar charity, read related magazines or live in a target area

Whilst it is impossible to predict response rates to any request for funds, the theory suggests that each level of the ladder is likely to respond three times better than the level below. The same mailing sent to X people at each level might produce:

- 1 response from suspects
- 3 responses from prospects
- 9 responses from customers
- 27 responses from clients
- 81 responses from advocates

'Advocates' and 'clients' at the top of the ladder will have a warm personal commitment – they will refer to you as "my charity" and must be treated as personal friends. These committed supporters expect acknowledgement, appreciation and recognition and will often be offended by standard mailings, gifts or incentives. The less committed 'suspects' and 'prospects' will be more influenced by offers, copywriting, graphics, premiums and incentives.

Treat With Care

First time supporters/customers are a special group who require individual treatment. They often feel that their gift is the initiation of a relationship. This makes them feel good about themselves. Cement the relationship with personal thanks and information (not a further request for money).

"as far as we can tell, this is your first gift and this makes you very special to us..." UNICEF

Talk to the Donor/Customer as a Friend

Become a "my" rather than a "the" organisation. Avoid formal letters and communications. It is more effective to use warm and friendly language in cards or notes. Talk to people as if you know them well.

Make it Easy to Respond

Today's donor/customer has a surfeit of choice. They will not take the trouble to look for your address if it is not immediately apparent. They will give up and try someone else if you do not answer the phone. They will lose interest if you do not accept credit cards, or their other favoured method of payment.

Maintain the Relationship

Learn everything you can about the donor and ask them what they want from you. People who described an organisation's customer relationships as "excellent" were likely to renew at the rate of 95% – those who described it as "good" renewed at 65% *(Judith Nichols on US charities at ICFM Conference)*.

Beware the Tip of the Iceberg

A high street retailer conducted a survey which suggested that for every customer who complains, a further 48 are left with a bad impression of the company. Only one in seven actually voices the complaint, but all seven go away dissatisfied and tell on average seven other members of their family or friends – the company has lost control of the process and suffers accordingly.

Donor Development Case Studies

Research by Burnett Associates 1993 showed that charities did not have the fast and efficient mechanisms for responding to legacy queries which they thought they had. The largest 50 charities were mailed with a letter suggesting that the writer was elderly and would make a good legacy prospect:

- *Six of the 50 did not acknowledge the letter.*
- *Of the 44 who replied, 21% took more than a month.*
- *Four got the name or personal details wrong.*
- *Three replies came from charities not written to!*

Lucky 13:

Following his research, Ken Burnett made 10 recommendations and The Antony Baxter Partnership have added a further three. You should aim to:

1. *be committed, believe totally in customer service*
2. *be properly resourced, with adequate staff and proper promotional materials*
3. *be consistent*
4. *be quick*
5. *be appropriate – look for clues in the correspondence you receive*
6. *be personal – use your database to achieve this*
7. *be known – advertise, give names and faces for people to relate to*
8. *be meticulous*
9. *be there when needed – often the biggest responses come between 6pm and 9pm – your customer service department should ideally be available until then*

10. *be open and honest – admit mistakes and be absolutely "up front"*
11. *look after your committed donors, make friends with them and become a "my" organisation*
12. *concentrate your resources where they will have most effect*
13. *don't imagine that because no-one complains everyone is happy*

The Five "I"s

The loyalty ladder is particularly relevant where the bulk of communication is by mail. An alternative or supplementary technique used widely in America for personal contact can be adapted for use in events, major gift and public fundraising.

Every person with whom the fundraiser has personal contact, and who might eventually give money to the organisation goes through a process called 'the Five "I"s'. It is the goal of the fundraising staff to lead donor prospects through these five stages of interest.

Identified: first the constituent is identified as a donor prospect. A board member might identify a local business, a volunteer might identify a neighbour, or the person might identify themselves by requesting information.

Informed: once identified as a prospect, the individual is fully informed of the organisation's distinctiveness and its need for funds.

Interested: once informed, prospects are then helped to decide that the project is important to them. When the prospect begins to react to the information he or she has received – asking questions, making comments, offering suggestions – it is clear that they are ready to become involved with the organisation.

Involved: interested prospects are invited to take some action in support of the institution. By attending a meeting or hosting a social gathering, the prospect signals that he or she is personally committed to the goal of the fundraising programme.

Invested: after the prospect's commitment is clear, then – and only then – can they be expected to contribute financially to the limit of their potential and interest.

"In the Pink"

The prospect grid which follows can be used to record each donor's level of interest and giving potential. The vertical axis shows an estimated giving capacity. The horizontal axis represents the level of interest or involvement in the organisation

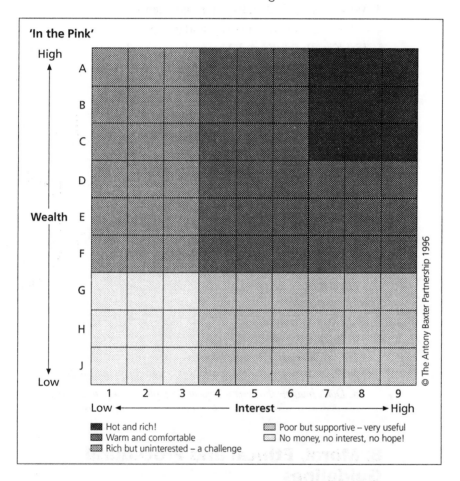

This is a fundraiser's version of an old sales technique known as 'in the pink'. Every donor or prospect you meet should be given a grid reference depending on their estimated giving capacity and their level of interest. A stockbroker with a Rolls who gives a large gift and attends events is a hot prospect and might be an A8 or B8. A suburban widow who gives regularly might be around E6. An unemployed student who regularly volunteers could be in the H7 or H8 area. Obviously you can't do a lot about people's income, but the aim should be to push people across the grid from pink to red by devising strategies to increase their involvement and interest.

Quiz

Questions

1. What is your most important resource?
2. Which group of people will respond best to your marketing?
3. What will motivate advocates and clients?
4. What will motivate suspects and prospects?
5. List Ken Burnett's and Antony Baxter's 13 recommendations

Answers

1. A committed donor

2. Advocates and clients

3. Personal acknowledgement, appreciation, recognition

4. Offer, graphics incentives

5. 1. Be committed

   2. Be properly resourced

   3. Be consistent

   4. Be quick

   5. Be appropriate

   6. Be personal

   7. Be known

   8. Be meticulous

   9. Be there when needed

   10. Be open and honest

   11. Look after your committed donors

   12. Concentrate your resources where they will have most effect

   13. Don't imagine that because no-one complains everyone is happy

8. Moral, Ethical and Procedural Guidelines

To achieve success a fundraiser needs the freedom to work with the minimum of supervision. To enable this to happen, 'no go' areas should be clearly defined, then the fundraiser allowed to work freely within the defined parameters. The Health Education Authority issues a series of guidelines as do the ICFM and other professional bodies. Reference should also be made to the Charities Act 1992, and the Data Protection Act.

Possible areas for inclusion in a moral, ethical and procedural policy

- organisations with whom a fundraising association is prohibited

(examples might be tobacco manufacturers, infant food stuff manufacturers etc.)

- organisations where special guidelines would apply (e.g. reference to a medical advisory panel)
- protection of copyright and exploitation of a charity's name and logo
- fundraising and public affairs codes of practice
- confidentiality and data protection
- misappropriation of funds
- standards of business conduct, gifts and hospitality, declaration of interest, relationships with contractors/suppliers, commercial ownership.

9. The Mouse Bites Back!

Gone are the days when all a fundraiser needed was a posh party and an address book. A sophisticated computerised database is almost certainly the most powerful weapon in today's fundraising armoury. You can still raise useful income through collections and events, but to access the big money there is no substitute for meticulous records and a planned strategy. With today's high powered computers and technical expertise this should be easy but after 15 years voluntary sector experience, I see just as many charities in total disarray because of computer problems: here are some do's and don'ts.

Do...

- decide in advance what you want the database to do – be sensible and create a list of essentials like name, address, phone, age, donation history, particular interests etc.
- have 'flags' which can identify and pick out or exclude sections of the database
- keep your demands simple and wherever possible buy a tried and tested package off the shelf
- keep proper back ups and security. Protect your data from unauthorised personnel
- 'clean' your data regularly and keep all data under your control
- personalise your mailings and make them relevant – use the power of computing to build a targeted list of people who are likely to respond to you.

Don't...

- allow an accountant or an administrator to plan your marketing database and don't demand everything you can think of like colour of eyes and date of last visit to Marks and Spencer. This information will never be used and will cost a fortune to design and maintain

- mail out "dear friend" letters to warm personal contacts and don't send specialist gardening info to people living in small London flats
- risk sending mailings to people who have specifically asked not to be mailed, or worse, people who have been notified as dead
- try to design a system from scratch however unique you imagine your needs – this can take years and thousands or even millions of pounds and rarely ever works satisfactorily
- allow open access or rely solely on your hard disk – 10 years' work can be wiped out overnight
- risk lots of independent databases developing over which you have no control and which can upset people by duplication of approaches
- waste your time on mass 'fridges to Eskimos' mailings.

The choice of hardware and software must remain yours, but remember that databases are demanding on memory. However much memory you need now, it will double within a year. Most systems work perfectly well on a Windows/PC based system and Apple Mac users have plenty of choice as well. For small applications, simple commercial relational databases by Microsoft, Lotus and other manufacturers can cost as little as a hundred pounds and work perfectly well.

Middle range systems like Raisers Edge can handle a mass of relational information and perform complex tasks like the administration of covenants – they generally cost around ten thousand pounds. For top of the range systems and custom built systems, the sky is the limit. But think carefully – do you really need this level of sophistication, or will it just lie idle and frighten people away?

Whatever your choice, training, training and more training is needed if you are to make full use of your technology. Software manufacturers estimate that the average user utilises less than 20% of the features available in any package.

10. Data Protection Act

The purpose of the Data Protection Act is to protect information about individuals which is held on computers and/or word processors. It is the responsibility of all employees and volunteers to make themselves aware of the specific purposes for which personal data is processed by the organisation and for which the organisation is registered. Under the terms of the Act it is an offence to use the data for purposes other than those registered. Employees or volunteers who have access to personal data are responsible for ensuring that this is observed.

In addition the following principles must be observed:
a. the information to be contained in personal data shall be obtained and processed fairly and lawfully
b. personal data shall be held only for one or more specified lawful purposes
c. personal data held for any purpose/s shall not be disclosed in any manner incompatible with that purpose or those purposes
d. personal data held for any purpose/s shall be adequate, relevant and not excessive in relation to that purpose or those purposes
e. personal data shall be accurate and, where necessary, kept up to date
f. personal data held for any purpose/s shall not be kept for longer than is necessary for the purpose or those purposes.

An individual shall be entitled:
a. at reasonable intervals and without delay or expense:
   i) to be informed by any data user whether he holds individual data of which the individual is subject;
   ii) to access any such data held by the data user
b. and where appropriate to have such data corrected or erased.

Appropriate security measures shall be taken against unauthorised access, alteration, disclosure or destruction of personal data.

11. Charities Act

This is dealt with more fully in *Chapter 3, Charity Law.*

In relation to fundraising, the 1992 Charities Act introduces controls over fundraising and in particular introduces the concept that it is unlawful for a professional fundraiser to solicit money for the benefit of a charity without an agreement with that charity. The Act defines a business/professional fundraiser as a business or individual, carrying on a business for gain, primarily engaged in procuring money for charitable purposes or soliciting money for property or reward.

The Act defines a commercial participator as someone who carries out for gain, a business which engages in promotional ventures suggesting that charitable contributions will be given to charity or applied for charitable, benevolent or philanthropic purposes.

In broad terms, the Act requires a fundraising business/ professional fundraiser or commercial participator to have an agreement in writing with the charity or charities represented; and to accompany each solicitation with a statement indicating the names of the institutions represented, the proportions in which each will benefit and the method of remuneration.

Professional fundraising is prohibited except by agreement with the charity concerned. It is the charity's responsibility to ensure that the agreement represents its best interests and agreements should only be signed by trustees or specifically authorised personnel.

Money (including cheques) acquired by the professional fundraiser or commercial participator should be paid gross to the charity (without deduction of fees or expenses) within 28 days of receipt.

The charity must include its full name, the words "registered charity" and preferably the charity number on all documentation which solicits money including letters, advertisements and raffle tickets.

All fundraisers should ensure that they understand the provisions of both Part II and Part III of the Act which regulates public charitable collections. The Directory of Social Change publishes a number of books on the subject and information can also be obtained from the ICFM.

12. Recruitment

The four main sources of fundraisers are:
- internal recruitment or promotion
- personal contacts
- external recruitment
- out-sourcing.

Beware of the term 'general all round fundraiser'. The skills needed to manage a capital appeal are quite different from those involved in revenue fundraising. It is often better to employ several specialists on short term or part time contracts than one 'Jack of all trades and master of none'.

Internal Recruitment

Doing it yourself is often the cheapest and will motivate staff, provide career paths and cut down on induction times.

Networking and Personal Contacts

Appointing someone you know is acceptable providing rigorous selection processes are used. Trying someone out on a temporary contract is common but beware of employing family or friends.

External Recruitment

Search and selection is cheaper if you do it yourself, but can be time consuming administratively and you may well make mistakes. Agencies use a variety of methods from Executive Search (head hunting) to advertising and selection or selection from a database. The cost is higher but choosing a reputable firm will save time and trouble and often produce a good outcome.

Out-Sourcing

The view that a small professional management team should buy in services rather than installing them in-house took root during the last decade. This has brought about a high growth in self employment and short term contracts.

Variously described as interim management, temporary executives or fundraising consultancy, this option may be appropriate when the problem cannot easily be managed in-house, or it is not feasible or political to recruit full time staff, or there is a gap between the leaving of one staff member and the starting of the next, or you need an input of a limited duration.

About the author

Antony Baxter is senior partner with the Antony Baxter Partnership, chief executive of Sandcliff AB Ltd, managing director of Fundraising Appointments Ltd and a director of Centrepoint Trading. He is a member of the Association of Chief Executives of National Voluntary Organisations and has held senior positions in national charities for 15 years.

CAMPAIGNING

2

Simon Hebditch

1. Introduction

Aims and objectives

This chapter is designed to enable students to learn about charities and the rights and wrongs of their campaigning activities. Over recent years it has been a matter of much controversy that charities campaign for the causes with which they are concerned. Some believe that voluntary bodies should just provide services to help the disadvantaged directly and that they shouldn't participate in the 'political debate' about the possible causes of distress and deprivation. Others have argued that charities have a responsibility to raise issues of concern and promote their views to Parliament and the public.

This chapter will enable the reader to:
- understand charity law in relation to campaigning
- learn about the different techniques that can be used to promote a successful campaign
- appreciate the different procedures of Parliament and government which can be employed to further a particular cause
- understand the need to win public support for changes in policy and practice – sometimes in difficult circumstances.
- learn about the importance of different publicity tools for pursuing a campaign – annual reports and general meetings, contacts with the press, video, the Internet.

Deciding whether to be a Charity

People come together to form 'associations' because they believe strongly in particular causes or needs. Such associations can either be geared towards providing services for those in need or campaigning for changes in law or social attitudes (or both).

Many of our principal charities try to combine both a service provision function and a campaigning role although this can sometimes be difficult to achieve. Such associations may wish to choose whether to become charities or remain voluntary organisations subject only to the common law. If you decide to apply for charitable status, certain benefits accrue. You can:

- show those who give you money that you are respectable and recognised by referring to your charity registration
- receive certain tax relief benefits that will undoubtedly help your financial position
- call upon the advice of the Charity Commission, which oversees the charity world, when considering all sorts of management and financial issues within your organisation. The Charity Commission is both the policeman and the counsellor of the sector – a difficult dual task to perform.

However, one of the possible disadvantages of charitable status is that you must abide by the guidance of the Charity Commission as to the legitimacy of any campaigning activity. A number of prominent organisations within the voluntary sector have therefore chosen not to be charities so that they can act with total freedom as long as they stay within the normal limits of the law. For example:

Amnesty International – a well known organisation dedicated to working for the release of 'Prisoners of Conscience' throughout the world – a task which means they must act without fear or favour and so often come into open conflict with national governments.

In this chapter we are referring to the issues facing charities when contemplating campaigning activity rather than those organisations which have steered away from charitable status and the regulation of the Charity Commission.

2. The Right and Duty to Campaign

It can be argued that charities not only have the right to campaign, but a duty to do so. In a democracy you have a right to stand up and speak your mind whether individually or with others in a group or organisation. A few examples give a flavour of the breadth of causes that can give rise to campaigning activity from the purely local to the international scene:

- a local community protesting about the lack of pedestrian crossings near a school
- a group calling for better pre-school playgroup provision in their area
- those concerned with the environment taking action to try and stop the building of by-passes
- organisations demanding better provision for elderly people, especially given the growth in those living beyond 85 years

- many groups speaking up for the homeless and demanding action to help people find affordable homes
- those working with international aid organisations helping to cope with hunger and famine, and the results of political repression or discrimination.

It is important to be clear about the different sorts of organisations within the charitable world. These are:

1. organisations which restrict themselves to providing services and which would not see it as their function to campaign
2. groups which are fully dedicated to campaigning and which would not claim to offer direct services to specific people
3. charities which combine both approaches and often argue that each function strengthens the other rather than dilutes it.

Of course the target of such campaigning action feel might feel very differently about it. Many politicians try to dismiss the views of organisations which don't offer services on the grounds that they have no real experience of the issues they are raising. It is certainly true that ministers of the government, of any political party, may find it more difficult to dismiss the considered arguments of charities which can show that their concerns arise directly from the experience they have in working with people and communities in distress.

Such charities also need to consider whether they do not have an absolute duty to campaign in such cases. If you are witnessing social or economic conditions every day which create severe distress, surely you would be failing in your duty to society if you failed to raise those issues with the powers that be? It is not enough just to apply sticking plaster! You may well have to argue for change as well.

Let's look at two examples:

Case Study – Age Concern England

Age Concern England is a national charity working with elderly people both to ensure that there are a wide variety of appropriate services for them and that the interests of elderly people are recognised. The latter impulse and the evidence of poverty, loneliness or neglect sometimes emerging from the first set of activities leads ACE into being a campaigning body. ACE will, for example, campaign for:

- *good quality day care*
- *high standards in residential homes*

- *effective advice and information services for elderly people locally and nationally*
- *adequate basic pensions for all.*

Such campaigns can be directed at local authorities, owners of residential homes, the Departments of Health and Social Security nationally and even the Treasury when arguments are flowing on the incomes of elderly people.

The issues raised and promoted by such campaigning come directly from the experience of local Age Concern groups in running services and often discovering the inadequacy of state provision. It would be a disservice to elderly people themselves if Age Concern simply felt that it should provide services and not comment on the conditions in which many people have to live.

Case Study – MIND

MIND (National Association for Mental Health) is one of the principal providers of mental health services through its network of local associations. Again the bedrock of MIND's experience comes from the activities of its local groups and supporters. It is a campaigning organisation which has long argued for better treatment of mentally ill people both from the point of view of the law and also in terms of the provision of local services for an often 'unpopular' group of people.

It is also an example of an organisation which has its work cut out trying to influence the views and opinions of the general public as much as the commitment of government ministers and officials. It illustrates a cardinal principle of campaigning – you must strive to change public opinion, not just the current views of local authorities and national government. MIND campaigns will be mounted on:

- *the treatment of patients in mental hospitals*
- *the desirability of discharging people from hospital who no longer need to be there*
- *development of community care facilities for people with mental illness*
- *the provision of a range of different forms of housing and care locally which are designed to ensure that all those in need have the right care at the right time in the right place.*

These examples demonstrate the challenge of campaigning to influence national government, local authorities and the general public. Campaigning is perfectly legitimate whoever you are and whatever your cause (as long as you don't break the law). You may well witness campaigns being undertaken against some of those outlined above. Hence the central importance of public opinion. You can imagine the difficulties often experienced by an organisation like MIND when it is proposed to open a hostel locally for people recently discharged from a mental hospital.

Exercise

Why not try it out for yourself? Draw up a list of arguments in favour of opening a hostel near where you live and then write down the disadvantages. Then see what your neighbours think. If you feel confident enough, you could test out these differing arguments on at least five different households where you live and find out the state of current public opinion.

3. Political Activities and Charities

Can you try to change policy?

Campaigning activity is often directed towards trying to obtain a change of policy at local or national level. If you are concerned with the size of the old age pension or the treatment of mentally ill people in hospital, you may well direct your efforts towards trying to shift the current policies of government – maybe criticising a White Paper which sets out government plans for a particular area of concern, or trying to get amendments to government legislation.

If you are trying to change policy, you are inevitably involved in the political process. One of the common misconceptions is that charities must 'not be political'. How can you not be political if you are trying to change policy?

It is absolutely true that charities must not be *party* political in that you must not ally yourself with any political party to the detriment of others. It is also important to make a distinction between political purposes and political activities. The Charity Commission has responsibility for defining the rules concerning campaigning activity – what is permissible and what is not.

Note: It is clearly not possible for a charity to be established for a political purpose, but any charity can participate in political activities if they are necessary for the achievement of its charitable purposes.

Defining political activity

Let the Charity Commission speak for itself on these difficult areas of definition: *"Charities must not be political organisations. But they are not precluded from all political activity. A distinction must be made between political purposes and political activities. The Courts have made it clear that a body whose stated purpose include the attainment of a political purpose cannot be charitable...*

"A body whose purposes are charitable... may nevertheless engage in activities which are directed at securing, or opposing, changes in the law or in government policy or decisions, whether in this country or abroad." (Political Activities and Campaigning by Charities. CC9, 1995.)

But what does this mean? Elsewhere, the Charity Commission defines political purpose and political activity. They conclude that:

"Political purpose in essence means any purpose directed at:- furthering the interests of any political party; securing, or opposing, any change in the law or in the policy or decisions of central government or local authorities whether in this country or abroad.

"Political activity means any activity which is directed at securing, or opposing, any change in the law or in the policy or decisions of central government or local authorities, whether in this country or abroad." (ibid)

It will already be apparent to you that there is some contradiction between the bald statement above that charities cannot be established for political purposes and the subsequent definitions. The safest course to take is to ensure that your charity is not furthering the interests of any particular political party.

It is perfectly possible for you to support arguments which lead to a particular policy solution for a problem or issue you have identified and it doesn't matter if a political party also happens to support the same conclusion – the rule of thumb in that case is to make clear that you are independent and have arrived at your conclusions independently of any political party.

Campaigning and Elections

Any general election poses a potential problem for charities. You must be extremely careful to ensure that any lobbying activity you engage in during a general election campaign cannot be interpreted as giving support to a particular political party. Many charities ensure that they don't undertake any such activity during the formal general election (usually a three or four week period up to polling day).

Again, current Charity Commission guidance on elections is useful:

"A charity may respond to forthcoming elections, whether local, national or to the European Parliament by analysing and commenting on the proposals of political parties which relate to its purposes or the way in which it is able to carry out its work, provided that it comments in a way which is consistent with these guidelines and complies with all the relevant provisions of electoral law.

"A charity may also bring to the attention of prospective candidates issues relating to its purposes or the way in which it is able to carry out its work, and raise public awareness about them generally, provided that the promotional material is educational, informative, reasoned and well founded.

"A charity must not seek to persuade members of the public to vote for or against a candidate or for or against a political party." (ibid)

Campaigning Must be Reasonable

Campaigners are obviously trying to change people's opinions and bring about specific changes in either law or practice. During the period when the Charity Commission guidance on political activities and campaigning was being developed, there was much argument about the legitimacy of charities trying to raise the emotional temperature on particular issues.

There was some concern that charities might whip up unnecessary or unhelpful emotion or seek to engage the public in supporting a particular cause, possibly inundating Members of Parliament with letters and petitions. But there has been some rethinking within the Charity Commission which was reflected in the guidance document:

"Provided all other requirements are met, material produced in support of a campaign may have emotional content. Indeed, the Commission accepts that in areas in which many charities work it is difficult engaging the emotions of the public. But it would be unacceptable (except where the nature of the medium makes it impracticable to set out the basis of the charity's position) for a charity to seek to persuade government or the public on the basis of material which was merely emotional." (ibid)

In other words, to remain within the law, your case must be based on well founded and well reasoned evidence, as well as emotional appeal, and expressed with a proper sense of proportion.

Most important of all, your campaigning must be relevant to your own work. That may sound obvious but 'political' comment on some issues may be interpreted by the Charity Commission or the courts as outside the concerns of your charity. Some charities have had to undergo intensive investigation by the Charity Commission, often following complaints by members of the public, about the legitimacy or otherwise of their campaigning activity and the suitability of their campaign material.

Case Study – Oxfam

Oxfam is a well-known international charity concerned with the relief of poverty, one of the fundamental charitable purposes. Some years ago the agency was working in Soweto, South Africa and in part of their literature took a position on apartheid as a governmental, economic and social system.

Oxfam felt that much of the poverty, disadvantage and deprivation they were addressing were attributable to the effects of apartheid – and they said so. A few members of the public complained that it was not part of Oxfam's charitable purposes to publicly express their views about the government of another country.

The Charity Commission rapped Oxfam's knuckles on some aspects of their campaign material but no formal action was taken against trustees of the charity. Put simply, the argument from Oxfam was that its campaign and material presented information about the apartheid system as it impacted on the people with whom the agency works. The contrary view would be that no charity has the right to pronounce on the governmental structures and policies of another country. In reality, of course, Oxfam would not have been able to operate effectively in South Africa without having a view about the apartheid system.

Interestingly, Oxfam also got into trouble over Cambodia when they were seen to be criticising one of its former leaders, Pol Pot, – criticisms which would have been shared by most of the civilised world.

Oxfam obtained a satisfactory result at the end of the day but the process of investigation is both time consuming and stressful for staff and trustees alike, the latter being finally responsible for ensuring that their charity behaves reasonably and within the confines of the law.

In evidence to the Charity Commission, the National Council for Voluntary Organisations (NCVO) said:

"Charities need to be sure when unfounded complaints are made against them that the Charity Commission will defend their campaigning robustly. Investigations, however informal, have a cost that ties up resources and inhibits campaigning. Lawful campaigning should not be impeded by unwarranted complaints. Charities should be fully informed of the substance and source of

complaints against them. Where investigations are warranted they should be initiated promptly and decisions made speedily so that charities' work is not frustrated by vexatious complaints. Once decisions are made, and charities found to have acted properly, the Commission should uphold and defend their continuing right to campaign."

Campaigning and Parliament

Parliament is naturally a regular target for a wide range of campaigns both by charities and other organisations. If you are trying to change government policy or influence other political parties you will want to direct some of your campaign material towards Members of Parliament and government officials. The strategies needed will be different depending on your target. You need to decide whether you are going to focus on government ministers or officials or other members of parliament.

If you are launching a campaign geared towards government be clear about the specific department you wish to approach and which minister in it has responsibility for your issue. As with all campaigning there are a number of dilemmas as to the best tactics to follow.

Case Study

Let's consider Parliament from the point of view of a charity operating in Newbury, Berkshire wishing to campaign against the bypass being constructed. Given that campaigning can be a long and wearisome business, what do you do?

a) Make sure that you have started early enough to try and influence the decision makers. Road plans can take years to get to fruition and you will need to ensure that you have a say at the relevant public enquiries and that you also track what all others are saying in their evidence.

b) Ensure that your case is well argued and that the research stands up to objective and hostile analysis. In this case, you must show that you have understood the case being argued for the bypass and that you can refute it on environmental, economic and traffic grounds.

c) Identify that the following departments would have a direct interest – Department of the Environment and the Department of Transport. But don't ignore the possibility that other departments might be persuaded to take up your case or at the least ask awkward questions of their colleagues in the Environment and Transport ministries.

Who to approach

There are specialist units it is very useful to approach with your views:

1. the Voluntary and Community Division (VCD) based at the Department of National Heritage
2. the Policy Unit at 10 Downing Street.

The Voluntary and Community Division has the responsibility within government for overseeing the general interests of the voluntary sector and ensuring that there is sufficient co-ordination between government departments concerning their own relationships with charities and voluntary organisations coming within their areas of interest. The VCD, therefore, has the ability to contact officials within the environment and transport departments to reflect the views they have received from charities.

Don't be put off by anyone saying – "Sorry, that's nothing to do with us. It's a matter for Environment or Transport". The VCD responsibility is to foster co-operation across Whitehall and oil the wheels of partnership between government and the voluntary sector.

There is also a junior ministerial committee, the Ministerial Group on the Voluntary Sector, which meets periodically to look at general issues across government affecting voluntary organisations and the services they offer. This committee is organised by the Department of National Heritage.

Equally, the 10 Downing Street Policy Unit might argue that it doesn't interfere in departmental priorities but it does have the job of keeping all government policy initiatives under review and it has a member who retains responsibility for the development of voluntary action and volunteering.

It is wise to try and engage senior department officials before approaching ministers for discussions. Going back to our example, you should ensure that you lobby the appropriate officials in all the relevant departments. There is a danger that you may be fobbed off or simply ignored.

At the right time you may then wish to write direct to the appropriate ministers either giving your views or seeking a meeting to discuss the proposed bypass. It is sometimes worth writing to the senior minister, the Secretary of State in the relevant department, so that he or she knows about it even if they delegate any meeting or response to one of their junior colleagues.

Summary

To sum up where we have got to so far. You should:

- research the full impact of the bypass and write a powerful case
- lobby senior officials in the principal departments of state, environment and transport
- keep the VCD and 10 Downing Street Policy Unit informed and ask them to convey their views to the principal departments
- write to the relevant Secretary of State and ask for a meeting to discuss the impact of the bypass.

Your own MP

It is also necessary to keep your own Member of Parliament informed, and try to influence his opinion. So you will also meet her/him either at the House of Commons or the local 'surgery' where they meet people from the constituency.

In general, MPs do respond to their post bag. They can assess the depth of feeling about any issue from the number of letters they receive. Therefore, you should organise a letter-writing campaign directed towards MPs, but the impact is much more powerful if members of the public write their own letters rather than simply sign up to a text which you have drafted.

Although no MP will ever admit to 'binning' letters from the public they are certainly tempted to do so if they receive sackfuls of identical letters. By all means provide all the relevant information to those willing to write, but then encourage them to write their own versions.

Of course, there will be some people who may well wish to support you but who can't write their own letters – in which case do it for them but explain that fact to the MP in a covering note.

How else can Parliament be used?

Now that you are building up your campaign around the bypass, Parliament can provide a number of avenues for promoting the cause:

You can ask MPs to table both written and oral questions to ministers about the bypass. Written questions can be submitted at any point during a Parliamentary session but there are set days for oral questions to be answered by particular ministers.

MPs have to apply to put oral questions so you need to know the dates for such questions, identify a supportive MP, draft a question with her/him and get it submitted – then hope s/he is successful in being able to put the question.

You can ask an MP to table an Early Day Motion, which is a device for MPs expressing views on any issue in the form of a resolution which is printed in Hansard, the official record of parliamentary proceedings, and which can be signed up to by other MPs. So you could draft a motion on the proposed by-pass, interest an individual MP in it, help her/him obtain three or four other signatories to get it started, have it tabled, printed in Hansard and then lobby other MPs to sign up to it. Such a device enables campaigners to show that a particular cause has from 20 to 200 supporters in the House of Commons.

You could approach the chair of both the Select Committees covering the environment and transport. These committees could decide to hold hearings into the bypass, call for written evidence and invite people to give oral evidence to them. Also, most importantly, they can require senior officials or ministers to attend and answer their questions. The Select Committee will then publish its report and recommendations. Of course, you have to risk the possibility that they might not agree with your case.

You could ask a sympathetic MP to table a Ten Minute Bill or apply to take part in the periodic adjournment debates. In the first case, an MP can apply to introduce a bill on any subject and gets the opportunity to speak to it for ten minutes near the beginning of a day's business. Again, it is purely a device to raise an issue. Nothing further happens about such a bill once the ten minute speech has been made. But it is another opportunity for promotion and publicity. An adjournment debate occurs at the end of each parliamentary session and again it is a period of time devoted to a topic of interest from an individual MP. Generally, an MP can speak for 30 minutes and a minister will be deputed to respond.

Finally, you could try the route of the Private Member's Bill. At the start of each annual parliament, usually in November each year, there is a ballot for a limited number of opportunities for individual MPs to introduce their own bills which do have the potential of going on to become legislation if enough support can be won. Potential bills have to be prepared carefully and you will have to enthuse an MP with your cause when many others will be attempting to do the same.

4. Campaigning in Coalitions

Working together with other organisations of like mind is often sensible and helps to convince those receiving representations that there is a wide body of support for a particular policy change. Let's take an example.

In 1988 a group of charities working in the field of health and community care came together to work for major changes in the delivery of community care policies and services. Eventually the group became Community Care Alliance of Voluntary Organisations hosted for many years by NCVO. Over 150 voluntary organisations joined this coalition and campaigned together on community care legislation being piloted in the early 1990's by Virginia Bottomley MP, at that stage Secretary of State for Health. Joint policy documents were adopted, delegations organised to see both officials and ministers, and lobbying material provided for MPs and local authorities.

Of course, there can be dangers in working with other organisations – especially coalitions which have a broad membership. How do you ensure that the campaigning work done by any part of the alliance conforms to charity law?

The Charity Commission provides advice on this point:

"A charity may affiliate to a campaigning alliance, even if the alliance includes non-charitable organisations, provided certain conditions are met. First, the charity must carefully consider the alliance's activities, and the implications of the charity's being associated with them, and should only affiliate if affiliation can reasonably be expected to further the charity's own charitable purposes.

"Second, since a charity may not undertake through an alliance activities which it would be improper for it to undertake directly, if the alliance engages in such activities the charity must dissociate itself from them and take reasonable steps to ensure that its name, and any funds it has contributed, are not used to support them." (Political Activities and Campaigning by Charities. CC9, 1995)

In other words: be careful who you are associating with; ensure that you have clear knowledge of the alliance's strategy, tactics and activities; and make sure that they all conform ideally within the limits of charity law but, if there are activities which cannot be defended from that point of view, disassociate yourself from them and insist that any campaign funds you make available only goes on political activities with which the Charity Commission would be comfortable.

5. The Powers of The Charity Commission

It may be useful at this stage to be clear what penalties the Charity Commission can impose if your activities are seen by it to be unlawful as far as charity law is concerned. The point is that if a charity is pursuing some illegitimate political activities, and presumably spending money on them, it would be mis-using those funds and the trustees of the charity would be liable. The Charity Commission states:

"The pursuit of improper political activities by charities is a misuse of charity funds and can lead to the loss of tax reliefs on funds applied for that purpose. It may also be regarded as amounting to the use of a charity as a vehicle for the personal views of its trustees. It can therefore bring about a loss of support for the charity and damage the good name of charities generally.

"...In the absence of a satisfactory explanation a range of possibilities arise, including simply giving advice to the trustees, taking proceedings against them for repayment of the funds applied on the activities in question (including any additional tax liability incurred as a result) and restricting future political activity." (ibid)

Naturally, you should take the above warnings seriously without being emasculated by them. The overall guidance provided by the Charity Commission is helpful and liberal in intention. The vast majority of organisations would be able to conduct their campaigns effectively with no risk of stepping beyond the bounds of acceptable behaviour. Details of the Commission's guidance is included in the list of additional materials.

Charities must have the confidence to campaign for what they believe in and to promote the interests of the people with whom they work or for whom they care.

6. Promoting Your Charity

People often forget that there are many ways of promoting your charity and the issues and causes on which you campaign. There are tools you have already and there may be the possibility of experimenting with new ways in which to get your message across. These methods include:

- exploiting your annual report and developing your public relations
- use of newspapers, radio and television
- videos and the Internet.

The Charity and Public Relations

Public relations is often regarded as a rather murky business. Why should you need to use public relations techniques when your charity is obviously doing a lot of good work with which people could not disagree?

Unfortunately, life is not as simple as that. One of the facts of life is that "the general public" remains amazingly ignorant of large segments of national or local life unless specific efforts are made to get through to them. One easy way to check that statement is to undertake a little market research exercise in your own area designed to find out:

a) how many people have heard of your organisation

b) what they think it does.

You may be somewhat depressed by the results.

'Public opinion' is often not sympathetic to your cause and you need to take specific action to try and educate people about your activities. One of the most difficult areas to tackle is that referred to earlier – the provision of a hostel for mentally ill people in the community.

Example

You are the organiser of Little Puddleduck Mental Health Association and as a result of extensive local research, your organisation is convinced that a number of people with mental illness who are currently living in Greater Puddleduck Mental Hospital should be able to live in a hostel in the community.

With the help of your local social services department and the local authority's housing section, you have identified an initial group of six men from the hospital who could live in a hostel. You have also found the building to be used – an empty property owned by the local authority and is part of a small council estate on the edge of Little Puddleduck.

What steps do you take? Being committed to the interests of the local community, you:

- prepare a leaflet and put it round the estate
- hold two consultation meetings in the estate's community centre.

You explain the needs of the men to be discharged from the hospital. You show how they will not pose a threat to the community. You illustrate how the estate could take a pride in absorbing people into their midst whom it is often difficult to house.

The first consultation meeting goes well – you feel relatively positive. But the results of the questionnaire are negative and by the time of the second consultation a head of steam has developed, with more people opposing the plan than supporting. What do you do next?

a) First, remember that your initial meeting may have been attended by a majority of local community activists. They are more likely to support you and cannot necessarily be relied upon to reflect the real views of the area!

b) Second, changing public opinion or prejudices is a long term business. Don't assume that what is obvious to you is sensible to everybody else. It is necessary to have a long term plan designed to ensure that you have enough public support to continue with the project. That means using all the public relations methods at your disposal:

(i) building on your own supporters and showing that you are a respectable charity with a clear purpose

(ii) cultivating local journalists not just for the news stories, but to encourage feature articles on 'mental illness and homelessness' and the unsuitable nature of the local mental hospital

(iii) working with other organisations to encourage the production of a newsletter for the estate which, amongst a wide range of issues, will regularly feature mental health matters and the needs of people in the area.

Exploiting the Annual Report

Annual reports can be used effectively as a tool for promoting your message. The requirement for an annual report often seems somewhat onerous and people then proceed to review their year's activities in a mundane and ritualistic way. But you could regard the publication of an annual report as an opportunity to put forward your main message to a wider audience. If you are a campaigning organisation, list your principal activities and show clearly what your priorities have been. What do such reports normally contain?

1. a statement by the trustees of your charity about the main activities you have been pursuing

2. lists of your trustees, members of staff, membership of any committees

3. the annual accounts showing your income and expenditure and balance sheet for the year in question.

The annual general meeting, at which the annual report is formally published, is often seen as a rather boring, staid occasion at which the requirements of the constitution are followed rather than being used as an opportunity to speak publicly about the issues that concern you most.

Annual general meetings are usually attended by important personalities and it is only sensible to use the time effectively. Therefore, see your annual report as a campaigning tool which can be launched publicly at an annual general meeting, when you may well be able to influence people who have a role in the local community. Make sure you invite:

- your local Member of Parliament
- the Director of Social Services of your local authority or other appropriate head of department
- the Chief Executive of your local authority
- the Chief Executive of your local health authority and Training and Enterprise Council (if applicable)
- representatives of local chambers of commerce or other business networks
- all your own members, users and beneficiaries.

Although an annual report is supposed to be a look back at your previous activities, there is no reason why you shouldn't have a section setting out your campaigning plans for the ensuing twelve months. A feature on 'Looking to the Future' may well produce good copy for your local newspapers, radio and television.

Using the Media

When we talk about the media most of us traditionally think of newspapers, radio and television. But there are plenty of opportunities for using different media now and in the future to ensure that information is transmitted about your campaign objectives. Video, CD-ROMS and the Internet provide increasing opportunities for people to find out about your aims and objectives.

Newspapers remain of vital importance especially at a local level. If you are a local organisation trying to affect public opinion, you must ensure that your local newspapers (including the free newspapers operating in some areas) receive your material regularly.

Don't be put off if press releases appear to be ignored sometimes. Persistence pays off and local newspapers and radio stations are often fairly desperate for news and information stories. So you should:

- provide regular press releases
- invite journalists to meetings and events
- establish a social relationship with local journalists so that you can confidently call on them to report your campaigns
- consider advertising sometimes.

It is just as important to cultivate local radio stations. National bodies can do this by making one tape recording of their 'story' and syndicating it round a range of local radio and television stations. A lot of them will use such a tape as it is an easy way for them to present a news story – with no effort having been expended by themselves.

Once again, local radio stations are always on the lookout for news stories. This would be in stark contrast to BBC Radio 4's 'Today' programme, for example, which is inundated with stories and where the opportunities to appear on it are few and far between.

Don't forget regional television. You should ensure that both the news teams and the forward planning staff at regional TV stations are kept informed of your activities as it may be possible to find a suitable 'regional' angle from time to time.

Video and the Internet

For some time it has been possible for charities to produce their own videos (assuming they could afford to do so) and use them for both promoting their own campaign messages and for training purposes. The main advantage of this approach is that the material and the message remain under your control – you are not dependent on how a journalist interprets your story. But the costs of producing videos can be prohibitive and so it is sensible to either try and find a sponsor – a company or trust which will pay for the video production and distribution – or try and put together a consortium of groups with similar interests who can thereby share the costs.

Example

There is much current controversy concerning refugees and asylum seekers entering this country. It would be possible to produce a video illustrating:
- the individual stories of political refugees
- their experiences in their home countries
- problems experienced when they arrived in this country
- the arguments for and against supporting such refugees.

Because the video would contain individual stories and be about real people, it would be likely to have a strong impact. Various refugee organisations could get together to either fund such a video themselves or approach a private company or charitable foundation to help.

The latest addition to the media that can be used both for information and promotion is the Internet – especially the World Wide Web. Information can be distributed quickly and effectively around the world via the Internet and will be of significant help to organisations such as the Refugee Council or Amnesty International in promoting the interests of the people with whom they work.

Of course, few organisations are geared up yet to use the Internet effectively to pursue their work but over the next few years this will change dramatically and news, information, publications, fundraising etc. will probably take place to a very significant extent through this medium.

Don't forget that the Internet can be used not only as another outlet for your own information but as a way of obtaining it from others so that your own campaign can be enhanced and supported. Organisations and individuals can be put together through the Internet and they can learn from each other's activities.

The Internet can also be useful for searching for funding to help support your campaigns. Find out which companies and trusts are putting information on the system setting out their criteria and policies. Assess whether they can be helpful to you and, once you are linked up to the system through your own computer, the world is your oyster. Charitynet is the Internet site of the Charities Aid Foundation (caf.charitynet.org).

7. Conclusions

What can we conclude from this exploration of campaigning?

First, many charities and voluntary organisations campaign in some way to try and achieve their objectives. Some are geared principally towards campaigning but they will probably have to decide not to be charities as such. The example of Amnesty International is a case in point.

The Charity Commission, which regulates charitable activity, believes that campaigning cannot be the principal activity of your charity – only a secondary and less important function in comparison to the services you are offering. If you wish to concentrate on campaigning then you should set up as a voluntary organisation or network and not seek charitable status.

Second, a charity can campaign as long as the case it is making is reasonable, based on research and analysis and is not too emotionally put. A charity can also:

- lobby Members of Parliament
- organise letter writing campaigns to MPs, local councillors, health authority members etc.
- seek to influence candidates in general elections and local elections so that they support the charity's aims.

As long as:

- the campaign is conducted fairly and reasonably – you do not call for support to be given to a particular political party simply because they have adopted your point of view
- it is not the main focus of your activities or services – any campaigns must be ancillary to your main purpose.

Third, any campaigning body should use all the available mechanisms to influence those in power or authority. For example:

- to influence MPs, remember to make use of the procedures of Parliament – oral and written questions, early day motions, ten minute rule bills, adjournment debates, Private Member's Bills
- if campaigns are directed towards local authorities or health authorities, find out what opportunities exist for addressing particular committees or the authority meetings as a whole
- make full use of newspapers, local radio and television to get your message across
- don't forget that the annual reports of charities, conferences, workshops and general publications can all be used to spread the word.

Finally, organisations working with or for people in need not only have the *right* to campaign but also the *duty* to do so. If you are involved in a charity working with homeless people, for example, you have the duty both to provide practical help and assistance (attempting to find suitable housing and caring for the homeless wherever they are attempting to survive), and to campaign on their behalf to try and change the policies or circumstances which may be causing homelessness.

Many organisations try to provide direct services and campaign at the same time for exactly that reason and this combination can also be attractive to the person on the receiving end of your campaign. If you were a government minister responsible for housing policy, for instance, you may be more likely to take notice of campaigners if they also have practical experience of trying to deliver direct services to homeless people.

This chapter will hopefully provide an opportunity for learning about campaigning activity and give the reader confidence to campaign reasonably and effectively. It is not meant to be in any way an exhaustive reader in campaigning. It provides a snapshot of the various issues those who wish to campaign must face, and suggests ways in which campaigns can be organised to increase their effectiveness. Most importantly, the chapter indicates what rules and regulations surround campaigning if a charity is involved and is, therefore, subject to Charity Commission rules.

Given this starting point, those wishing to enter the campaigning field should consult a Council for Voluntary Service in their area or similar co-ordinating body which has the job of providing advice and assistance to charities and voluntary organisations.

Quiz

Questions

1. Are charities able to campaign for changes in national or local policies?
2. Can charities support particular political parties which may be promoting the same cause?
3. Can charities campaign during a general election campaign?
4. If a charity is running a national campaign and seeking a change in the law, who are the people they should seek to influence?
5. What mechanisms of influence in Parliament could a charity use?
6. How else can a charity affect public opinion?

Answers

1. *Yes, but it has only been made clear relatively recently that it is possible for charities to try and change policies or influence MPs for example. (See Charity Commission Guidance Note CC9, Political Activities and Charities).*
2. *No, a charity will risk losing its charitable status if it supports a specific political party to the detriment of the others. Your job is to win wide acceptance of your views from politicians of all persuasions.*

3. *Yes, there is no reason why you shouldn't pursue your campaign during the actual weeks of a general election as long as your meetings and lobbying are directed at all candidates, and you are not favouring one over any other. Your meetings can be used to allow candidates to reveal their own views but it is not your job to suggest how people should vote.*

4. *Members of Parliament; Senior officials in the relevant government departments; the Voluntary and Community Division of the Department of National Heritage; Members of the 10 Downing Street Policy Unit.*

5. *Parliamentary Written Questions; Parliamentary Oral Questions; Early Day Motions; Ten Minute Rule Debates; Adjournment Debates; Private Member's Bills.*

6. *By using their annual reports and annual general meetings, keeping the press well informed of their campaigns, producing their own promotional material both on video and in general advertising and, if they have access, using the Internet as a means of spreading information far and wide!*

About the author

Simon Hebditch has worked in the voluntary sector for the last twenty years with a variety of organisations. He is currently Policy Director for the Charities Aid Foundation and provides policy development support to the Council for Charitable Support.

CHARITY LAW : 3

Jeffrey Lever

1. Introduction

Aims and Objectives

This chapter will introduce you to the law[1] relating to charities[2]. It should also be helpful to anyone involved or contemplating involvement in charity matters, especially charity trustees.

Although the chapter draws on the body of knowledge which is part of the expertise of professional lawyers, interested lay people involved in charities should be able to develop some understanding of the operation of charity law and its significance. Please note that all suggested reading is listed at the back of the book on *page 364*.

This chapter explains:
- the reasons for the legal regulation of charity
- the chief sources of charity law
- the nature of the activities that the law considers to be 'charitable'
- the role of the Charity Commissioners
- how to form and register a charity
- the duties and responsibilities of charity trustees
- certain specialist transactions that a charity may encounter
- when and how to alter the purposes of a charity.

Why is law relevant to charities?

We often think of the law as something to turn to when things have gone wrong. Since charitable activity is one of the more benevolent expressions of human behaviour, why should law be relevant to it?

---

1 This chapter is based on the law in England and Wales. In Scotland and Northern Ireland the law relating to the legal definition of charities and the duties of charity trustees is quite similar. However, the registration and regulatory roles of the Charity Commission which pertain to England and Wales are the responsibility of the Inland Revenue in Scotland and Northern Ireland.
2 In addition to specialist charity law, activities undertaken by charities are also subject to the general law, such as contract (governing legally binding agreements), tort (including the duty of care not to cause damage or harm to other people or their property) and criminal law. For example, when contemplating whether to provide alcohol on its premises a charity may have to pay attention to the law relating to licensing, food regulations, building regulations, town & country planning, fire regulations, land, insurance, rating, companies, and taxation (also see *Providing Alcohol on Charity Premises*, Reference CC27, Charity Commissioners, July 1996).

Probably the main reason is the size and complexity of present-day society. In smaller, simpler communities in earlier times, charity took the form of direct gifts to needy people. However, in more complex societies, special organisations are required, through which charity is channelled, because direct gifts from individuals to those in need may be impossible or inappropriate. This may be because:

- the gift is too small to be of help on its own
- it is too large a sum of money to be given to one person
- the gift is not money but some other asset (e.g. a building)
- it has been left in a will
- the donation is for a *purpose* rather than a person (e.g. to assist a school or museum, or to provide a service)
- it has been given for a *category* of needy persons (e.g. the homeless)
- it is intended for a special purpose that requires premises, equipment and trained staff (e.g. medical research)[3]
- it is a gift to an institution.

The need to be familiar with charity law

As this more organised charitable activity has developed, laws have grown up to regulate it, so that modern philanthropy is subject to quite detailed legal regulation.

Naturally, at certain times, you may need to seek assistance from qualified solicitors with experience of advising charities. However, a familiarity with the basic principles of charity law will reduce the number of instances where you require such advice on everyday or smaller matters. It will also make you more aware of the important occasions where specialist advice is required, enable you to approach your legal adviser on a more knowledgeable footing, and so get fuller or more relevant advice for your charity's money. It may also help you to steer your organisation clear of legal difficulties, and increase your expertise, effectiveness and confidence in running the charity.

The special legal meaning of 'charity'

The law gives a special meaning to the word 'charity' that is different in some ways from the ordinary meaning of the word and also from similar words, such as 'benevolent' or 'philanthropic'. It is important to know when the law recognises a purpose as charitable, because the *charitable status*[4] of an activity

---

3 Chesterman, 1979, p. 23.
4 Most of the legal words printed in italics in this chapter are explained in the Glossary of Terms: see Section 11 of this chapter.

can be of value in encouraging donors. It is also a qualification for claiming a number of valuable tax reliefs, and enables you to comply with the legal requirement to register as a charity with the Charity Commission.

Trustees

English law regards those who are responsible for a charity as 'trustees', with a particular legal responsibility to use the funds and assets of the charity in a proper manner. Charity trustees can be held personally liable to make good any loss suffered by their charity, if it has been caused by their lack of due care. It is therefore in the interests of both the charity and its trustees that they should make themselves aware of the standard of conduct legally expected of them. In certain circumstances, a similar standard of care is also expected of the employees of a charity, so this knowledge can be relevant to them too.

2. What is a Charity – The Legal Definition

In English law, 'charity' is a word with a technical meaning that is in some ways wider but in some ways narrower than the everyday meaning of the word. This legal meaning[5] is based on several sources, having evolved over a long period since the thirteenth century, when the ecclesiastical courts began to enforce a legacy for *"pious causes"*.

At the end of the reign of Queen Elizabeth I, we find a landmark in this evolution when the Statute of Charitable Uses 1601[6] was passed. The preamble to the statute, which reflects Tudor[7] concern to secularise charity and prevent the prevalent abuse and misappropriation of charity property, is an early source of the modern legal definition of 'charity'. It includes a detailed list of acceptable charitable purposes, from the "relief of aged, impotent [i.e. disabled] and poor people" to the "repair of bridges, ports, havens, causeways, churches, seabanks and highways".

The preamble was not intended to be an *exhaustive* list of the purposes which were regarded as being charitable in 1601, and so the courts have always discussed whether any particular purpose

---

5 The outline given here of what the law regards as charitable should be regarded as indicative only. In borderline cases, it will be necessary to seek professional legal advice.

6 Commonly known by this name, the formal title of the legislation was an "Act to redress the Misemployment of Lands, Goods and Stocks of Money heretofore given to Charitable Uses"

7 "No other single period of English history is so important in the formation of the modern legal concept of charity." (Chesterman, 1979, p. 28.)

lies within the *spirit* of the preamble. Thus it has become incorporated into the case law[8] which derives from it,[9] even though the legislation itself is no longer in force, having been repealed in 1888.

Case Law

Case law consists of the principles and rules of law which have emerged from the decisions taken by judges in court cases. Parliament[10] is the supreme law-making body in the United Kingdom. Thus in any particular case judges look to any relevant Acts of Parliament as the paramount source of the law which they have to apply. However, in applying the legislation to the particular circumstances of litigants, judges have had to interpret it.

Where there is no applicable legislation, it has been up to the judges to state the law. In carrying out these duties, the judges too are law makers. In order to achieve some consistency and predictability to this judge-made law,[11] the past decisions of courts in particular cases have been generalised over a period of time by successive generations of judges, and the resulting statements of principle are treated as setting the legal standard in later cases.

So, despite the repeal of the 1601 Act, the effect of the courts deciding controversies under its influence for nearly four centuries has been to infuse the case law with references to it. For a gift to be charitable it must still fall within the "spirit and intendment"[12] of the 1601 preamble.[13] However, it need not be for one of the purposes actually listed in the preamble. It needs only to be charitable in the same sense.[14]

Lord Macnaghten's "four categories of charity"

The most frequently cited modern legal description of 'charitable' comes from a court judgment late in the nineteenth century, in

---

8   i.e. the law created by the courts in successive decisions on disputes involving the concept of charity.

9   This was confirmed by the House of Lords in *Scottish Burial Reform and Cremation Society* v *Glasgow City Corporation* [1968] AC 138.

10 More accurately "the Queen in Parliament", signifying that a statute becomes law only when it has been approved by both chambers of Parliament and received the Royal Assent.

11 Known as the "Common Law" from its origins as the earliest system of law to be applied throughout the country.

12 *Incorporated Council of Law Reporting in England and Wales* v *Attorney-General* [1972] Ch 73.

13 But see Chesterman's argument (1979, pp. 6061) suggesting that modern judges have only "paid lip-service to the Tudor concept", while fundamentally altering it.

14 *Re Strakosch* [1949] Ch 529, at 538. Thus, providing relief to mentally-ill people is charitable, even though not expressly mentioned in the preamble. It is charitable in the same sense as other purposes mentioned in the preamble, such as relief to physically ill or maimed persons. But, for example, support for a political purpose, such as "promoting understanding between different nations", is not charitable because it is not within the spirit or contemplation of the preamble, even though it may be for the public good.

which Lord Macnaghten updated the illustrations of charity contained in the 1601 preamble:[15]

"Charity in its legal sense comprises four principal divisions: trusts for the relief of poverty; trusts for the advancement of education; trusts for the advancement of religion; and trusts for other purposes beneficial to the community not falling under any of the preceding heads."[16]

So if a gift falls within one of the four categories it is, *prima facie*[17] charitable, provided it satisfies two additional tests. To be legally charitable a gift must be *wholly and exclusively* charitable. It must also be of *public benefit*, unless it is for the relief of poverty. We shall consider these additional tests later. First let us consider the scope of each of Lord Macnaghten's categories in more detail, for although the court has not ruled out new charitable purposes which may not fall neatly into one of the headings,[18] they are a convenient and authoritative classification.

1. Trusts for the relief of poverty

You don't have to be destitute to be poor

Traditionally, the law has not regarded 'poverty' as an absolute concept: it is quite broadly interpreted. The courts consider that the poor include people who have to 'go short' in the ordinary sense of that term.[19]

This lack of an absolute definition of poverty has served usefully to broaden the category of people whom a charity for the relief of poverty may help. For example trusts for 'distressed gentlefolk',[20] and for 'aged and decayed actors',[21] have been considered to be charitable, even though such people were not completely penniless. However, the court would not consider charitable a trust to provide dwellings 'for the working classes and their families'[22] nor to contribute to the holiday expenses of 'work people',[23] because the 'working classes' are not all necessarily poor. The 1601 preamble refers to 'relief' (not benefit) of the poor, implying that

15 Lord Macnaghten, without acknowledging it, was himself putting forward a revised version of a description which Samuel Romilly, a renowned barrister of liberal opinions, and friend of Jeremy Bentham, had suggested in argument in a case 86 years previously: see *Morice* v *Bishop of Durham* (1805) 10 Ves 522, at 532.
16 *Income Tax Special Purposes Commissioners* v *Pemsel* [1891] AC 531, at 583.
17 I. e. "on the face of it", in the absence of any evidence to the contrary.
18 See Lord Wilberforce in *Scottish Burial Reform Society* v *Glasgow City Corpn* [1986] AC 138 at p. 154. For a "new expanded classification" thought to reflect developments since *Pemsel* see Picarda, 1995, p. 11.
19 "... due regard being had to their status in life and so forth" Evershed MR in *Re Coulthurst* [1951] Ch 661.
20 *Re Young* [1951] Ch 344.
21 *Spiller* v *Maude* (1881) 32 Ch D 158.
22 *Re Sanders' Will Trusts* [1954] Ch 265.
23 *Re Drummond* [1914] 2 Ch 90.

the poor who are the intended recipients must have some *need* to be alleviated. On the other hand, the court has regarded gifts for the construction of hostels for working men as charitable,[24] because accommodation in a hostel implies someone who is 'going short' insofar as they lack a home.

You can provide more than the bare minimum

In the modern welfare state, social security aims to provide a subsistence level below which no-one should fall, at least in theory. By continuing to apply a *relative* definition of poverty, the courts may be endorsing the idea that charity given for the relief of poverty ought not to be restricted to duplicating provisions for which the state has accepted responsibility, but can usefully *add* to what the government provides for those in need.

2. Trusts for the advancement of education

'Education' means more than just classroom teaching

Although the 1601 preamble mentions various forms of education which qualify as charitable, the courts have extended this category beyond simply teaching activity to include a broad range of activities concerned with the imparting and disseminating of knowledge.

Any educational institution can be charitable, even a private one, provided it is not profit making. Many types of gift which encourage or assist learning are also charitable, for example the provision of prizes for the study of academic or commercial subjects,[25] the establishment or maintenance of public libraries or museums, and gifts to learned institutions and professional bodies for the promotion of their knowledge and skills.[26]

Recreation and sport, when linked with an educational purpose

Even the promotion of recreational[27] activities which are considered to be of educational value, such as choral singing,[28] or the playing of chess[29] has been regarded as charitable by the court. Similarly, although a gift merely for the promotion of sport is not charitable,[30] it can be if it is linked with education by, for instance,

---

24 *Guinness Trust (London Fund) Founded 1890* v *West Ham Corporation* [1959] 1 WLR 233.
25 *Re Mariette* [1915] 2 Ch 284.
26 *Royal College of Surgeons* v *National Provincial Bank Ltd* [1952] AC 631.
27 See also, below, discussion of *Recreational purposes*, under Lord Macnaghten's fourth category, Trusts for other purposes beneficial to the community.
28 *Royal Choral Society* v *IRC* [1942] 2 All ER 101.
29 *Re Dupree's Deed Trusts* [1945] Ch 16.
30 *Re Nottage* [1895] 2 Ch 649.

encouraging the physical education of students at schools and universities.[31]

Research can be charitable provided it is educationally useful

This may be so if it is of educational value to the researcher, or is aimed at discovering something which would contribute to education.[32] Research is charitable only if its results are disseminated rather than being kept private.

3. Trusts for the advancement of religion

The courts have extended the scope of this category far beyond merely the repair of churches alluded to in the Statute of Charitable Uses. The law considers two issues: what is 'religion'? and what amounts to 'advancing' it?

What is religion?

The court holds that a religion requires a belief in and worship of a supreme being,[33] and activity to promote that belief, such as services, rituals, pastoral and missionary work.[34] Thus all Christian denominations are included, for example the Church of England, Roman Catholicism, and Baptists as well as the Salvation Army.

Non-Christian religions are also included. *"As between different religions the law stands neutral, but it assumes that any religion is at least likely to be better than none,"* it was said in a case which established that the promotion of Judaism is charitable.[35]

However, defining religion is not a simple matter. For instance, the Freemasons, despite their assertion of belief in a divine spirit, have not been successful in acquiring legal recognition as a religion, since they neither conduct religious services nor impart religious instruction.[36] Attempts to equate *ethics* with religion have also failed.[37]

On the other hand, two trusts associated with the Unification Church (the 'Moonies') have been registered by the Charity Commissioners, and remain so despite unease that this

---

31 *IRC* v *McMullen* [1978] 1 All ER 230.
32 *Re Hopkins' Will Trusts* [1965] Ch 669. Compare *Re Shaw* [1957] 1 All ER 745.
33 *Re South Place Ethical Society* [1980] 3 All ER 918.
34 *United Grand Lodge of Ancient Free and Accepted Masons of England* v *Holborn Borough Council* [1957] 3 All ER 281.
35 *Neville Estates* v *Madden* [1962] Ch 832. Hindu, Sikh and Buddhist temples have also been treated as charitable by the Charity Commission.
36 *United Grand Lodge of Ancient Free and Accepted Masons of England* v *Holborn Borough Council* [1957] 3 All ER 281.
37 *Re South Place Ethical Society* [1980] 1 WLR 1565.

organisation may be more accurately characterised as a personality cult than a religion.

What is the 'advancement' of religion?

It seems that it is sufficient for charitable status that the religion is being promoted to people in general, even if it is unlikely that this will succeed. Thus a gift for the publication of the sacred works of Joanna Southcott, who claimed she was pregnant by the Holy Spirit and would give birth to a second Messiah was considered to be a trust for the advancement of religion, even though the court acknowledged that she had very few followers.[38]

However there are many more conventional activities which are regarded as amounting to the advancement of religion. These include gifts to build, maintain or repair religious buildings, including graveyards, preaching sermons, saying public masses for the dead, the provision of Sunday School prizes, and supporting a church choir.

4. Trusts for other purposes beneficial to the community

This is a very wide category covering numerous charitable purposes which are dissimilar to each other. For a purpose to come within this category it must be not merely beneficial to the community; it must be beneficial to the community in the sense of the *"spirit and intendment"* of the 1601 preamble. This may be so by analogy with a case that has already been decided.

In cases of uncertainty, the court will have to decide objectively in light of all the available evidence. However, in some circumstances the court is faced with a need to weigh 'conflicting moral and material utilities',[39] as was the case when it refused charitable status to the work of the National Anti-Vivisection Society on the grounds that the suppression of vivisection was not beneficial to the public. In this case the court had to weigh opposing arguments both of which are doubtless supported by many reasonable people. Where the Charity Commissioners are doubtful of the benefit to the community of a proposed charity, they usually ask for evidence of its beneficial impact.

Because of its very wide scope, the nature of this category is best illustrated by some examples.

38 *Thornton v Howe* [1862] 31 Beav 14.
39 *National Anti-Vivisection Society v IRC* [1948] AC 31.

The relief of the sick

The 1601 preamble refers to *"relief of... impotent... people"*, and relief of the impotent[40] includes those suffering physical or mental illness, or as a result of injury or disability. Bear in mind that it is the *relief* of the sick etc. which makes the purpose charitable, so if a money payment were made to a sick but very wealthy person, this would not be charitable, since it does not cater for any *need*.

Protection of human life

Trusts for emergency services such as ambulances, lifeboats, mountain rescue, fire brigade or police are charitable. Trusts for the relief of disaster (e.g. the flooding of a town) are charitable only if the number of persons affected by the disaster is large enough to make them a section of the public for the purpose of the test of public benefit (which is discussed further below). Failing that, a trust for the relief of disaster is charitable only if it is restricted to relieving financial need or poverty caused by the disaster.

Children

While trusts for the advancement of education cater in part for the *"education and preferment of orphans"* mentioned in the 1601 preamble, the funding of other provision, such as children's homes, is also charitable under this community benefit heading.

Elderly people

The preamble refers to the *"relief of aged... people"*. This includes the provision of suitable accommodation or nursing homes, provided they are not for profit. Also included is financial assistance to aged people in need, but not to the wealthy elderly, since money is not 'relief' to them.[41]

National heritage, conservation, public works and buildings

These are within the 1601 preamble's reference to *"repair of bridges, ports, havens, causeways, ... seabanks and highways"* and include contributions towards public libraries, museums, parks and cemeteries, nature conservation, zoos and organisations such as the National Trust.

Trusts encouraging 'moral welfare'

This category *does* include a trust to encourage ethical principles (excluded from the category of 'Advancement of Religion' as

---

40 The word "impotent" in the seventeenth century meant physically disabled.
41 *Joseph Rowntree Memorial Trust Housing Association Ltd* v *Attorney General* [1983] Ch 159.

mentioned earlier). Also included in this category are trusts for the welfare of animals, and it is important to note that the charitable nature of animal welfare is based on its humanising affect on *people* by promoting *"feelings of humanity and morality"* and *restraining an "inborn tendency to cruelty"*.[42]

Recreational purposes

A gift of land for public recreation has been held to be charitable.[43] The Recreational Charities Act 1958 also deems charitable the provision of facilities for public recreation where they are in the interest of social welfare. The Act specifies that the interest of *"social welfare"* is satisfied if the facilities are provided with the object of improving the condition of life of the persons for whom they are primarily intended, *and* are either provided for the public at large, or female members of the public at large, or for people who have a special need for those facilities by reason of their youth, age, infirmity or disablement, poverty or social and economic circumstances.

The Act spells out that it applies to the provision of facilities at village halls, community centres and women's institutes, and to the provision and maintenance of grounds and buildings for recreational purposes.

Other civic purposes

Other purposes which the courts or the Charity Commissioners have found to be charitable are as diverse as the promotion of efficiency in the armed forces,[44] promoting agriculture, and the provision of a public memorial to a well-respected person. A gift for a particular village, town, district or country is regarded as charitable by implication[45] so that even though no specific charitable purpose has been specified, a scheme will be agreed to use the gift for charitable purposes.

Can political purposes be charitable?

It is not hard to see why a trust to support a particular political party or its doctrines is not charitable.[46] It lies outside the spirit of 1601 preamble, and the court is not willing to decide whether a political purpose is or is not for the public benefit. To do so would risk its impartiality. Unfairness would also arise if a group could

---

42 *Re Wedgwood* [1915] 1 Ch 113. Compare with *Re Grove-Grady* [1929] 1 Ch 557.
43 *Re Hadden* [1932] 1 Ch 133.
44 *Re Good* [1905] 2 Ch 60.
45 *Williams' Trustees* v *Inland Revenue Commissioners* [1947] AC 447.
46 *Re Jones* (1929) 45 TLR 259.

fund their politically partisan activities partly from the public purse, by availing themselves of the substantial tax reliefs available to a charity.

Apart from the clear-cut case of political parties, there is some difficulty in determining the legal relationship between political purposes and charity. The twentieth century has seen a significant growth in the complexity of society and its problems, in the size of the population, and of business corporations and other economic institutions. The task of regulating and ameliorating the problems of our time is beyond private initiative alone.[47] This being the case, charity workers may think that there are needs which they can relieve to some extent, but which only the government can tackle decisively.[48] For example:

- the renovation of the hospitals in your area, may be so expensive that only the government has the resources to make a significant impact on these needs
- the improvement of the welfare of many children may require the reform of the law relating to young people, divorce law, or adoption law, or increases in the level of welfare benefits
- procuring the abolition of torture or inhuman or degrading treatment or punishment might require changes in the law or government policy of United Kingdom or of foreign countries.

It is not always easy to decide which of these non-party political purposes might be charitable. The promotion of peace has in the past been regarded as an acceptable charitable aim,[49] but as one learned author points out, the resolution of any specific area of conflict depends on arriving at peace terms which involve a political decision.[50] On the other hand to promote peace by educational means, might be charitable: a course in 'Peace Studies' at a university promotes education, and is therefore charitable.

Organisations for the promotion of international friendship or understanding are not charitable, because trying to promote a view of one nation by another is considered sufficiently controversial to be political.[51] However the promotion of greater

47 "One of the magnificent failures of our history is the endeavour made by these charities, more particularly in the late eighteenth and early nineteenth century, to provide by private effort universal services of schools, hospitals, dispensaries, almshouses, orphanages, pensions for the aged and relief for other categories of the 'deserving poor'." (*Report of the Committee on the Law and Practice relating to Charitable Trusts* (1952) Cmnd 8710, 1952 (known as the Nathan Report)). Only the welfare state of the twentieth century has been able to tackle these needs universally.

48 The Nathan report considered that "some of the most valuable activities of voluntary societies consist ... in the fact that they are able to stand aside from and criticise state action, or inaction, in the interests of the inarticulate man-in-the-street."

49 *Re Harwood* [[1936] Ch 285.

50 Picarda, 1995, p. 154.

51 *Anglo-Swedish Society* v *IRC* (1931) 47 TLR 295.

understanding between nations may be charitable if it is a purpose which is carried out ancillary to a primary purpose such as the advancement of education, in the context of which the relevant ideas are discussed in an objective way without political bias.[52] In the past it was thought that the promotion of good race relations was a political purpose, and therefore not charitable.[53] Now, however, there is legislation based on the clear understanding that racial harmony is of public benefit. Thus promoting good race relations is charitable, including, for example, working to eliminate racial discrimination in employment, education and housing. The same position applies to sex discrimination.

Campaigning to change the law or to oppose change in the law

If one of the *main* objects of an organisation is to obtain a change in the existing law, it is political and not charitable. Since the court's prime role is to uphold existing law, it is reluctant to be drawn into making a ruling which implies that a change in the law is in the public interest, or to usurp the role of Parliament and other bodies in debating law reform.

However, if an organisation furthers the *enforcement* of the law, this is not political, since everyone has a duty to observe the law. Therefore, for example, an organisation assisting homeless people which promotes the prosecution of landlords who illegally evict tenants is charitable. *(See also chapter 2.)*

Political purposes which are ancillary to primary charitable aims

If advocating or opposing changes in the law is only a minor part of an organisation's objects, and is merely *ancillary* to its main, charitable purpose, this will not thwart its charitable status. Thus a charity for the promotion and improvement of agriculture was not compromised merely because this included monitoring and advising on legislation affecting farming.[54] Likewise, a polytechnic students' union was not barred from its status as an educational charity merely because its constitution included, among a wide range of aims aimed at enriching students' educational experience, the development of political activities among the students.[55]

52 *Re Koeppler's Will Trusts* [1986] Ch 423.
53 *Re Strakosch* [1949] Ch 529.
54 *IRC* v *Yorkshire Agricultural Society* [1928] 1 KB 611.
55 *Attorney General* v *Ross* [1985] 3 All ER 334.

5. The further requirement of public benefit

Charities must satisfy further requirements. One of these, which applies to all categories except the relief of poverty, is that its purpose must be *"for the benefit of the community or an appreciably important class of the community."*[56]

There must be benefit...

It has to be demonstrated that any given purpose is beneficial. For example, since the advancement of religion is charitable, an organisation such as a religious fellowship may well be a charity. However, an order of *cloistered* nuns isolated from the public was not judged to be a charity by the court, since it was not possible to show clearly how the public would *benefit* from the nuns' activities.[57]

...to the community or a significant class of the community

Whether the persons at whom the benefit is directed comprise *"an appreciably important class of the community"* is not merely a question of how numerous they are. This point was well illustrated when a fund was proposed to provide for the education of the children of employees or former employees of British American Tobacco, numbering more than 100,000 people. The court considered that although there were numerous potential beneficiaries, they were a private grouping, linked by their personal, contractual relationship to the same employer. The benefit was not available to members of the public.[58]

One underlying policy behind this rule might be to prevent companies or private groups from contriving to obtain a 'fringe benefit' for themselves, subsidised by the taxpayer via the tax immunities enjoyed by charities.

Trusts for the relief of poverty

Trusts for the relief of poverty among groups of persons do not have to be for the public benefit. Thus a trust for the donee's poor relatives[59], and a trust for a company's poor employees[60] have been declared charitable. However a trust for specified *individuals* is not regarded as charitable in law.

56 *Verge* v *Somerville* [1924] AC 496.
57 *Gilmour* v *Coats* [1949] AC 426.
58 *Oppenheim* v *Tobacco Securities Trust Co Ltd* [1951] AC 297. See also *Re Compton* [1945] Ch 123. Similarly, a mutual benefit society such as a friendly society or a trade union is not a charity.
59 *Re Cohen* [1973] 1 All ER 889 (but not restricted to next of kin only).
60 *Dingle v Turner* [1972] AC 601.

6. The further requirement that a purpose is wholly and exclusively charitable

To be valid as a charitable trust, its funds must be not merely *available* for charitable work, they must be *confined* to such purposes. So a trust claiming to relieve poverty will not be regarded as charitable if it can benefit rich people as well as poor people. For example, a trust was established to provide knickers for boys of a certain age who were sons of residents of Farnham. This did not qualify, as rich boys were eligible to benefit.[61]

A problem may occur where the statement of the purpose of an organisation or gift links the word 'charitable' with other words such as 'benevolent' or 'philanthropic'.[62] Then the court will have to construe whether the phrase used connotes an *exclusively* charitable purpose. Usually an expression such as 'charitable *or* benevolent' will fail this test, but 'charitable *and* benevolent' will pass, since such a purpose *must* be charitable.

7. Points to note

In considering the legal definition of 'charity', the most important points to bear in mind are:

- the word 'charity' has a technical, legal meaning which is not always the same as in everyday speech
- this special meaning is significant when drafting a statement of the aims of any activity or organisation which it is intended should be charitable
- it is also important when the trustees of an established charity are considering any activity which goes beyond the purposes which they have usually promoted.

For a purpose to be charitable it must:

1. be within the spirit and intendment of the 1601 Preamble as interpreted in the *Pemsel* case and other court decisions
2. **and** be for the public benefit (or for the relief of poverty)
3. **and** be wholly and exclusively charitable.

4. Charitable Status

The advantages of charitable status

Charities enjoy considerable social, financial and legal advantages which may warrant the work and expense involved in setting them up.

---

61 *Re Guyon* [1930] 1 Ch 255.
62 These do not always mean "charitable".

Public goodwill

If you depend on the public as a source of funding[63] and/or on volunteer helpers, then the fact that your organisation has charitable status will reassure the public that their support is going to a good cause. Public support is hard to attract without it.

Official support

Grant-giving bodies such as local authorities[64] or foundations which are themselves charities prefer to sponsor an organisation which is a registered charity. The Charity Commission issues many informative advisory publications and will give free advice to charity trustees on any matter affecting the performance of their duties.

Regulation

Charities are regulated by the Charity Commissioners, and their purposes are enforceable by the Attorney General. This official supervision gives supporters the confidence that their help is unlikely to be abused.

Tax advantages

Charities enjoy certain exemptions or reliefs from Income Tax, Corporation Tax, Capital Gains Tax, Inheritance Tax, Stamp Duty, Value Added Tax, and Business Rates.[65] This amounts to a significant element of financial support from the state and encourages donations, since benefactors are encouraged by the thought that their gift will trigger additional support to their chosen charity from the tax authorities.

Administrative convenience

Unlike private trusts whose trustees may be compelled to act by unanimous decision, charitable trustees may make their decisions by a majority vote. And if a charity becomes defunct, usually funds given to it can be reallocated to another similar charity.[66]

The possibility of perpetual existence

Private trusts are prevented from existing in perpetuity for policy reasons which lean against the idea that assets could be tied into a trust forever. However, charitable trusts are free of this rule, and

---

63 19.9% of the income of charities was made up of donations in 1990 (Posnett, *Charity Trends*, 15th. edn., 1992).

64 Government grants comprised 6.2% of charities' income in 1990 (*ibid.*).

65 Details of these are given in the separate chapter on charity taxation elsewhere in this book.

66 This is known as the *cy près* doctrine (originating from the French *si près,* or *ici près* or *aussi près* = so near, as near).

there are charities which have been in existence for centuries and will continue indefinitely.

The ability to pursue a purpose

Private trusts are not valid unless the beneficiaries are identifiable people or corporations. A charitable trust is not subject to this restriction: instead it is set up for a *purpose* which will benefit people who cannot yet be identified.[67]

Are there disadvantages to charitable status?

In view of the privileges they enjoy, perhaps it is not surprising that charities are subject to a degree of restriction and regulation to ensure that public confidence in them is not misplaced.

Restrictions on activity

Charitable status is available only to those organisations whose purposes are legally charitable. You may wish to carry out activities which are not charitable, such as political activity which is more than merely ancillary to your main charitable purpose. If so, you will have to organise and fund these through a parallel organisation which is completely separate from your charitable one. If a charitable organisation engages in non-charitable activity, sanctions can be imposed. In minor cases the Charity Commissioners might issue a warning, but in serious cases they can intervene to safeguard the charity's assets. The tax authorities may withdraw exemptions.

Personal liability of trustees

Charity trustees assume a serious responsibility, and may become personally liable for wrongful expenditure by their organisation. In the above example of a charity which has wrongfully engaged in non-charitable activity, trustees personally might have to refund non-charitable expenditures to the charitable trust. In the event of their charity becoming insolvent, they may also become personally liable for contracts they have entered into on its behalf.

Not for profit

Profits of a charity may not be distributed to members, nor are its trustees usually allowed to receive a salary from the charity.

---

67 Indeed, a charitable trust *must* be for a charitable purpose, and not merely for the benefit of an individual.

Regulation and reporting

All charities, other than the smallest, are required to register with the Charity Commission (unless they are under some alternative form of supervision, such as the Church Commissioners). Registered charities must complete an annual return for the Charity Commission containing prescribed information. Those with a gross annual income of £10,000 or more must also provide the Commission with a copy of their annual report and accounts. These are open to public inspection, and enable the Commission to monitor the charity. The Commission has the power to investigate a charity, and the Inland Revenue also has a significant supervisory role.

5. The Charities Acts 1992 and 1993

The Charity Commission

The 1601 legislation authorised the setting up of county charity commissions to investigate mismanagement of charity assets.[68] After these local commissions became defunct a Royal Commission[69] led, in 1853, to the replacement of the Elizabethan county commissions by the first central, permanent Board of Commissioners for England and Wales.[70]

The Charities Act 1960

The early drafters of charity law could not have foreseen how social provision would expand. In the nineteenth century the expenditure of charities had far exceeded state spending under the poor law. In the twentieth century, this relationship was reversed: the state grew to be the dominant partner in welfare provision, culminating in the sweeping welfare state reforms[71] introduced by the Labour Government after 1945.

Following a new committee of enquiry,[72] the Charities Act 1960 reconstituted the Charity Commission and enhanced its powers. The Commission's function was newly defined. It was to promote the effective use of resources by encouraging better administration,

68 "Over 950 such investigations were set up between 1660 and 1742, but only six were created from 1743 to 1818." (Alvey, 1995, p. 16)
69 The "Brougham Commission" instigated by Henry Brougham, a barrister and Member of Parliament.
70 The new Board was established by the Charitable Trusts Act 1853.
71 Education Act 1944, National Health Service Act 1946, National Assistance Act 1948.
72 The Committee on the Law and Practice Relating to Charitable Trusts, set up in 1950 and chaired by Lord Nathan a respected lawyer and active member of the House of Lords. The other important study of this period was Beveridge's *Voluntary Action*, 1948.

investigating and checking abuses, and advising trustees. The Charity Commission acquired a jurisdiction, in parallel with the High Court, over the content of charity constitutions, the appointment and removal of trustees and other charity officials, and the transfer of charity property.

A central register of charities was set up, to be run by the Commission. Local Authorities too were empowered to register and review charities in their own areas, to promote the co-operation of charities with each other and with the local authority.

Charities Act 1992

After 1960 admission to the central register informed the Commission and the public of some of the particulars of charities, but could not in itself guarantee the legitimacy of a charity or the good standing of its trustees. There was a material expansion of charitable activity in the post-war decades,[73] so that by the mid-1970s it was realised that the Charity Commission did not have sufficient resources to oversee such a large and expanding component of the economy.[74] Many charities were failing to submit accounts to the Commission, and it was clear that the Commission needed additional powers of enforcement.[75]

Strengthening the regulatory structure

The Charities Act 1992 reinforced the supervisory powers of the Commission,[76] and more resources were allocated to its work. Parts II and III of the Act concern the controls on professional fund-raising and on public collections (*see Chapter 1, Fundraising*).[77] The remainder of the 1992 Act was consolidated with earlier legislation to become the Charities Act 1993.

---

73 " ... by 1992 there were over 170,000 registered charities with a total turnover of about £17 billion more than the whole output of Britain's largest industry, agriculture." (Alvey, 1995, p. 43). Another estimate put the total income of registered charities at £16.175bn, comparable to 3.4% of Gross Domestic Product (Posnett, in *Charity Trends*, 15th. edn., 1992).

74 Concern about the effectiveness of the charity sector and its regulation was raised in *An Efficiency Scrutiny of the Supervision of Charities*, 1987 (Woodfield Report); *Monitoring and Control of Charities in England and Wales*, National Audit Office, HC Papers (198687) No. 380 & (199091) No. 13; and *Sixteenth Report from the Committee of Public Accounts*, HC Paper (198788) No. 116.

75 See *Charities: A Framework for the Future* (Cm 694, 1989).

76 See Section 6 of this chapter.

77 See also *Charities and Fund-raising, A Summary*, Reference CC20(a), Charity Commissioners, March 1995.

6. The Charity Commission – Function and Powers

Constitution of the Charity Commission

The Charity Commissioners are civil servants appointed by the Heritage Secretary. There is a Chief Charity Commissioner and four other commissioners, of whom two must be barristers or solicitors, who lead a staff of about 700 people. The Commission acts independently of the Department of National Heritage, but submits an annual report to the Heritage Secretary.

General function

The general function of the Commission is to *"promote the effective use of charitable resources by encouraging the development of better methods of administration, by giving charity trustees information or advice on any matter affecting the charity and by investigating and checking abuses."*[78]

This remit includes helping to modernise charities whose purposes require alteration to enable them better to meet current welfare needs, and supervising charities to uphold honesty and efficiency.

Registration

You might have gained the impression that all decisions on charitable status are made by the courts. This is not the case. While the courts determine the law in this area through a few decisions a year on contested matters, the process of registration involves the Charity Commission in over 4,000 such decisions annually.[79]

The Commission maintains a computerised register of charities, and this also involves the Commission in its *quasi-judicial* function of evaluating the charitable status of all organisations applying to register. In addition, certain categories of persons are not allowed to become charity trustees, including undischarged bankrupts, those convicted of offences involving dishonesty or deception and anyone previously removed from charity trusteeship on grounds of misconduct or mismanagement.[80]

---

78 Charities Act 1993 s. 1(3).
79 Moffat, 1994, p. 646.
80 CA 1993 s. 72(1).

Advice

The Commission publishes an extensive range of advisory booklets and leaflets, written in a straightforward style, and dealing with many different charity issues. Most are available free of charge to the public. In addition, any charity trustee may apply in writing to the commissioners for their advice on any matter affecting the performance of the trustee's duties.[81]

Custodian trustee of charity property

The Commission can act as a *custodian trustee* for land owned by a charity. This may be convenient, since it is therefore unnecessary to alter the title to the land whenever there is a change in the charity's trustees. This custodian function can also be exercised to protect the property of any charity from misconduct or mismanagement.[82]

Common investment funds

The Commission is empowered[83] to establish common investment funds for charities whereby the participating charities pool their investments, and receive returns of income and capital in proportion to the value of their contribution. This is especially convenient for charities with small investments. One of these, the Charities Official Investment Fund, is open to all charities.

Monitoring charity accounts

Charity trustees have a duty to submit to the Commission an annual report on the activities of the charity, together with a statement of accounts[84] and the report of an auditor or independent examiner.[85] Every registered charity must also submit an annual return to the Commission containing information about its trustees and the charity's activities. Charities that fail to comply will be approached by the Commission, and may be investigated. Persistent failure to submit the required reports and accounts is an offence.[86]

---

81 CA 1993 s. 29. Trustees acting on the commissioners' advice are deemed to have acted in accordance with the trust and are therefore protected from any complaint that they have acted in breach of trust.

82 CA 1993 s. 18.

83 CA 1993 s. 24.

84 The preparation of charity accounts is discussed in a separate chapter in this book.

85 CA 1993 s. 45. A professional auditor is required where the gross income or expenditure of the charity exceeds £100,000; otherwise examination by a competent independent person is sufficient: s. 43. Anyone contemplating the latter task should read *The Carrying Out of an Independent Examination: Directions and Guidance Notes*, Charity Commissioners, March 1996. Exempt charities are not subject to these reporting requirements, although they have to keep proper accounts and retain them for at least six years: s. 46.

86 CA 1993 ss. 47(2), 49.

Corporate charities need not submit their accounts to the Commission, since they have to submit them to the Registrar of Companies.[87] However, the commissioners can appoint an auditor to conduct an independent investigation into the accounts of any charity.[88]

Sanctioning problematic transactions

Sometimes trustees wish to carry out some action in the administration of the charity which does not appear to be authorised by the terms of the trust. The commissioners are empowered to sanction such a step if it appears to them to be *"expedient in the interests of the charity"*.[89] (*See Section 10 of this chapter.*)

Instigation of proceedings to enforce a charitable trust

The Charity Commissioners are among those (including the Attorney General and other individuals) who are authorised to instigate proceedings against defaulting trustees.[90]

Modernising defunct charities

If a charitable purpose fails for some reason to meet modern needs, it may be possible to use the assets for similar charitable purposes[91] (*See Section 8 of this chapter*). The commission has jurisdiction to authorise such modernisation schemes as may be proposed by charity trustees, and in some cases in can initiate them itself.

Modernising, amalgamating or ending small charities

The Commission can authorise the trustees of any small charity whose existing purposes no longer provide a *"suitable and effective"* application of the charity's resources to alter the purposes to new ones which are *"as similar in character... as is practicable in the circumstances"*, or to transfer the charity's assets to another charity which has purposes which are *"as similar as is reasonably practicable"*.[92] The Commission can also authorise the winding up of a charity with a very small endowment which does not include land.[93]

---

87 Companies Act 1985 Part VII.
88 CA 1993 s. 43; including a corporate charity: s. 69.
89 CA 1993 s. 26(1). See also CA 1993, s. 27 and *Re Snowden* [1970] Ch 700: the Commission may authorise payments outside the terms of the trust if there is a strong moral reason for the payment.
90 CA 1993 ss. 32 & 33.
91 Either by modifying the charity's purposes under the *cy près* doctrine, or by changing the administration of the trust.
92 CA 1993 s. 74.
93 CA 1993 s. 75.

Receiving information and complaints

The Commission's monitoring role is supplemented by complaints and information it receives from the public, the police, the Inland Revenue,[94] concerned members, employees or trustees of a charity, and from the media.

Conducting inquiries

The commissioners have the power to make enquiries of individuals[95] and of charities[96] and can:

- require anyone to provide information they have which relates to any charity
- scrutinise and copy any documents relating to a charity[97]
- require anyone to attend an enquiry and give evidence on oath
- require anyone to produce accounts and other documents
- publish a report of their findings.

Protecting charity property

Where misconduct or mismanagement of the charity is found, or it is necessary or desirable to act to protect charity property,[98] the Commission may:

- appoint or remove trustees[99]
- deliver or transfer property[100]
- suspend any trustee, officer, agent or employee of the charity pending consideration of their removal[101]
- transfer charity property to the Official Custodian[102]
- restrict any dealings in charity property,[103] including freezing bank accounts
- appoint a receiver or manager of the charity.[104]

Where there has been maladministration and it is also necessary to act to protect the charity's property, the Commission may remove any of the people involved with the charity and establish a scheme to administer it.[105]

94 Normal confidentiality is waived where the Inland Revenue suspects a charity of applying its funds or activities for non-charitable purposes: CA 1993 s. 10(2).
95 CA 1993 s. 9.
96 CA 1993 s. 8.
97 Other than an exempt charity.
98 CA 1993 s. 18(1).
99 CA 1993 ss. 16(1), 18(1)(ii), 18(4)(5).
100 CA 1993 s. 16(1).
101 CA 1993 s. 18(1)(i) & (11).
102 CA 1993 s. 18(1)(iii).
103 CA 1993 s. 18(1)(iv) & (vi).
104 CA 1993 s. 18(1)(vii) & s. 19.
105 CA 1993 s. 18(2).

Other regulatory bodies

This array of duties and powers makes the Charity Commission the principle agency monitoring and regulating charities, supported by the court. However, further supervision is exercised by the Inland Revenue, who require accounts and other supporting documents to be submitted by charities claiming tax relief. The Inland Revenue may withdraw tax relief if charity funds are not being used exclusively for charitable purposes.

A charity may also be asked for detailed information about its management, finances and activities by any grant-making public bodies with whom it deals. It may co-ordinate its work with a local authority, with whom it may have involvement through a local index of charities, or because the local authority gives it grant aid, or acts as a custodian trustee, or appoints trustees to the charity's governing body, or is asked to permit certain types of local fundraising, or is consulted about altering the trusts of the charity.

7. Setting Up a Charity

The process of forming a charity

Setting up a charity comprises a number of steps.
1. The decision to form a charity is made.
2. The purposes of the charity are decided.
3. The form of the charity is determined.
4. Unless the charity is *exempt* or *excepted*, application is made to register the new charity. *(See definitions on pages 107 and 108.)*
5. The Charity Commission considers the application.
6. What happens if the application to register is unsuccessful?
7. What happens after the charity is registered?

Step 1. Deciding whether to form a charity

Is your purpose charitable?

You, and the other *promoters*, will have some purpose in mind which you wish to promote. You must now consider whether this purpose is *wholly and exclusively* charitable in law.[106] If your purpose is not charitable you should not attempt to form a charity, since you will be prevented from pursuing your non-charitable purposes.[107]

---

106 See Section 2 of this chapter.
107 See Section 6 of this chapter.

If your purpose is only *partly* charitable, then consider hiving off the non-charitable work to a parallel, non-charitable organisation which is organised and funded separately from the charitable one.

Is it beneficial to form a charity?
Does a similar charity already exist?

If your purpose is charitable, you should weigh the disadvantages of forming a charity against the advantages.[108] Also look at the possibility that there is already an organisation doing similar work after all there are already more than 150,000 registered charities. Using the Charity Commission's computerised register, it is best to find out whether there is an established organisation with whom you should work, rather than duplicating effort and competing for funds with them.

2. Deciding the purposes of the charity

At this stage it is necessary to determine with some precision what are to be the objects of the charity, so that the promoters of the charity are clear about their objects when they come to decide how the charity should be organised.[109] This will allow you to state the organisation's objects authoritatively in its *governing document*, and to answer the searching questions about the purposes of your organisation in the application form for registering the charity with the Charity Commissioners.

3. What form of organisation should the charity take?

The main options

The legal form of your organisation will affect who will run it, who will take legal responsibility for its decisions and financial liabilities, how it will be run, including any internal rules concerning meetings, voting and control of funds, how can these rules can be changed, or the people running the organisation be replaced, and how the charity can be wound up.

In due course, these crucial issues will, to a large extent, be settled in the organisation's governing document. Generally the promoters' choice of an organisational structure is between a *trust*, an *unincorporated association*, and a *company limited by guarantee*.

---

108 See Section 4 of this chapter.
109 "Organised" in the sense of its *form* of organisation, discussed later.

A trust

What is a trust?

When a charity operates as a trust, a number of individuals, the trustees, hold the legal ownership of the charity's property (such as money, equipment, land) and are under a strict duty to administer these assets to advance the purposes of the charity, and for no other purposes.

When is it suitable?

The trust is appropriate when the charity is to be run by a small group of people, and is not going to rely on a membership to run it.[110] Compared with other organisational forms, the trust offers simplicity of administration, requiring only the vote of a majority of the trustees to decide issues.

Disadvantages of the trust

Trustees act in person, and are therefore legally liable for transactions they enter into in the course of charity business. For example, if equipment is acquired or a lease entered into, the trustees have a personal responsibility to pay the agreed price or rent. If the charity's funds fall short of what is necessary to make these payments, the trustees might have to make up the shortfall from their own pockets. However, this risk very rarely materialises in practice, provided trustees take care not to over-commit themselves.

Governing document

The organisation's governing document defines its purposes and method of administration. In the future running of the charity, and especially if any doubt or dispute should occur, this *instrument* will be a central point of reference, and could determine the legality of any proposed course of action which is being contemplated by those running the charity. You may be able to form an initial view on the necessary content of your governing document from advice published by the Charity Commission,[111] or from seeing a copy of the governing documents of other charities which have been accepted in the past by the Commission.[112]

---

110 More detailed advice on this point can be found in *Guidance on when to use a Trust Deed*, Reference INF 5, Charity Commissioners, August 1996.

111 *Minimum Requirements for Governing Documents*, Reference INF 2, Charity Commissioners, August 1996. Also useful is *Preparation of Governing Document checklist*, Reference INF 7, Charity Commissioners, August 1996.

112 *Standard Governing Documents*, Reference INF 8, Charity Commissioners, August 1996.

However, it is usually advisable for a solicitor experienced in charity law to be involved in the drafting of this document.

The trust deed

The governing document of a trust is known as the *trust deed*, or *declaration of trust*. The Commission has published a model of such a document which will help you to consider the matters you wish to cover in your own trust deed.[113]

An unincorporated association

What is an unincorporated association?

An association is an organisation consisting of a group of people who have agreed to work together to foster the agreed purpose and activities of the organisation.

Unlike a company (which is incorporated) an *unincorporated* association is not a legal person in its own right, but acts through its individual officers and other members. For example, when an unincorporated association decides to purchase equipment or make an investment, it will have to appoint individual members or officers to carry out the purchase or hold the investment asset on behalf of the association. By contrast, a company is regarded by the law as carrying out such transactions in its own name.

When is it suitable?

Where the goal is to create a membership organisation whose participants carry out voluntary work for the charity and periodically elect officers from among themselves to be its trustees, the unincorporated association may be a suitable structure. It is also convenient where the society is to be the local branch of a national charity which has a standard constitution for all its branches. This form also allows the organisation to admit as members local residents, users of the facilities, funders and any other groups whose opinion the charity wishes to see represented in its democratic processes.

Disadvantages of the unincorporated association

The need to adhere to its constitutional requirements may make the unincorporated association more cumbersome to run than a trust, but this may be a small price to pay for the advantages

---

113 *Model Declaration of Trust for a Charitable Trust*, Reference GD2, Charity Commissioners, January 1995.

brought by the participating membership. Since the unincorporated association acts through its officers, who are the charity trustees as long as they hold office, the trustees assume personal liability for transactions they enter into on behalf of the association. In this respect they run a similar risk to the trustees of a charitable trust, discussed earlier.

Governing document

The governing document of an unincorporated association is called a constitution. As with the charitable trust, there are many national charities that have standard constitutions which may serve as a model for your own. If you use the Commission's own model constitution[114] this will allow the Commission to process your application more speedily.

A company limited by guarantee

What is a company?

The law regards a company as a *"legal person"* which, for legal purposes, has the same standing as a natural person or individual. A company can therefore own property and enter into contracts in its own right; it does not have to carry out transactions in the names of its officers. The company and its members are regarded as *separate* legal persons, and it continues to exist notwithstanding changes in its membership or officers.

What is 'limited' in a limited company?

Since any debts or other liabilities incurred are therefore those of the *company* and not of the individuals who are participating in the company, the *insolvency* of the company does not normally lead to its members or officers being required to pay its debts from their own personal resources. The liability of company members towards the company is limited to paying to the company only such sums as have been agreed, upon joining the company, as payment for shares[115] or by way of guarantee.[116] This 'limited liability' protects a participant's personal assets from commercial risk, unless the company's inability to pay was caused by deliberate wrongdoing by that person.

What is a company 'limited by guarantee'?

A commercial company exists ultimately to distribute annual

---

114 *Model Constitution for an Unincorporated Association*, Reference GD3, Charity Commissioners.
115 Companies Act 1985 s. 1(2)(a).
116 Companies Act 1985 s. 1(2)(b).

profits to its members, and any remaining assets on its dissolution. A member will have bought shares in the company, and this ownership stake will entitle the member to receive such distributions in proportion to the value of his/her shares. A member's liability to the company is limited to any sum still owed by him/her to the company in payment for his/her shares, hence this liability is said to be 'limited by shares'. A charitable company ought not usually be owned in this way, because charity assets must be applied for charitable purposes and not be distributed to members for their private gain. Most companies limited by guarantee are charities or other non-trading companies. In a company limited by guarantee each member undertakes to pay a specified amount, usually nominal, if the company is wound up while he/she is a member (or within a year of ceasing membership). Hence the liability of its members is limited to the amount of this guarantee.

When is it suitable?

Since the chief advantage of a limited company is the protection of participants' personal assets from commercial risk, it is a suitable form if a charity is to be quite large, employ many staff, or regularly enter into commercial contracts.

Disadvantages

Because a company is subject to company law and the requirement to file accounts and other information with the Registrar of Companies, it may be more complex and costly to set up and administer than a trust. Nevertheless, this drawback may be decisively outweighed by the benefits of limited liability and the independent legal status[117] of a company.

Governing document

The governing documents of a company are its memorandum and articles of association.[118] In addition to standard versions produced by some national bodies, the Commission has a model upon which yours can be based.[119]

---

117 It is also possible to incorporate the trustees of a charity without forming the charity itself into a company. This allows the trustees to conduct transactions and hold property in the name of the incorporated body, but without the charity itself being formed into a company. For further details see *Incorporation of Charity Trustees*, Reference CC43, Charity Commissioners, September 1995.

118 See *Guidance on when to use a Memorandum and Articles of Association*, Reference INF 4, Charity Commissioners, August 1996.

119 *Model Memorandum & Articles of Association for a Charitable Company*, Reference GD1, Charity Commissioners, January 1995.

The governing document is settled

Once agreed, the governing document should be executed, adopted or incorporated, as the case may be, depending upon whether it is a trust deed, constitution or memorandum and articles of association. The Charity Commission will not usually consider an application from an organisation whose governing document is only in draft form. Their experience has been that applications from promoters who have not clarified the ways in which they will carry out their charitable objects are usually time consuming and often abortive.

The type of case where the Commission might make an exception to this rule is where a disaster appeal needs to be launched, and it is urgent to establish its charitable status.

4. Registering the charity

Which charities must register?

All charities subject to the *jurisdiction* of the High Court are required to be registered with the Charity Commissioners except:

1. exempt charities
2. charities excepted by order or regulations from registration
3. 'small' charities (i.e. any charity which has neither any *permanent endowment* nor the use and occupation of any land and whose income from all sources does not in aggregate amount to more than £1,000 a year
4. a charity in respect of any registered place of worship.

The jurisdiction of the High Court

A charity will fall within the jurisdiction of the High Court if it is established in England and Wales, and in addition: all or most of its trustees are resident in England and Wales, or all or most of its assets are held in England and Wales, or if the charity is a company, it is incorporated (i.e. registered as a company) in England and Wales.

Exempt charities

These are listed in Schedule 2 of the Charities Act 1993, and are exempt from many provisions of the Act and from the supervision of the Charity Commissioners. They include certain universities, museums and art galleries, the Church Commissioners and the British Library. The reason for their exemption is that they are supervised and protected by other legislation.

Excepted charities

These are excepted from the obligation to register, but are otherwise subject to the supervisory powers of the Charity Commission. The exceptions can be authorised either by regulations made by the Heritage Secretary or by order of the Charity Commissioners. They include every university which is not an exempt charity, certain voluntary schools, boy scout and girl guide charities, non-conformist and other religious charities, trusts for the upkeep of graves, and charities for the promotion of efficiency of the armed forces.

'Small' charities

It would be administratively inconvenient to register all the smallest charities. Therefore any charity which does not have a total income from all sources of more than £1,000 per year, nor have any permanent endowment (i.e. assets which are required to be held as capital and may not be spent as income), nor own or occupy land or buildings for which it is responsible for paying rates to the local authority (or would be had the local authority not granted rate relief), is considered too small to be eligible for inclusion on the register, and is therefore not required to register.

Submitting the application

The application form for registering a charity (Form APP 1) is clearly set out, and includes many helpful explanatory notes. Along with the completed form, trustees are also asked to submit a declaration (Form DEC 1) which confirms that they have read certain Charity Commission leaflets,[120] and that none of them is disqualified from acting as a charity trustee.

If for any reason the application is unsuccessful, the Commission will write to the applicants explaining the reasons why. The applicants then have an opportunity to reply, explaining why they disagree with the decision, or clarifying any points which they feel the Commission might have misunderstood. The application will not be rejected for a second time unless a more senior or legal officer of the Commission has reviewed the case. A further review may be conducted by the Board of Commissioners, and an appeal against their decision can be made to the High Court.

---

120 This is to ascertain that the trustees understand the commitment which they are making. The leaflets are: *Responsibilities of Charity Trustees*, Reference CC3, March 1996; *Political Activities and Campaigning by Charities*, Reference CC9, July 1995; *What is a Charity?*, Reference CC21(a), March 1996; *Registering a Charity*, Reference CC21(b), March 1996; and *What Happens after Registration?*, Reference CC21(c), March 1996.

After the charity is registered

If the application is accepted, the Commission will write a letter advising that the organisation has been registered. This is significant, since the Charities Act 1993 declares that a registered organisation is conclusively presumed to be a charity at all times when it is on the register.[121]

8. Altering the Trusts of a Charity

The problem of the *ultra vires* rule

Normally, charity trustees must use the resources of their charity for the purposes described in their governing document, and not for any other purposes, even charitable ones. The *ultra vires* rule is fundamental to the proper control of all organisations managed by persons whose powers are limited by law.[122]

However, a problem therefore arises if money or property has been donated for a charitable purpose but, for some reason, it cannot now be used for that purpose. The trustees are then faced with the difficulty that there is, apparently, no lawful way in which their funds can be used. Examples of when this may happen are where:

- an existing charity has fulfilled its purpose or become defunct, and there are surplus funds left over
- a charity's original purpose is now provided for in other ways, for example by the welfare state
- the assets of a charity are too small for it to be practicable to carry out its purpose
- money is left in a will for a charity which turns out not to exist, or to have been wound up prior to the death of the donor.

How charities may be altered or modernised

In this type of case the *cy-près* doctrine may allow a solution to this problem. The charity may be allowed to alter its governing document to take on new charitable purposes as similar as possible to the existing ones, or one charitable organisation may amalgamate with another, or the money or property might be allocated to another but similar charity.[123]

---

121 S. 4(1).
122 Such action is also likely to be in breach of trust, rendering trustees liable to make good any loss to the charity caused by unauthorised expenditure.
123 For information on how a church hall may be used for other charitable purposes if it is no longer needed exclusively for church purposes, or on selling or letting the property if it is no longer needed, see *Use of Church Halls for Village Hall and Other Charitable Purposes*, Reference CC18, Charity Commissioners, March 1996.

If the legal conditions for this type of solution are satisfied,[124] the Charity Commission or the court will formulate a *Scheme* for the application of the funds to another charitable purpose as near as possible to the original purpose.

A scheme for changing the administrative machinery (as distinct from the purposes) of a charity can also be approved without invoking the *cy-près* doctrine where it is shown that such a change would be expedient.[125] This might be necessary, for instance, to change the constitution of the charity's governing body where this is no longer appropriate, or to enable the trustees to take some action which their governing document does not presently empower them to do (e.g. to sell or invest charity assets).

Therefore, if a charity's purpose or constitution cause the trustees difficulty in running it, an approach should be made to the Charity Commission to consider a solution, which might include the making of a Scheme to authorise the necessary changes.

9. The Responsibilities and Liabilities of Charity Trustees

What is a charity trustee?

A trustee is a person who holds property on *trust* for another, known as the *beneficiary*: this obligation of trust has been recognised by English law since the 15th century. Traditionally, a charity trustee has meant a trustee of a charitable trust. However, the Charities Act 1993 has enlarged the concept of a charity trustee. Section 97 extends the obligations imposed upon charity trustees by the Act to *everyone* who manages a charity.[126] So, for the purpose of the legislation, all those on the governing body of a charity is are charity trustees, even if they are referred to by a different title, such as directors, governors, or committee members.

Who can become a charity trustee?

A responsible office

Even though working for charity can be personally very satisfying, the Charities Acts of 1992 and 1993 have made the charity

---

124 Traditionally this was determined by case law, but nowadays CA 1993 ss. 13 & 14 cover most circumstances. See also s.74.

125 *Re J W Laing Trust* [1984] 1 All ER 50 is an example.

126 "[i]n this Act, except in so far as the context otherwise requires 'charity trustees' means the persons having the general control and management of the administration of a charity ..."

trustee's role more demanding than in the past. Modern charity trustees have to submit audited accounts, manage the investments of their organisations, submit to supervision by the Charity Commission, and even raise funds though entering into contracts for services rather than receive grant aid as in the past. The responsibility of a trustee of a medium to large charity is today is somewhat closer to that of a company director or local authority councillor than it was in the past. Therefore no-one should accept trusteeship lightly, nor only as a mark of honour.

Eligibility

Only an adult (i.e. over 18 years old) of sound mind may be a trustee. The following are disqualified[127] from being a charity trustee:

- anyone convicted of an offence of dishonesty (unless the conviction is spent under the Rehabilitation of Offenders Act 1974)
- undischarged bankrupts and anyone who has entered into an arrangement with creditors and has not been discharged in respect of it
- anyone whom the court or Charity Commissioners have removed from trusteeship of a charity on grounds of misconduct or mismanagement of a charity
- anyone disqualified from being the director of a company under the Company Directors Disqualification Act 1986 or under insolvency legislation.

Appointment of trustees

Usually, the charity's governing document lays down the procedure for appointing trustees, including how many there are to be and for how long they should hold office. In the unusual event that it does not, then the Trustee Act 1925 contains statutory provisions which will apply in default.

Similar provisions regulate the retirement of trustees. Usually, when one trustee retires, a successor is appointed. A trustee may not retire without the appointment of a successor if this would leave less than two remaining trustees (or a *trust corporation*). The Charity Commission consider it advisable to have at least three charity trustees.

---

127 By Charities Act 1993 ss. 7273. Acting as a trustee while disqualified is a criminal offence punishable by fine and/or imprisonment: s. 73. The Charity Commissioners can waive disqualification if this is in the interests of the charity concerned, except for those disqualified under the Company Directors Disqualification Act 1986.

Trustees' duties and standard of conduct

Non-professional unpaid trustees

A trustee's main duty is to manage the charity, including a duty to ensure that, in relation both to income and to capital, the right amounts are paid to the right persons. In doing so, the standard of care which he/she should exercise has been defined by law as being that which an ordinary businessman or woman would take in managing his/her own affairs. Trustees must therefore play an active role, ensuring that they are aware of the purposes, constitution, property, and personnel of their organisation, and in control of its activities.

Professionally qualified trustees

Those such as solicitors, accountants and trust corporations must exercise a higher standard of diligence and knowledge, because they hold themselves out as capable of providing an expertise as trustees.

Duty to protect trust assets

Once appointed, trustees must make themselves aware of the terms of the governing document, check that the charity's property is under their proper control, and that any investment of charity funds complies with the terms of the governing document.

Trustees must not profit from their office

Trusteeship is normally a voluntary, unpaid office. Only in exceptional cases may remuneration of a trustee be authorised by the governing instrument, or by the Charity Commission if it is satisfied that it is in the best interests of the charity. An example would be where only remuneration would make it possible for a trustee with special skills to accept appointment. On the other hand, a trustee is entitled to be reimbursed for reasonable out-of-pocket expenses incurred while on charity business.

Conflict of interest

All trustees should act exclusively in the best interests of the charity. Therefore a trustee must not allow a situation to arise where his/her duty as a trustee conflicts with his/her own personal interest. Examples of a conflict of interest include: a trustee who performs work in return for payment by the charity; a trustee who participates in a decision that the charity will assist him/her; and a trustee who buys, sells or rents something to or from the charity (e.g. goods, land or a building).

There would also be a conflict of interest if any close family members or business associates of a trustee were affected by these transactions.

It is important to appreciate that it is immaterial whether the charity ac*tually* loses, or the trustee profits, by the transaction. The point is that there must be *no opportunity* for the trustee to be influenced by his/her own personal interests while engaging in the management of the charity. The trustee must ensure that the only possible factor influencing his/her role in the charity is the best interest of the charity.

Therefore, where a decision has to be made in which a trustee's personal interest (or those of his/her family or business connections) is affected, he/she should declare the interest and not participate in the taking of that decision.

Decisions

Charity trustees must meet regularly enough to ensure that they retain control over the running of their organisation. Decisions are taken by a simple majority vote of those trustees present and voting at the meeting, unless the governing document makes some provision such as a casting vote for the chairman or woman, or a greater majority for decisions on certain issues. It may be practical for the governing document to specify a quorum for trustee meetings, otherwise meetings will not be valid unless all trustees are in attendance.

Documentary transactions

Where a transaction requires the execution (signing) of a document, the trustees may authorise any two or more trustees to do so on behalf of all of them.

Advice

When faced with a difficult or complex decision it is advisable for trustees to seek out competent advice. This may be from professionals such as a solicitor or accountant. The Charity Commission's many advisory booklets are also a valuable source. In addition, charity trustees should bear in mind the advice service offered by the Commission in response to written queries on any matter affecting the performance of the trustee's duties.[128]

---

128 CA 1993 s. 29. Trustees acting on the commissioners' advice are deemed to have acted in accordance with the trust and are therefore protected from any complaint that they have acted in breach of trust.

10. Specialist Transactions

Certain transactions by charities require professional advice and/ or the authorisation of the Charity Commission or the court. They are only briefly mentioned here to alert you to this need.

Investment

Generally, the resources of a charity should be deployed in furtherance of its charitable purposes. However, where there are funds which are held as reserves or which are not to be used for some time, the trustees have a duty to invest these, since not to do so would be to subject the fund to unnecessary erosion by inflation, thereby causing loss to the charity.

When setting up a charity you should ensure that the governing document gives the trustees wide powers of investment, otherwise the trustees will be constrained by a restrictive regime imposed by the Trustee Investments Act 1961, now regarded as archaic and in the process of being reformed.

In making investments trustees are expected to exercise a standard of care that a prudent person of business would take when making investments on behalf of others for whom he/she feels morally bound to provide. If you take expert advice on your investment activity, as indeed you should for all but the simplest investments, you are expected to exercise due care in selecting your advisor.

Permanent endowment

Permanent endowment means charity property, which may include land, which is subject to a restriction on the expenditure of capital.[129] If permanently endowed property is sold, the charity is not allowed to spend the proceeds of the sale on day-to-day expenses. Instead, these have to be reinvested or used to buy other property, which in turn will also be permanent endowment. You should take advice on whether any property is permanent endowment, and on how to manage any contemplated transaction involving such property. In some cases the Charity Commissioners can authorise transactions which appear to them to be expedient in the interests of the charity but are not within the normal powers of the trustees.[130]

Land transactions, including mortgages

Land and premises may be freehold or leasehold. They may have been acquired to carry out the charity's objects, or alternatively

---

129 Charities Act 1993, s. 96(3).
130 Charities Act 1993, s. 26.

as an investment, or to accommodate the offices of the charity. The purchase may have been funded from the charity's own resources, or by raising a loan. The charity may also wish to borrow money against the security of its land. Clearly, dealings in land (which may or may not be permanent endowment), and the management of premises are specialist activities on which you should seek professional advice.

11. Glossary of Terms

Case law consists of the principles and rules of law which have emerged from the decisions taken by judges in court cases. *See Section 2* of this chapter for further discussion of the nature of case law.

Charitable purpose A charitable purpose is a purpose recognised by the law as charitable. *See Section 2* of this chapter.

Charitable status The legal status of an organisation (whether corporate or not) of being charitable, because it operates solely and exclusively for *charitable purposes*. All charities are required to be registered with the *Charity Commissioners* except (1) exempt charities, (2) charities excepted by order or regulations from registration and (3) any charity which has neither any *permanent endowment* nor the use and occupation of any land and whose income from all sources does not in aggregate amount to more than £1,000 a year. In addition, no charity is required to be registered in respect of any registered place of worship.

Charity Commission See *Charity Commissioners*

Charity Commissioners are a statutory body (i.e. who draw their authority from Parliamentary legislation) which administers charities, secures the effective use of charity property and investigates abuses, removing trustees from office where necessary.

Charity trustees Traditionally, this has meant the trustees of a charitable trust. However, the obligations imposed upon charity trustees by the Charities Act 1993 are extended to *everyone* who manages a charity, by section 97, which states that *"in this Act, except in so far as the context otherwise requires 'charity trustees' means the persons having the general control and management of the administration of a* *charity...*" This will be the case even if, in the charity's *governing document*, they may be referred to as directors, or governors, or committee members, or some other title. Thus we may now refer to charity trustees in the traditional sense and in the statutory sense, respectively. See also *Trust*.

Court judgment The decision of a court, including the judge's explanation for the decision. When a court judgment is legally significant because it offers a clarification or new interpretation of the law, or changes what was hitherto regarded as accepted law, it is reported as a *law report* in a series of which there are several well-accepted periodical publications.

Custodian trustee is a trustee whose sole role is to hold the legal ownership of trust property, but without any powers of management.

Cy-près doctrine (originating from the French *si près*, or *ici près* or *aussi près* = so near, as near) a rule developed by the Court of Chancery and liberalised by legislation (now Charities Act 1993 ss. 13, 14. See also s. 74) permitting a charity's funds or property to be reallocated to a different but similar charitable purpose, or to another charity, in certain circumstances.

Donor A person or organisation who gives money or other assets.

Excepted *See definition on page 108.*

Exempt *See definition on page 107.*

Governing document Any document setting out a charity's purposes and, usually, how it is to be administered. It may be a trust deed, constitution, Memorandum and Articles of Association, *will*, conveyance, Royal Charter, Scheme of the Commissioners, or other formal document.

Insolvency inability to pay debts. A condition where the debts of an individual or company exceed his/her/its assets.

Instrument a formal legal document in writing, such as a deed, *will* or the *governing document*, of a charity.

Jurisdiction the power of a court to hear and decide on a case by reason of some territorial or other legally valid criterion.

Law reports Publications reporting the courts' more important decisions.

Lawyers Professional lawyers, who may hire themselves for legal advice, advocacy and other work, comprise solicitors and barristers. A solicitor may have as a client any member of the public or a corporation. A barrister, also known as 'counsel', is usually hired at the behest of a solicitor to carry out advocacy in court or to give specialist legal advice. There are also academic lawyers, who teach law and carry out academic research and writing about law, but they may not hire themselves out to give legal advice to the public unless they are also a solicitor or barrister.

Legacy A gift of personal property made by *will*.

Legislation, for the purpose of this chapter, refers to the making of laws by Acts of Parliament, (also known as *statutes*) or by regulations made by a government minister acting with the authority of Parliament.

Permanent endowment Property, including land, buildings, investments or cash, which may not be spent by the trustees as if it were income.

Promoters in the context of this chapter means those persons who are intending to set up a charity.

Quasi-judicial akin to judicial. For example, someone making a quasi-judicial decision should do so not arbitrarily, but in a way similar to a judge. This involves ascertaining the facts by means of evidence presented by the people who are affected by the decision, considering the legal arguments, and making a decision based on a finding of the facts (if they are disputed) and an application of the law to the facts as found.

Scheme A Scheme is legal document propounded by the Charity Commissioners or the court to amend or replace a charity's governing document.

Solicitor *See lawyers.*

Statute *See legislation*

Trust An obligation which imposes on a person, known as the *trustee*, certain duties of dealing with property held and controlled by him or her for the benefit of other persons, known as the beneficiaries. In a charity there are often no such named beneficiaries, and then the trustee must deal with the property in fulfilment of the *charitable purpose* of the trust.

Trust corporation A corporation which is authorised to act as a trustee.

Trustee One who holds property on *trust* for another, known as the beneficiary: this obligation of trust has been recognised by English law since the 15th century.[131] See also *Charity Trustees*.

***Ultra vires* rule** A rule affecting the actions of companies, public bodies and anyone whose powers are defined by a governing document or legislation. Acts which are *ultra vires* ('beyond the powers') are void. Thus a charity formed to carry out purpose A cannot validly tackle purpose B.

Will A declaration, usually in writing, of the intentions of the person who writes it concerning the disposition of his/her property after his/her death. It is common for people to leave money or other property to a charity in their will.

---

131 Milsom, SCF, Historical Foundations of the Common Law, 2nd ed, Butterworths, London 1981.

ADMINISTRATION : 4

David Prescott

1. Introduction

Aims and objectives

Generally speaking charities, or the work they carry out, appeal to the emotions (the heart) and yet charity administration must be a matter for the head. Charities need effective management and good administration, not only to ensure that funds are spent with the greatest effect but also to encourage support for the charity (donations). This is particularly important in the light of a 1993 survey by Loughborough University which showed that:

- 40% of non-donors to charities believed that charities are run by disorganised amateurs
- 59% believed that there is corruption in charities
- 78% didn't believe that donations reached the beneficiaries of a charity.

This section demonstrates the need for effective administration and the skills and competencies demanded by increasingly complex charity organisations. By the end of the chapter readers will have learned:

- that a charity cannot survive without effective administration
- the importance of cost ratios as an indicator of a charity's efficiency
- how to conduct meetings and handle minutes
- the need for effective office administration and management
- the uses of information technology in administration
- the importance of adequate insurance cover
- an administrator's statutory responsibilities
- the efficient purchasing of goods and services
- internal control and audit
- performance measurement.

2. Administration is for All

Survival depends on it

A charity cannot survive without administration (as indeed no organisation can). If you get it right your charity will be effective;

get it wrong and the consequences could be costly, painful and – not least – time consuming. The success of a charity will be improved if administration is seen not only as an exclusive job of the administrator/s. Fundraisers, welfare officers, care staff and indeed, any functional head of department should have some training in business administration. Administration must be an integral part of the organisation – not just incidental to it.

A survey carried out in 1992 by the ICSA (Institute of Chartered Secretaries and Administrators) found that in any organisation an administrator deals with matters at all levels: routine, operational and strategic. Matters dealt with can be either easy and straightforward, technical (e.g. IT) or complex in nature.

The job of an administrator varies enormously between organisations – there are no well-defined boundaries. As a result, the purpose and value of administration are often undervalued to the serious detriment of organisations.

There is no one 'right' way of carry out administration. But administration will hold a valued place in organisations (especially charities) only if it is seen to provide value for money.

The Skills Needed

A charity's administrative staff will need many skills to enable them to be competent and make a positive contribution. These include:

- planning, organising and monitoring work, including use of materials and equipment
- developing and maintaining effective working relationships with colleagues and external contacts
- researching, supplying and preparing information
- drafting and preparing documents e.g. minutes
- developing and maintaining procedures to meet specific needs e.g. distribution of grants to individuals
- influencing and facilitating decision making by trustees and Committees e.g. by preparation of management information
- entering and integrating data using computer systems
- developing staff to improve performance of individuals and team as a whole
- preparing and updating operational plan, implementation and monitoring of results
- planning and creating systems to meet the organisational needs of the charity, agree systems and procedures with management
- negotiating contracts for the supply of goods and services
- dealing with legal and regulatory requirements (compliance) which affect charity e.g. health and safety.

Checklist

☐ Does your charity organisation achieve effective administration?

☐ Are you working towards creating a common level of expectation of administration standards?

Does effective administration in your organisation:

    ☐ (a) reduce the margin of error?

    ☐ (b) achieve satisfied "customers" e.g. donors, beneficiaries?

    ☐ (c) achieve real cost savings?

    ☐ (d) motivate employee to higher achievement?

    ☐ (e) help to recruit and train staff?

    ☐ (f) assist in achieving initiatives towards quality assurance e.g. ISO 9000 or Investors in People?

☐ Does your organisation assess staff performance at work and identify training and development needs?

☐ Do you have job descriptions in your organisation; are they reviewed on a regular basis?

☐ Do you have a structured training programme for administrative staff?

3. Office Organisation and Management

The Role and Objective of the Office

The Offices, Shops and Railway Premises Act 1963 defined the following terms:

- Office Purposes: include the purposes of administration, clerical work, handling money and telephone operating. (In 1997 this would also include information technology, fax etc.).
- Clerical Work: includes writing, book-keeping, sorting papers, filing, typing, duplicating, machine calculation, drawing and editorial preparation of matter for publication.
- Office Premises: means a building, or part of a building, the sole principal use of which is an office for office purposes.

The basic functions of office work are receiving and/or producing information, processing information or creating information from data, storing or communicating information e.g. word processing, copying, mailing etc. and control – inspection, supervision, audit etc.

Objectives and effectiveness

The overall objective of a charity's office is to provide an efficient, effective service to management (trustees and executive staff) and other information users throughout the organisation e.g. donors, users of the charity's services etc. Its effectiveness is measured by the extent to which the activity fulfils its purpose and meets its users' (e.g. beneficiaries') requirements. Its efficiency is measured by the extent to which resources are utilised without wastage in the pursuit of effectiveness.

Resources of the office include finance, materials, equipment and not least, human resources of time, effort, skills and knowledge. Achieving and maintaining efficiency will involve elimination of delays in the provision of office services and keeping to resource budgets. See the office as an 'Open System' connected to and interacting with its environment; whilst being stable, it is continually changing or evolving.

The office environment

Office location is vital to a charity's work and depends upon the nature of its business e.g. the need to be in London. Other factors influencing location include cost – rental charges, availability of grants etc.; communication and transport links; whether there is a sufficient 'pool' of labour; and surrounding facilities e.g. bank, post office etc.

Example

In 1966 National Charity re-located its H.Q. adjacent to its nursing and residential centre; a new building in the grounds was 'paid for' within 10 years from savings on renting office space in central London.

The internal environment is also important. Office accommodation should have the following basic features:
- economical use of space (space costs money)
- arrangement for efficient work flow (easy movement of people and documents)
- arrangement for supervision
- provision for security (as necessary) and safety of occupants.

The different types of office layout also have advantages and disadvantages:
- small closed offices linked by corridors offer privacy and security but supervision and communication may be hindered
- open plan offices offer ease of communication and supervision, flexible arranging of furniture and equipment, economic use of heating and lighting, but lack privacy, and there may be

distraction from noise and movement and loss of status for managers

- landscape offices offer a variation of open plan, using acoustic screens
- mixture of closed and open offices may combine some or all advantages/disadvantages
- charities may not have a choice of layout as space may be donated, or the cheapest solution found.

Office management – Principles and Practice

The responsibility for office work will vary depending upon the size and type of charity. In a medium sized or small charity the role of office manager will be undertaken by the Secretary or Accountant. Large charities may have a separate office services department.

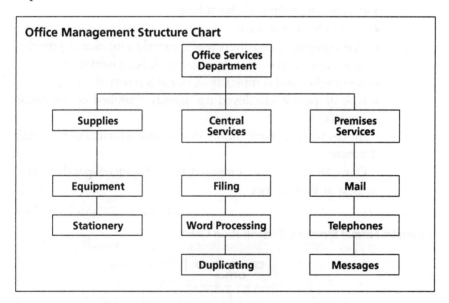

Office Management Structure Chart

- Consider issues of authority, responsibility and delegation in the office environment.
- Consider the centralisation or decentralisation of office services, decide what is best for the charity.

The Role of the Manager

The manager:

- plans and formulates: policy, including setting objectives, forecasting, analysing problems and opportunities, making decisions
- organises: decides activities necessary to achieve objectives of

charity, allocates work and assigns it to different groups and individuals

- motivates: inspires staff to contribute to achievement of purpose of charity (Job satisfaction is often major motivation in charities)
- controls and measures: seeing that targets are met and objectives achieved
- communicates: ideas, decisions, instructions and results, both within and outside the organisation essential to all the roles of a manager.

Organisational Structure

It is important that the line of authority from trustees and Chief Executive of a charity down to all employees is clear to all concerned. This is known as the 'chain of command'.

The chain of command depends upon:

- size of the organisation
- type, complexity and diversity of the services the charity provides
- its geographical spread e.g. regional, UK or worldwide
- the number and complexity of controls required
- type of people employed e.g. mainly unskilled or technical experts.

Consider whether your charity should have a formal or informal structure

Consider supervision, management and leadership styles in the context of your charity.

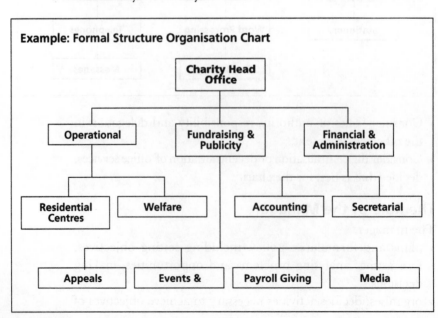

Example: Formal Structure Organisation Chart

Charity Head Office

Operational — Fundraising & Publicity — Financial & Administration

Residential Centres — Welfare — Accounting — Secretarial

Appeals — Events & — Payroll Giving — Media

Office services

All charities will have to consider how information is produced, reproduced, stored and retrieved. You will need to consider the use of equipment and automation (computerisation of systems) in your organisation.

Office efficiency

Some general advice may help you to get into the habit of efficiency in your office

a) use window envelopes

b) use message forms to record phone conversations

c) use carbon paper instead of time and ink

d) word process rather than type (reduces time in correcting errors)

e) sort out work in batches e.g. documents requiring copying

f) avoid having to cross the room to retrieve items used regularly

g) use the phone rather than 'off chance' visit

h) design forms, filing systems and desk top layout for ease and speed of information retrieval

I) don't work in ways or places that will tire you more quickly

j) don't duplicate tasks which you could do once

k) don't do tasks that you needn't do at all.

4. Cost Ratios

The relationship between the expenditure on meeting the charity's objectives and that spent on administration and raising funds (appeals and publicity) is of major concern to donors. They ask "how much of my gift will go directly to the cause?", e.g. to relieve poverty. Donors often feel that the less a charity spends on administration and fundraising, the more effective it will be. However, in fact this may not be so.

The Charity Commission, in its 1989 report, commented *"The cost of administering charities is a matter which arouses strong feelings and varied opinions. It is sometimes assumed that people who work for charities should do it for nothing, or at most, for a pittance. Donors often express a wish that their money should go exclusively to the object of their beneficiaries and not towards the cost of administration... such attitudes, however imply that administration is a bad thing and that the ideal administration cost is nil. If carried into actual practice, such an attitude can only lead to badly administered charities and to inefficiency and abuse."*

In 1990, the Commission said: *"Effective and efficient administration cannot be bought on the cheap..."*

Policy and Practice on Expenditure Ratios

The ratio of funds used for administration and fundraising cannot be used as a measure of the overall efficiency of a charity. The relative efficiency of different charities cannot be compared, due to varying methods of accounting and allocation of costs. The level of spending on administration and fundraising will depend largely on the individual circumstances of each charity:

- a charity with large endowments generating substantial investment income may spend little on fundraising.
- a charity relying on canvassing a large number of supporters, with regionally based teams of paid fundraisers will have a relatively high cost fundraising strategy.
- a charity funded by endowment income or several large grants will cost less to administer when compared with a charity handling thousands of small donations and covenants.

Example

A charity with a caseload of 3000 families, employing 12 support staff and 75 volunteers. In addition to financial aid, advice, advocacy and emotional support is given to beneficiaries. Trustees currently consider all the departments' expenditure as direct charitable expenditure. Figures for 1994/95:

Grants	£462,000	67%
Salaries	£168,000	24%
Other Costs	£ 63,000	9%
Total	£693,000	100%

However a major grant-making trust refused an application for funds due to the level of welfare salary costs; even though all these costs were assisting and supporting needy people in accordance with the "hands on" approach of the charity.

A positive approach

A charity physically providing a number of services e.g. residential homes and day centres will cost more to administer than a charitable foundation making grants to other charities. Inconsistencies are caused by differing accounting policies used by charities e.g. allocation of cost between fundraising and publicity (education). But it is possible to adopt a positive approach to cost ratios for both administration and fundraising:

- promote the idea that 'good administration has to be paid for'
- promote fundraising costs as an 'investment for future funding' e.g. £10 can raise £50 for the charity.

Example

The administration, management and fundraising costs of Motor and Allied Trades Benevolent Fund have remained relatively consistent over a 10 year period:

1987	-	17.5% of £2.9m	=	£ 500,000
1996	-	17% of £6.8m	=	£1,150,000

The Effect of SORP on Cost Ratios

SORP (*See Chapters 5 and 6 for more detail*) contains the following definitions:

a) *"Fundraising and publicity costs comprise the costs actually incurred by a charity, or by an agent, in inducing others to make voluntary donations to it."*

b) *"Administration and management would include: central management and administration: investment management: internal & external audit: costs of compliance: trustee meetings: annual general meetings: valuations fees."*

What this means is that costs should be apportioned on a reasonable, consistent and justifiable basis e.g. premises costs allocated on basis of floor area used by each department at H.Q. No part of costs which are directly attributable to one category should be allocated to another. And costs which are not direct charitable expenditure and not fundraising or publicity should be allocated to management and administration.

However, the SORP does not solve the problems of comparing cost ratios between charities.

Checklist

☐ Do administration and fundraising costs effectively contribute to meeting the objects of your charity?

☐ Does your charity have a clear policy on cost ratios?

☐ Are your trustees aware of the cost ratios of other similar charities?

☐ If so, are there reasons why your charity is different than its peer group?

☐ Have you re-considered allocation policies in the light of the SORP?

5. Meetings and Minutes

Meetings are an essential part of the administration and management of a charity, enabling decisions to be made by a group collectively. The minutes become a permanent record of the activities of a charity. The content of this section will provide information and practical advice on types of and function of committees, forming committees, meetings – law, procedure and administration, preparation of minutes.

Types of Committees

The main committee of a charity is its governing body, trustees of an unincorporated association or directors of a charitable company. Its role is to control and manage the affairs of a charity. If permitted by the constitution, this body may delegate tasks to other committees for one or more of the following purposes.

1. Management e.g. 1) executive committee, 2) finance & general purposes committee.
2. Functional – to co-ordinate and plan activities e.g. 1) fundraising committee, 2) grants committee, 3) project committee, say to plan and develop a building.
3. Advisory – to gain specialist advise on technical matters e.g. 1) medical committee.
4. Consultative – to obtain views and opinions from a wide field e.g. 1) geographical region.

General Advice – Terms of reference for each

Terms of reference for each committee are absolutely essential and must define: purpose, specific task/s, limits of authority composition and frequency of meetings. Sub-committees should report to governing body e.g. by circulation of minutes. Sub-committees should have at least one member from the governing body since this is good for communication.

The aim of a committee should be to reach sound decisions reasonably quickly after adequate discussion of all relevant factors.

Case study

Specimen Terms of Reference for a Sub-Committee distributing grants to individuals:

Terms of Reference
a) *the Sub-Committee shall be responsible to the Management Committee for the consideration of all applications for assistance*
b) *it shall determine amounts granted to beneficiaries by gift, loan, charge on property or otherwise, subject to overall budget approved by the Committee*
c) *the Sub-Committee shall determine from time to time the maximum amount that the Welfare Officer may give as an individual emergency*

grant to a needy applicant, such grants, made at the discretion of the
Welfare Officer, to be ratified at the next meeting of the Committee

d) the Welfare Committee at its discretion may delegate powers to the
Director of Welfare Services to authorise payments to beneficiaries
within maximum as determined by the Management Committee, such
grants to be ratified by the Sub-Committee

e) the Welfare Committee shall consider the types of assistance given to
beneficiaries in their own homes and make recommendations to the
Management Committee as necessary

f) it shall advise the Management Committee on policy matters which
affect beneficiaries in any way

g) the Sub-Committee shall delegate to Director of Welfare Services the
executive action needed to implement their decisions.

Constitution

Membership: *The Chairman and Deputy Chairman shall be appointed*
annually by the Management Committee.

Sub-Committee shall consist of a panel of 12 members
who shall be appointed by the Board.

Whilst periods of service and age- limitation of Sub-
Committee members are not defined, they shall retire
automatically at the date of the Annual General
Meeting of the Fund. In reviewing appointments, the
Management Committee shall take into consideration
age, length of service, contribution and attendance
record.

Quorum: *4*

Meetings: *Monthly or as necessary.*

Expenses: *Generally speaking travelling and out-of-pocket*
expenses incurred by Sub-Committee members shall not
be met by the Fund. However, the Management
Committee will sympathetically consider exceptions.

Forming a Committee

The main considerations are:

- key appointments e.g. Chairman, Vice Chairman and Secretary
- selection of members
- role of permanent staff
- size – dependent upon:
  a) constitutional requirements e.g. maximum number may be
  limited

b) type of committee

c) quorum and availability to attend meetings

d) efficient and effective conduct of business i.e. must not be unwieldy

e) the minimum number considered reasonable to make decisions on behalf of the full committee.

Conduct of Meetings

The Law

The main legal requirement is that meetings are properly convened and constituted and held in accordance with the rules of the charity (incorporated in the Articles of Association of an incorporated charity). Section 81 of the Charities Act 1993 states that notices may be sent by post. In this case notice is deemed to have been given by the time at which the letter containing it would be delivered in the normal course of post.

Procedure and administration

Various factors can influence the frequency and timing of meetings, these include:

a) the type and amount of work involved e.g. a finance committee would require regular meetings fixed a year in advance

b) volume of work needed between meetings e.g. research by staff or obtaining estimates

c) the effect on the operational tasks of the charity

d) cost of holding meetings

e) the availability of committee members: frequency is an important consideration for potential members.

Role of secretary

In a large charity the Secretary will attend meetings as a senior member of the management team, with assistance by a staff member who may be responsible for 'servicing' several committees under the Secretary's supervision – including production of agenda, minutes and other papers.

Before a meeting: adequate secretarial support is important; all or some of the following will need to have been done:

• confirm availability of the venue, arrange refreshments if necessary

• prepare agenda and supporting documents (involving Chairman) as appropriate

- brief the Chairman concerning the business and conduct of the meeting, prepare briefing notes if appropriate
- distribute the agenda and papers to members at least one week before a meeting
- remind members who are due to present a report to the meeting, also any external consultants (e.g. Investment Manager) who is to attend
- ensure that a quorum will be present.

The Agenda

It is very important that the agenda structures the meeting. Its format will depend upon type and size of committee – the following example of an agenda for a governing body can be adapted to meeting particular requirements.

Example Agenda

1. Apologies for absence.
2. Minutes of previous meeting (circulated).
3. Matters Arising (not listed on agenda).
4. Other Operational Matters e.g.:
   minutes from sub-committee (matters needing ratification)
   periodic reports e.g. review of a policy
   departmental reports e.g. fundraising.
5. Financial Report including as appropriate:
   Investment Manager's Report
   Management Accounts
   cash flow/bank balances
   approval of capital expenditure
6. Development Plans e.g. new project.
7. Personnel Matters e.g. appointment of staff.
8. Any other business.
9. Date and venue of next meeting.

During the meeting the Secretary will notify apologies for absence; check that the meeting has been properly convened and that a quorum is present; provide additional information relevant to the decision making process; be alert to see that any matters are not overlooked, also advising the Chairman of any deviation from the committee's powers; if necessary, clarify the result of any discussion with the Chairman (important for accuracy of minutes).

Minutes

It is important that minutes are drafted as a legal record as soon as possible after a meeting and (if appropriate) approved by the Chairman. If preparation of minutes is delayed, it could affect accuracy and delay implementation of decisions. Minutes must be recorded accurately and where appropriate, include a summary of background information. Major points which indicate why a particular decision was reached may also be included.

Minutes are the official record of the charity and should be kept securely in a bound volume or numbered loose-leaf binder.

General Meetings

The constitution of a charity will usually require an annual general meeting (AGM) of members. If a charity is incorporated under the Companies Act 1985, general meetings are convened as prescribed by the Articles of Association.

The formal business of an AGM is to:
- consider the annual report and accounts
- consider the report of the auditors
- elect (or re-elect) trustees/directors
- appoint auditors and fix their remuneration.

Any meeting other than the AGM is an extraordinary general meeting (EGM).

Checklist

☐ Purpose of meetings
☐ Types of committees
☐ Forming a committee
☐ Meetings – the law
☐ Meetings – procedure
☐ Meetings – duties of Secretary
☐ Preparing the agenda
☐ Preparing the minutes

6. Information Technology

Most charities can benefit from the use of computers and information technology, ranging from the use of a single word processor in small charities to complicated multi-user systems in larger organisations. Many charities handle large volumes of detailed information (data), often having 'high volume, low item value' transactions e.g. list of subscribers.

It is important that a charity use and develop IT solutions to improve operational efficiency and provide 'marketing' information which will promote its work. This section will include strategic planning, IT application, selecting systems, glossary of terms and case study.

IT Strategy for Charities

Without a strategic plan for introducing computers (or replacing old systems), there is a tendency to purchase IT systems on a piecemeal basis. Such lack of planning leads to the creation of several incompatible systems, even within a single department. Before starting any form of computerisation (or expansion of existing systems), it is important to develop strategy at the outset.

Ensure that new systems complement the charity's 'culture' (unless you want to change it deliberately!). Carry out a thorough review of all systems used by the charity (computerised and manual) and decide which areas would benefit from computerised applications.

Determine priorities as costs may be high and need spreading over a period, e.g. two years. Adopt a co-ordinated approach: consider the effects of computerising one department on another, e.g., accounting/grant giving. A charity's IT strategy must be consistent with and form part of the charity's business strategy.

An effective IT strategy can achieve many benefits, including:
- optimising investment in IT (value for money)
- ensuring that systems satisfy needs of a charity, including best use of staff resources
- ensuring management knows what is feasible and practical
- assisting decision making i.e. improving and streamlining information flow
- the co-ordination of systems delivery to meet objectives
- give a 'competitive' edge in the charity market place e.g. supporting fundraising appeals.

IT Applications to Charities

As part of the IT strategy, a charity should identify where the most effective use of computers can be made. The most frequently used systems are:
- donor/subscriber systems, including mailing and covenanting. This forms a database
- accounting, including investment ledger, management accounts, purchase ledger, VAT

- office systems (word-processing, electronic mail)
- personnel/salary systems.

Other specialised systems used by charities include:
- fees and rents billing and debt analysis (residential homes)
- grant making, including beneficiaries' records
- payroll giving schemes
- communication and marketing
- sales and stock control (charity trading company).

The objective of IT systems must be to improve the charity's efficiency and effectiveness.

To maximise benefit from systems, applications should be integrated wherever possible, using common data. The need for integration highlights the importance of understanding the use of information throughout the organisation.

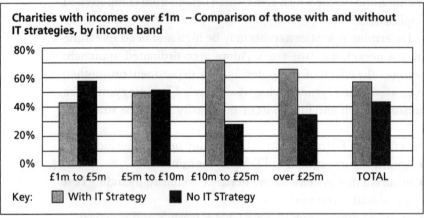

Charities with incomes over £1m – Comparison of those with and without IT strategies, by income band

Key: With IT Strategy — No IT STrategy

Source: Survey into use of IT in charities, Clark Whitehill (September 1994)

Selecting a New System

If a large or complex system is required, obtain an independent consultant's help. Good advice should ensure that specification and procurement are handled properly. Beware – the use of hardware or software suppliers as consultants is not recommended (a conflict of interests is possible). The main stages of a computerisation project are as follows:
- preparation of specification is perhaps the most vital part of the process
- specification defines the scope of a project and details user requirements
- specification forms the basis of a tender documentation and will form part of the contract

- staff preparing specifications will require business analysis and IT skills.

Consider whether to use a specifically designed system (bespoke) or 'off the shelf' package. Decide whether to use an 'in-house' system or use a computer bureau – the latter reduces the need for IT skills within the charity. Before making a selection, a charity should obtain references from existing users.

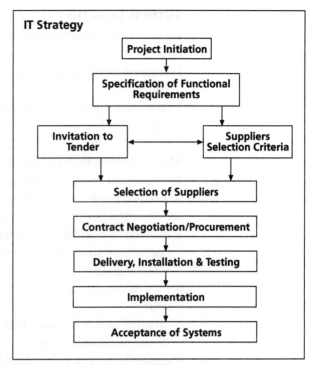

Example

The introduction of a new computer system at BEN has led to requests from staff for IT equipment, particularly from fundraising managers (outworking). A simple IT capital proposal has been devised for the purchase of additional equipment not included in the scope of current major projects. These will include new fundraising and welfare systems.

Checklist

Requirements Specification

Have you:

☐ initiated a study/study group to really find out what is wanted and set objectives?

☐ listed those wants perhaps under the headings – *essential, would be nice, could easily do without* (particularly when reviewing against budget)

☐ developed a list of wants into functional descriptions and details of Data Flow to form the basis of the requirements specifications (for external evaluation purposes and invitation to tender)?

☐ ensured that a correct budget is set?

☐ evaluated cost and possible benefits?

☐ formed basic implementation strategy?

N.B.: You will now be ready to talk to suppliers and review software.

System Selection

Equally as important as the software itself are the suppliers of the software. Have you:

1. ensured they have a good reputation, are they professional and ethical?
2. found out whether they can modify software, not just support it?
3. taken up references?

Matching the software available to your specification. Have you:

1. ensured all *essential* facilities are available?
2. weighted each item on your *wish list* and scored each product?
3. discovered how easy is it to modify or tailor the system?
4. ensured (if possible) the product is compatible with up to date operating systems and written using an up to date development tool/language?
5. established that the software is flexible enough to grow with you?
6. established that it is easy to implement, (especially conversion of current data), and use?
7. ensured that you visit at least two sites of current users of the system?

7. Insurance

Charity trustees have a duty to ensure that adequate insurance cover is maintained against physical loss or damage. Cover is required for a wide range of items including property (land, buildings, equipment, furniture), cash, its liabilities to employees, volunteers and the public, motor insurance and special events.

This section will deal with types of cover which might be needed in the course of a charity's work. It will also help to identify potential risk and discuss administration and selecting an insurance broker. An insurance checklist is also provided.

Buildings and Contents (Property)

Ensure all the charity's property is insured to its full value against all risks, including fire or theft. The charity must disclose all the facts in relation to risk being undertaken by the insurance company. Non-disclosure of information may invalidate the insurance e.g. evidence of subsidence. Trustees of a charity could be personally liable to compensate any loss or damage if insurance is invalidated.

Obtain advice from an insurance broker or independent surveyor on the sum to be insured. Insurance cover can be on an indemnity basis or reinstatement basis. On an indemnity basis the insurers (in the event of a claim) agree to pay the actual loss sustained. Reinstatement cover means that the insurer will meet the cost of reinstating what has been destroyed to its original condition. Cover should be on the basis of rebuilding costs, plus the cost of demolition, site clearance and professional fees. A charity should also consider seriously insuring any costs which result from the disruption to the activities of a charity as a result of a fire for example. This is called consequential loss.

Example

A charity running nursing and residential centres is covered for 'increased cost of working' following loss or damage to its homes. This will cover additional costs of providing alternative accommodation for its residents whilst the building is being repaired for a period of up to 12 months.

The contents of premises should be covered by an 'all risks' policy which covers all items against loss or damage. Ensure that your contents policy covers items on hire or loaned to the charity. Theft or loss of money is usually covered separately. An up to date inventory of all property, furniture and equipment must be kept.

Insurance for liability as an employer

Trustees are required by law to insure against any liability for personal injury or illness sustained by their employees as a result of their employment. Everyone who has an employment contract with the charity must be covered. Cover can be extended to people who are on Executive Work Placement Schemes and other government or local authority training schemes.

The premium payable will be assessed on the number of employees and the total annual cost of salaries and wages. A copy of the employer's liability insurance certificate must be displayed at each workplace. Insurance can be arranged to provide cover against losses relating to employment matters e.g. costs arising from an industrial tribunal award. Trustees may consider insuring against staff absence due to sickness or accident i.e. to cover the cost of sick pay. If your employees (or volunteers) handle cash, a charity should take out fidelity insurance to protect against dishonesty.

Professional indemnity cover should be considered if the staff (or trustees) give advice to the public or other organisations. This will afford protection against claims for incorrect advice.

Insuring for liability to members of the public

A charity occupying premises has a duty to its lawful visitors to ensure that they are reasonably safe; this is called the 'common duty to care'. Public liability insurance is therefore essential to cover for any injury, illness or damage to property incurred by members of the public as a result of the activities of the charity. 'Members of the public' include the charity's volunteers, including trustees and committee members. Volunteers must be informed about the extent of cover given to them by the charity e.g. volunteers over the age of 70 may be excluded when working in charity shops.

Example

A charity employing over 400 people (including contractor's employees) with extensive premises including 275 residential bed spaces and 110 sheltered housing units is insured for £5 million for any one incident.

Exception: fundraising events (covered separately)
Extensions: use of electrical wheelchairs
              staff children on premises.

Trustees insurance against personal liability

If trustees act lawfully, prudently and in accordance with the charity's constitution, any liabilities incurred as a trustee can be met from charity funds. Trustees wishing to use charity funds to insure themselves must have specific power to do so. The Charity Commission only allows a charity to use its funds to pay for liability insurance in respect of:

- acts which are properly undertaken in the administration of a charity
- acts in breach of trust (e.g. making unlawful payment to a trustee) made as a result of an honest mistake.

Trustees cannot cover themselves for acts which they know were wrong, or for actions taken recklessly in disregard as to whether they were right or wrong.

Other types of insurance a charity might need

- Engineering – to cover plant and machinery used by a charity e.g. lifts, boilers.
- Fundraising events – many charities organise special events at which staff, volunteers or the general public are subject to risk e.g. go-karting, assault courses. Exhibitions may also need separate insurance.

- Motor cars – comprehensive insurance cover should be arranged for all vehicles owned by the charity. It may be also necessary to insure volunteers' vehicles for occasional business use, e.g. visiting beneficiaries.
- Computer equipment – if a charity has extensive computer facilities it will be necessary to have a special policy to cover the equipment (hardware) and the programmes it uses (software); this should also cover for increased cost of working in the event of a loss of data.

Selecting an insurance broker

It is important that you are 'comfortable' with selected broker in terms of capability, working relationship and cost. View the broker as an extension of your direct administration.

Allow sufficient time for the selection process, say three to six months. Seek the views of other charities and business associations.

Clarify the broker's role – the broker will be involved in the following activities: placing cover, documentation, invoicing, reporting and handling claims.

The invitation letter

Invite a manageable number of participants (maximum six). The letter should include details of: nature of business; copy of annual report and accounts; insurance to be reviewed; current insurance register (remove premium details); timetable; size of report required; issues to be addressed e.g. claims processing; selection process; risks and claim history; whether site visits are permitted and finally a confidentiality agreement (you will be disclosing confidential information about your charity).

Appoint a selection committee. It is advisable to select only one or two finalists to obtain quotes on the insurance market. The achievement of better or more appropriate cover, at lower cost and with enhanced service will make the process worthwhile.

Insurance checklist
Trustees

☐ Does the charity need to review its procedure to ensure adequate cover?
☐ Does the charity review cover annually?
☐ Has the charity received advice on the sums insured?
☐ Is the charity satisfied that all important conditions have been met?

☐ Does the charity meet its legal requirements in respect of employees' liability?

☐ Have the trustees discussed the need for personal liability insurance?

Administrator (responsible to trustees)

Responsibilities:	Who will make decisions?
	Who will identify risks?
	Who will monitor risks?
	Who will report to management and when?
	Who will determine the first proportion of potential losses to be borne?
Accounts:	How will premiums, rates and any charity discounts be checked?
	How will accounts be settled?
Records:	Will records systems cover details of policies, policy expiry dates?
	Are there any long-term agreements? Premiums and adjustments and loss/claims records, etc.?
Procedures:	Have you ensured that all incidents likely to lead to a claim are reported to management for investigation and future prevention?
	What procedure has been arranged to notify incidents and claims to brokers/insurers?
	Has the procedure been agreed with brokers/insurers?
Valuations of buildings and contents:	Who will value buildings for insurance purposes?
	How will valuations be updated to cover building alterations and inflation?
	Who will list and value contents of buildings and other items?
	How will lists and values be updated?
Professional advisers and negligence:	Clarify basis of fees and remuneration.
	Check adequacy of adviser's professional indemnity insurance.
Existing buildings leased:	Clarify own and landlord's insurance obligations.

Existing buildings owned and occupied:	Is fire cover to be on reinstatement or indemnity basis?
Building under construction:	Check contractors' insurance covers. Monitor 'hand-over' date to ensure continuity of cover.
General	Each charity should compile a checklist of potential causes of losses.

8. Statutory Matters and Responsibilities

In addition to the law and regulations which relate directly to charities, there are many other statutory duties and responsibilities relating to business generally – including charities. This section covers the main areas of concern and their application to charities; it also covers legislation which applies to particular types of charities.

The regulatory framework

The Inland Revenue: controls and regulates covenants and gift aid, payroll giving schemes, charity tax policy and charity tax claims branch.

Local Authorities: are responsible for granting of mandatory (80%) and discretionary reliefs from business rate, maintaining a register and conducting reviews of local charities, appointing trustees of local charities and registering lotteries under £20,000.

Government Departments involved in supervising charities are: Department for Education and Employment (educational charities), Department of Health (NHS Charities), Department of Social Security (community homes), Department of National Heritage (charity legislation, appointment of Charity Commissioners, and charities connected with probation, Prison Service and Voluntary Services Unit).

Other Public Bodies: Housing Corporation (charitable housing associations), University Funding Council (universities).

Companies House (Charities registered as a company limited by guarantee). (*See Chapters 5 and 6.*)

Responsibilities as an employer – *(See Chapter 9.)*

Health and Safety: The 'umbrella' legislation is the Health & Safety at Work Act 1974. Under the Management of Health & Safety at Work Regulations 1992 a charity is required to:
- conduct risk assessments to identify preventative and protective measures
- put into practice action needed following risk assessment
- provide appropriate health surveillance
- set up emergency procedures including fire drills and evacuation of premises
- provide information to staff and volunteers on health and safety
- provide training for staff.

Various Workplace Regulations (1992)

A charity must adhere to requirements covering:
- working environment e.g. temperature, lighting etc.
- general safety e.g. passage of pedestrians and vehicles, falling objects, floors etc.
- provision of facilities e.g. toilets, changing facilities etc.
- housekeeping, including maintenance of workplace, equipment etc. deadlines etc.

Health and Safety (Display Screens/Equipment) Regulations 1992

Requires employers to:
- assess display screen equipment workstations and reduce any risks e.g. by use of special spectacles
- ensure that workstations meet minimum standards
- plan work so that breaks and changes in activity can be included
- provide users with information and training on health and safety issues.

Charities also have to consider their responsibilities under the Manual Handling Operations Regulations 1992 and Personal Protective Equipment at Work Regulations 1992.

Charities providing or serving food must comply with the Food Safety Act 1990 and associated regulations (1995).

Example: Office Risk Assessment				
What Risk	**When/Where**	**Why**	**Remedial Action**	**Residual Risk**
1. VDU Screen	Using long periods	Causes eye strain	Written procedure	Small
2. Photocopier a) Fire risk b) Health	Paperclips/ staples in copier	Set on fire	Written procedure	Small
3. Lifting	Moving files, equipment etc.	Personal injury due to unsafe	Safe lifting policy Mandatory training	Small
4. Fire exits/ doors	Obstruction	Fire/personal injury risk	Written procedure	Small
5. Passenger lifts	Breakdown	People trapped	Written procedure Maintenance contract	Small
6. Slips and falls (external)	Car park/ entrances	Slippery surface in wet/icy weather	Written procedure	Small

Suggested Action Plan
- **Audit** the workplace under your control
- **Liaise** with other tenants and landlords if the charity is using shared accommodation.
- **Develop** a programme for good standards.
- **Consult** staff on programme.
- **Implement** and audit the programme.
- **Monitor** your management system.

Data Protection
Many charities use computers to collect, store, process and distribute information. Personal data i.e. information held on computer about living, identifiable people, is subject to the Data Protection Act 1984. Every data user who holds personal data must be registered. The Act declares that data shall:
- be obtained and processed fairly and lawfully
- be held only for lawful purposes
- be adequate, relevant and not excessive in relation to purpose
- be accurate and kept up to date as necessary
- be held no longer than necessary for purposes
- be surrounded by proper security.

Typically charities hold data on current, past and potential claimants /beneficiaries, members and supporters, residents and tenants, donors and lenders, etc.

Trade Marks

A charity's name is a valuable asset that can be underrated. A charity has a responsibility to protect its name and any trade mark it uses e.g. a logo on clothing. Consider whether you need to register trade marks. If you are registered, check that registration is valid. Ensure that copyright of the registered trade mark is in the charity's ownership and use the name and logo consistently to establish usage.

Special Statutory Responsibilities

Charities operate in a wide field of activity and are governed by legislation and regulations in their specialist area. Some examples are: the Social Welfare: NHS and Community Care Act 1990, Registered Homes Act 1984, Housing Acts 1985 and 1988, Children Act 1989, Health and Handicap: Health Services and Public Health Act 1969.

Checklist

- [ ] Does your charity comply with the regulation to account to Companies House (incorporated only)?
- [ ] Do your trustees need to review its statutory responsibilities?
- [ ] Is a review of procedure to ensure compliance with employment law needed?
- [ ] Does your charity meet the requirements of health & safety legislation?
- [ ] Have you registered under the Data Protection Act?
- [ ] Have you considered registering your logo as a trade mark?
- [ ] What special legislation applies to your charity?

9. Contracts/Suppliers

Charities are involved in two distinct areas in the contracting environment; firstly they contract to *carry out services which meet the objective of the charity* e.g. care for children for payment. Secondly they contract to *purchase the goods and services needed for the running of the charity*. This section will consider both areas.

Contracting charities

With the introduction of community care legislation and a move towards a 'contracting culture', grants are or have been replaced by contracts. Contract fees paid to the voluntary sector increased by 154% between 1990/91 and 1993/94, mainly in the fields of community care and personal social services.

Generally speaking, contract conditions are much more structured than those for grants – they can be less flexible and the charity is held accountable. Purchasers of services can be government departments and agencies (quangos), local authorities or other public bodies.

Contracting to provide services involves risk. If a charity breaks a contract it may have to pay compensation for failure to deliver service. Contracting could lead to a loss of independence, i.e. an excessive reliance on statutory funding through contracts. Charities which are contemplating contracting or setting up as providers of services:

- should know the philosophy of purchasers – do they wish to drive down costs or are they seeking genuine diversity of provision?
- should think carefully about contracting, its impact on staff policy, and independence issues. Will donors subsidise contract price? Has the charity any choice?
- should develop a contract strategy consistent with the charity's mission and objectives
- should not lose sight of their philosophy in the rush to get funding
- should choose the purchasing authorities with which they can work, not chase contracts for the sake of short term gain
- should consider client groups, location and the overall effect on the charity – will the contract cause growth?
- should assess financial risk and establish a monitoring system. Beware of effect on the charity's overall cost structure
- should ensure that a proper contribution to the charity's overheads is included in any contract.

The Transfer of Undertakings Regulations 1981 (TUPE) will apply if employees previously delivering a service for example in a health authority are transferred to a charity.

The contract

Funding bodies usually prefer to use their own standard contract. Unless you are a very large charity you are unlikely to influence this. If possible, join an alliance with other charity contractors to change standard contracts. For example: VOICES (Voluntary Organisations Involved in Caring in the Elderly Sector; ARC

(Association Residential Care) and VODG (Voluntary Organisations Disability Group) were involved with local authority associations in preparing Guidelines for Residential Care Contracts.

If you are dealing with many funders, try and get your own standard contract accepted.

Main Clauses in Contract:

a) term of payment – argue for realistic terms e.g. not all in arrears

b) VAT – although many services are exempt from VAT, always check whether price is exclusive of VAT

c) price increases e.g. Retail Price Index if appropriate

d) indemnity clause – seek to limit liability

e) the funder's input – specify what the funder will provide in addition to cash e.g. accommodation, and 'lock' it into the contract

f) reporting of information to funder

g) clause preventing sub-contracting

h) penalties, disputes and arbitration.

Dealing with suppliers

Formulate a purchasing strategy appropriate to your charity. Develop a purchase order system, ensuring that authority to purchase is given at different levels – set several spending limits, for example. Negotiate and get the best deal for regular suppliers, but still obtain check quotes from time to time. Obtain at least three estimates when purchasing equipment, repairs etc. For large items, invite contractors to tender e.g. major repair to buildings; professional help such as an architect or surveyor may be needed.

Review the use of suppliers on a regular basis following the simple but effective format used for supply of goods and services (*see below*).

Remember that your professional advisers are also under contract. Review the effectiveness of your solicitors, accountants, auditors, investment manager, bankers and other consultants as appropriate at least every five years.

Contracting out services

For many years the private sector has contracted out 'in house' services such as works canteen, cleaning etc. Recently the legislation requiring local authorities to adopt compulsory competitive tendering has encouraged providers of services to pursue contracts in the charity sector. Main areas for 'out sourcing' in charities are catering and domestic services.

Survey of Contractors

Location: ☐ HEAD OFFICE ☐ REGIONAL OFFICE
          ☐ LOCAL OFFICE ☐ OTHER
          (Tick as appropriate)

Name of Contractor:

Service Provided:

Estimated amount spent in full year: £

Quality of work (marks out of 10)   ☐

Quality of service (marks out of 10) ☐

How competitive (marks out of 10)   ☐

Attitude (marks out of 10)   ☐

TOTAL POINTS   ☐

Any other comments:

Signed: **Date:**

Charities contemplating sub-contracting (such as catering in residential homes) should assess the reasons for taking this step. Determine key issues in relation to services and the degree of control required over the sub-contractor. Obtain competitive tenders based on pre-determined specifications. Assess contractors on a value for money basis. It is important that the charity retains residual rights to enforce standards, with an option to terminate if the contractor fails to deliver.

Checklist

☐ Has your charity assessed the risks associated with contracting to provide services?

☐ Has your charity compromised its independence by contracting?

☐ Does your charity have a purchasing strategy?

☐ Are your charity's suppliers reviewed on a regular basis?

☐ How often does your charity review its professional advisers and consultants?

☐ Has your charity considered out-sourcing?

☐ If applicable, have you considered the effects of the TUPE regulations?

10. Internal Control and Audit

The 'management' of a charity, both trustees and executive staff, are responsible for ensuring that the assets (material and human) and liabilities are managed with economy, efficiency and effectiveness. Charities are accountable to their stakeholders – donors, volunteers, staff and beneficiaries – and to society as a whole. Recent development, both in charity law (Charities Acts 1992 and 1993) and the Report of the Cadbury Committee on corporate governance (1992), have focused attention on the need for effective internal control systems. This section will cover the principles and practices of internal control and audit, including interface with external auditors or independent examiners.

Internal controls

Effective controls are important because they protect charity property for the benefit of current and future beneficiaries, and give confidence to potential donors, grant makers and contractors for services that a charity is well managed. They also reduce the risk of abuse of charity property.

Special problem areas for charities are:
a) achieving a sensible balance between maximising security and the availability of resources
b) the sensitivities of establishing effective controls over enthusiastic and dedicated volunteers.

Smaller charities may have particular difficulties over cost and lack of expertise. Many charities are 'cash based' i.e. they rely on public collections, lotteries etc.

Defining internal control structures

Charities should prepare a comprehensive record of existing control systems, consider whether they address real and potential risks and ensure:
• that they meet the major objectives
• that the charity's objectives are efficient and effective
• the charity complies with relevant laws and regulations
• the charity's financial information is reliable.

Ask the following questions and consider what control structure is the most appropriate, bearing in mind the size and complexity of your charity.

1. Which laws and regulations materially affect your charity's operation? How is compliance monitored?
2. What procedures are in place to ensure efficiency and effectiveness?
3. What procedures are needed to communicate conduct standards to staff?
4. Are there clear lines of accountability and is delegation of authority documented and understood? Do you have an organisation chart?
5. Are there procedures for identifying, assessing and minimising or mitigating risk e.g., health and safety policy and insurance?
6. Are there effective financial and management reporting controls such as measuring actual against budget monthly? Are the trustees and executive staff involved in monitoring on a regular basis?
7. What operational controls are in place – for example accounting procedures manual, security of computerised systems? Are controls updated?

Basic Elements of Controls

Separation of duties. One person should not record and process a complete financial transaction. Separation of duties reduces the scope for abuse.

Precise job descriptions. Staff should know the scope and limits of their responsibilities.

Professional qualifications and / or skills. Work should be carried out by staff who have the appropriate qualifications and ability.

Professional Advisers. Should have the relevant experience to enable them to discharge their responsibilities, i.e. detailed knowledge of the charity and its sector.

Formal Procedures for Income and Expenditure. These should include:

- security from interference and controlled opening of mail (by two persons) and immediate diarying of cash
- regular banking of income, safe custody of cash and cheques
- independent checks/verification – cash and cheques should match bank statement

- proper authorisation of expenditure and checks on supporting documentation e.g. purchase order
- reliable payment system
- safe custody of cheque books and strictly controlled signing of cheques by authorised persons
- the proper recording of all cheque and cash expenditure.

Bank or Building Society Accounts. These should be strictly controlled and supervised.

Personnel Records. Should be kept for all staff and kept separately from pay records. Also:

- checks of personnel record against pay record and physical checks should be made to prevent payment to fictitious employees
- all staff should have proper contracts of employment and not be self-employed (possible liability for unpaid tax and National Insurance contributions).

Internal auditing

"Internal auditing is an independent appraisal function established within an organisation to examine and evaluate its activities as a service to the organisation. The objectives of internal auditing are to assist members of the organisation in the effective discharge of their responsibilities. To this end, internal auditing furnishes them with analyses, appraisals, recommendations, counsel and information concerning the activities reviewed. The objective includes promoting effective control at reasonable cost." (*See also Chapters 5 and 6*).

Whilst external examination is usually concerned with accounts, the role of internal auditing is much wider and requires employees or consultants of a charity to conduct searching examinations of all aspects, including personnel. Internal audit must make a positive contribution to a charity and be a supportive and enabling resource. To be effective, an internal audit system must have official recognition, adequate resources and status in the charity.

Role of Independent Internal Auditor

1. To assess the risks a charity might face.
2. To prepare an annual plan of campaign to be agreed by the trustees or audit committee.
3. To examine the adequacy and effectiveness of internal controls per the plan above.
4. To review quality of performance.

5. To check that the systems operated by the charity are:
   defined, communicated and fully understood
   being controlled and operated correctly
   complied with standing financial instructions etc.
   achieving objectives.
6. To report results to the management and help trustees meet their responsibilities in a cost effective way.

Checklist

☐ Have your financial policies and standing instructions been agreed?

☐ Are branches/projects visited regularly to ensure that they are operating correctly?

☐ Are you sure that all information presented to the trustees is reliable, complete and consistent?

☐ Are you confident that the charity's resources effectively meet objectives?

☐ Is there scope for improvement in efficiency?

☐ Is an internal audit necessary in your charity and are you comfortable that the external auditors are sufficient?

12. Performance Measurement

The management of a charity – trustees and executive staff – can have no idea whether their charity is providing value for money, nor can they know whether its performance is improving without some measurement or evaluation process. It is relatively easy for a charity to demonstrate its financial integrity or that an activity has actually taken place. Performance measurement goes beyond this and sets out to demonstrate that a charity achieves its objectives.

"If we cannot measure performance of non-profit making organisations, we cannot know if we need them at all or whether we would be better off without them... we cannot tell whether they are being managed well or badly, or not at all." John Argenti (1993)

Performance measurement provides information on what is being achieved by the charity (**outputs**) and at what cost (**inputs**). It:

• helps to prevent allocation of resources on the basis of subjective judgement, personal whim or fancy, or under 'political' pressure

• informs managers of the extent to which operational activities are contributing to the effectiveness and efficiency of the charity

- tells managers when diagnostic intervention is necessary e.g., something needs to be put back on course and how performance has changed over time
- provides a method of comparing performances of charity project with similar project elsewhere and improves the value given to customers e.g., users of a day centre
- is needed to justify existence, allows charity to meet criticisms e.g., accusations of bad management
- motivates and enables managers to take effective and appropriate action.

For more information on performance measurement, refer to *Performance Measurement of Charities*, David Wise, ICSA.

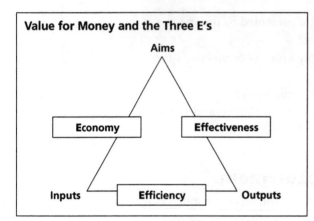

Value for Money and the Three E's

Value for money concept

Charities cannot be judged on the criteria of profitability and return on capital as in the commercial sector. (*See Chapters 5 and 6*). Assessment of charity performance requires consideration of both financial and non-financial outcome e.g., occupancy of beds, quality of life.

As assessment of value for money must take into account the interests of beneficiaries of a charity and donors/funders who make a charity's work possible. Value for money analysis relates these various factors to each other. Performance cannot be measured by a single indicator – it must be approached by looking at individual elements of the three E's (*economy, efficiency* and *effectiveness*). A value for money analysis relates these factors to the aims and outputs as achieved by inputs (*money, staff*).

Importance of Vision, Mission & Objectives

Performance has to be considered at both strategic and operational levels. (*See Chapter 7*). Whilst strategy is usually expressed through a mission statement, this requires long term assessment; operational performance has to be monitored on a day to day basis. The process from vision via mission through to individual objectives is illustrated below.

The process allows training and staff/volunteer development

needs to be identified. It also provides feedback from individuals into the objective-setting process. The mission and strategic objectives of a charity using the 'cascade' are converted into specific operational targets and budgets. Objectives should be: *specific, measurable, achievable, relevant* and *time related*.

Economy, Efficiency & Effectiveness

It is important to establish a system to get hold of and quantify inputs and outputs. *Inputs* are usually recorded in value terms but can also be in non-financial terms e.g., use of volunteers. *Outputs* are not easily expressed in value or financial terms e.g., welfare visiting/counselling service, with the exception of fundraising. Procedures must therefore be capable of measuring physical outputs e.g., number of visits

The Objectives Cascade

Vision → Corporate Mission → Corporate Values

Corporate Mission → Strategic Objectives → Critical Success Factors → Key Corporate Goals

Strategic Objectives → Divisional / Departmental Objectives → Action Plans → Budgets

Divisional / Departmental Objectives → Individual Objectives

made. Outcomes are measured less frequently as part of a strategic review because by nature they are imprecise. Measures of performance must be designed from consideration of objectives, inputs and outputs. Use a small number of key ratios e.g., percentage occupancy of beds.

Economy – internal procedures should encourage economy e.g., tender procedures for major items and elimination of waste.

Efficiency – The efficiency of an operation is usually expressed in terms of key outputs per unit of key inputs e.g., for every £100 spent we can support five families for one week. At a strategic level, the measure of efficiency may be the amount spent on meeting the objectives as a percentage of the total income e.g., 85% charitable objects, 10% fundraising & publicity and 5% on administration.

Effectiveness – Measurement is difficult and can only be used in non-financial terms to measure outputs with objectives, i.e. is the work of this charity achieving the objects, such as relieving need.

Checklist

☐ Has your charity considered performance measured principles?
☐ Do you understand the concept of value for money?
☐ Do you understand the meaning of economy, efficiency and effectiveness as they relate to your charity?
☐ Do you understand the relationships between inputs, outputs and outcomes?

About the author

David Prescott is deputy director of BEN – the Motor and Allied Trades Benevolent Fund. He has been chairman of the Charities Group of the Institute of Chartered Secretaries and Administrators since 1983 and in 1994 was elected to the Council of the Institute.

FINANCIAL MANAGEMENT : 5

David Wise

1. Introduction

Aims and objectives

Trustees are all responsible for the proper financial management of their charities. This chapter is therefore written for the reader interested in charity management in general and for the reader with a special interest in finance. Those with specialist knowledge will naturally move quickly through the unit. For non-specialists, finance and accounting often seem obscure because of the terminology used. For this reason the text explains the meaning of financial jargon as it arises – often by way of examples or self assessment activities.

By the end of the chapter you should be able to:
- appreciate what is covered by the term 'financial management'
- appreciate how financial management of a charity differs from that of a business
- review the duties and responsibilities of a financial manager
- assist in planning a charity's operations
- help to prepare and co-ordinate charity budgets
- monitor financial performance and advise on control
- discuss matters of accounting and finance with managers and external experts
- help appraise the financial effect of capital expenditure proposals
- advise trustees on performance measurement and evaluation.

Financial management is not only a technical subject. Above all it is about communication and decision-taking across the charity as a whole. The successful financial manager must have a broad understanding of all aspects of the charity, of the strategic aims and objectives of the trustees and of the needs of other managers in the charity.

2. What is Financial Management?

Financial management is a wide term. It means looking after the cash – cash control in a voluntary organisation is just as or perhaps even more important than in a commercial business. But there is much more to it than this. The Chartered Institute of Management Accountants (CIMA) defines financial management as that part of management accounting concerned with setting financial objectives, planning and acquiring the optimum finance to meet them, and seeing that fixed and working capital are effectively managed; while management accounting is defined as an integral part of management concerned with identifying, presenting and interpreting information used for:

- formulating strategy
- planning and controlling activities
- decision taking
- optimising the use of resources
- disclosure to [shareholders and] others external to the entity
- disclosure to employees
- safeguarding assets.

Financial management is sometimes divided into two aspects; the aspect of accountability, explaining and accounting for what has happened in the recent past; and the more forward-looking aspect of helping management to take decisions about future actions.

Sometimes this is formally recognised in an organisation by the appointment of a financial accountant or treasurer, whose prime responsibility is financial accounting and reporting, including cash management, investment and relationships with external stakeholders; and a management accountant or comptroller, whose main role is internal, assisting management in its important tasks of decision-making, planning and control.

In any case, financial management is an essential part of the communication process among managers and between managers and trustees; finance provides a common language for measuring most resources and for monitoring many aspects of a charity's performance as well as providing, through the budget process, a framework for planning and controlling activities.

3. What Does a Financial Manager Do?

Rather than spend too much time trying to define financial management, it may be useful to consider what we might reasonably expect a professional principal finance officer to be able to do. CIMA lists nine key roles:

1. to provide management accounting services and systems, which

includes the specification and development of information and communication systems

2. to manage accounting staff, which includes the control of staff levels and their direction, motivation and development
3. to assure the quality of services and systems, which implies operational and internal audit functions
4. to plan and arrange finance, which includes the management of cash flow, working capital, project finance and taxation implications
5. to utilise intelligence from external sources, which includes the identification and analysis of relevant data and advising management on its impact
6. to provide planning services, which includes forecasting and budget activity
7. to guide management decisions, including making a contribution to the appraisal of major projects and strategic plans, and recommending improvements to operational efficiency and effectiveness
8. to analyse, report and interpret the organisation's performance to management
9. to present reports and accounts to [shareholders] external stakeholders.

Self Assessment Activity 1 *(for answers see page 177)*

Consider the nine roles listed above and the extent to which the principal finance officer in your organisation is expected to fulfil them.

a) In a large organisation, suggest, with the use of an organisation chart, how the roles might be grouped for responsibility and reporting purposes.
b) Not all the roles above are generally considered to be within the definition of financial management. Which are the principal activities you would regard as within the scope of financial management?

In this chapter we do not intend to dwell in detail on all the nine roles outlined by CIMA, as some are covered elsewhere in this book, but will concentrate on those roles central to financial management. In particular we will explore the ways in which the financial manager analyses information, particularly on costs and income, so as to improve decision taking and preparing for future action. We will consider the process of budgeting, an important activity which completes the planning cycle in an organisation and starts the process of financial control. We will be looking at methods of evaluating risk and return and how to balance the – often conflicting – needs of the present and the future. Finally we will consider the difficult question of how to assess performance in organisations which are not established for the purpose of profit.

4. Why is it Different in a Charity?

The four major roles of financial management recognised by CIMA, planning and arranging finance, providing planning services, guiding management decisions, and analysing, reporting and interpreting the organisation's performance to management, all apply both to charities and to commercial businesses. But there are important differences of emphasis and philosophy.

Cash is essential to both but in the case of a not-for-profit organisation it is merely the means to an end, whereas in a profit-seeking organisation cash flow available for the owners is arguably an end in itself as well as a means to that end. In a commercial enterprise there are two cash cycles:

Short term working capital cycle whereby cash is converted into stock and work in progress, thence into finished goods and services for sale to the customers or debtors who in due course pay cash back to the organisation. The sale of goods and services at a value which exceeds the cost of supplying those goods and services is vital to earning profit, replenishing the cash and ensuring the life of the organisation.

Longer term corporate finance cycle whereby capital provided for the business by shareholders or lenders is invested in

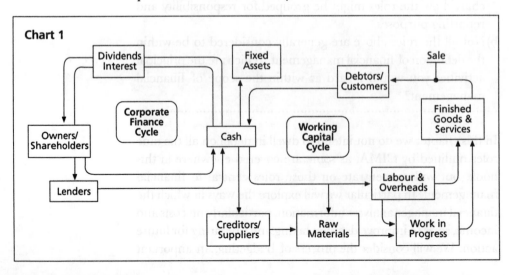

Chart 1

all the fixed and working capital assets which are used to generate the cash, which in time is available to reward the investors by way of interest, dividends or capital gains.

These two cycles are the principal concerns of corporate financial management, both from the point of view of planning and arranging finance and measuring performance in terms of profit.

Self Assessment Activity 2 *(for answers see page 178)*
....
The business cash cycles provide a model of points which require attention in business financial management. The movement of cash is not necessarily the same as profit, of course.
- At which point on the *working capital cycle* is profit calculated?
- Why is profit different from cash?
- What actions can be taken to improve profit?
- How does this model differ from that in a charity? Try drawing a charity cash model.
- What are the implications for charity control procedures?
....

Commercial operations
In some ways financial management of a business is more complex than that of a charity because of the need to understand corporate finance concepts and the need to maintain or increase shareholder value. This involves not simply questions of trading profitability but also structural questions such as whether it is better to borrow or to use shareholders' funds; whether it is better to retain profit or to pay dividend; whether to use profits to grow internally, acquire other companies or return surpluses to shareholders; and so on.

However, the finance director of a charity, which itself may be incorporated, may well have to control trading subsidiaries and associated companies. So an understanding of commercial operations is essential for many financial managers in the larger charities.

Most large charities will also have large investments which need to be actively managed so that a good knowledge of investment principles and practices is required. Moreover the charity sector has special requirements for separate legal funds to be identified, segregated and separately accounted for in a way which does not have the same application in business financial management. Finally, the lack of the discipline of a bottom line profit or loss raises special problems of motivation, performance measurement and control for the not-for-profit sector.

The lack of the closed business cash cycles means that security and verification procedures require particular care and attention; expended resources must be accounted for in business by a receipt of equivalent value and cash receipts are balanced by an equivalent liability, but these points of verification are often absent in a charity.

There is a further point which makes financial management in charities more onerous than in a commercial operation – the need to be accountable to such a variety of different stakeholders. Shareholders are of prime importance in a company, but in a charity there are likely to be (sometimes in addition to shareholders) trustees, donors, the charity commissioners, government departments, beneficiaries, volunteers and staff, and the general public who may properly require financial information from the charity.

5. Preparing for the Future

Forecasting

Management is about decision taking and this means making assumptions about the future circumstances in which the decisions will take effect. The financial manager needs to devote a considerable amount of his or her time to attempting to predict what will happen under different circumstances in order to optimise the availability and use of resources and to guide decisions towards desired but realistic objectives.

Forecasting is necessarily a preoccupation of financial management and we will consider this briefly before looking at budgeting. The terms 'forecasting' and 'budgeting' are sometimes used interchangeably. But in the sense used here, forecasts imply a passive estimation of what will happen rather than the more active process of budgeting, which implies a calculation of how we wish to react with, and to influence, events in the future. Indeed, it is the comparison between the forecast of a likely future position and the position which we wish to achieve which helps us to plan our strategy and prepare budgets for action.

This comparison between a forecast and a desired future is called gap analysis and is one of the techniques employed in strategic planning.

Self Assessment Activity 3 *(for answers see page 180)*

Consider how we go about forecasting a regular activity, say a source of income. Make a list to include at least three different methods of forecasting which may be used.

Trends

Churchill is reputed to have said that it is only by studying the past that we can hope to foretell the future and so the main method of forecasting is the extrapolation of historical figures. One of the services which a financial manager provides is the identification of past trends because, other things being equal, the past trend may be expected to continue. It is sometimes said that a trend goes on until it stops!

But great care must be exercised in projecting past trends, since they will be sure to stop in time. The second service which the financial manager can provide therefore is guidance on when previous trends are likely to be discontinued.

In practice, trends are rarely straight lines but rather follow S-shaped curves. A new source of income may be projected to take off as a straight line but it is more likely to rise slowly at first before rising rapidly. When rising rapidly it may be projected to continue; it is more difficult, but often vitally important, to forecast when the rise will flatten out and start to decline again.

Keeping track of trends in order to get as early a warning as possible of changes in trend is then an important routine to be followed. A helpful way of doing so is by way of moving annual totals. These smooth monthly or short-term fluctuations and eliminate any seasonal fluctuation because they always contain twelve months' figures.

Self Assessment Activity 4 *(for answers see page 180)*

Collections for an area are as follows:

1996	£142,000	audited
1997	£150,000	audited
1998	£156,000	draft accounts

Forecast collections for 1999.
What additional information would you like to have?

Your forecast based on annual figures in Self Assessment Activity 4 is going to be much less reliable than if it is based on monthly figures which will naturally give earlier warning of any change in trend.

The answer to Self Assessment Activity 4 shows how moving annual total figures are calculated and how they show the trend clearly. If you plot the 1998 figures by month, cumulative and moving annual totals on a graph you will produce what is called a 'Z-chart' (for obvious reasons). Plotting an actual Z-chart as the year progresses on top of an annual budget Z-chart will soon show any divergence of trend from that assumed when preparing the budget.

Regular income

Analysis of trends is particularly useful when considering regular income. Sales forecasts are usually the first step in approaching business budgets. For a charity, forecasts of regular income are often a first step in the budget process since they will give an indication of what additional fundraising efforts will be needed and/or what restrictions may have to be placed on charitable work.

A knowledge of how certain future income streams are likely to be is also essential to management's judgement on the degree of risk faced by a charity. Where income can be predicted with a high degree of certainty, a correspondingly high proportion of income can be committed to expenditure; but, where income is less certain, management will need to seek ways of protecting the charity from risk by reducing commitments and increasing reserves.

Reserves

The question of reserves poses a matter of fine judgement for the trustees of a charity. The Charity Commissioners have made plain the fact that it is for the trustees to decide whether their charity needs to pursue a policy of building up or maintaining reserves of income.

Either way, trustees must be able to justify their decision. The financial manager will assist in this decision by verifying that:

- trustees have the legal power to retain income
- reserves are appropriate and affordable in view of other commitments
- the size of reserves is proportionate to the costs of the purpose for which the reserve is being built up.

Suitable purposes, which would need quantifying, have been classified as including:

- project and programme funding
- future spending programmes
- repair and rebuilding funds
- working funds, to cover seasonal or other peaks and troughs in income/expenditure
- providing for budgeted future deficits
- commitments and contingencies
- potential resource demands
- protection against a decline in income
- windfalls, or unexpected large receipts which cannot be spent immediately.

6. Costing Matters

Before moving on to the budget process it may be useful to consider how management accountants classify costs and the relationship of costs to activity levels.

Costing is a form of accounting which takes into account both quantity measures as well as financial ones and is an early example of the principle, increasingly recognised, that financial accounts need additional quantitative or qualitative data to assist in their proper interpretation – especially true in the case of charities where the true worth of outputs is not a financial one.

Businesses make an effort to calculate their unit costs. Such costs are an aid to controlling profit and pricing policies and they also give a measure of efficiency. One way of securing competitive advantage is to try to achieve lower costs than competitors. Comparative unit costs, over time or between businesses, are an important performance indicator.

Charities do not usually need to establish a profitable selling price for their services. Consequently it is rare to find well designed costing systems which show the unit cost of services provided. Yet, without such a concept, it is hardly possible to talk of cost effectiveness at all.

Costing Terminology

Management accountants often classify costs as being direct or indirect.

Direct costs are those which can be attributed directly to the service being costed, for example in costing a project it is usually easy to recognise all those costs which relate specifically to that project. On the other hand there are many costs, telephone charges and printing for example, which are required to service projects but which cannot be directly attributed to specific projects and will need to be allocated on some reasonable basis such as the direct costs or number employed on the project.

General overheads – running the head office for example – are even more remote from projects. It may be fair that projects should bear a reasonable proportion of such overheads, in which case they would need to be apportioned to projects on a more or less arbitrary basis – but a basis which is consistent and which allows the accounts to show a true and fair view.

The Charity SORP requires expenditure to be analysed under two main headings: *Direct Charitable Expenditure* which includes grants payable and other direct expenditure on charitable objectives, and *Other Expenditure* which includes fundraising and publicity costs, together with administration and management costs and those other costs which cannot properly be treated as direct charitable expenditure.

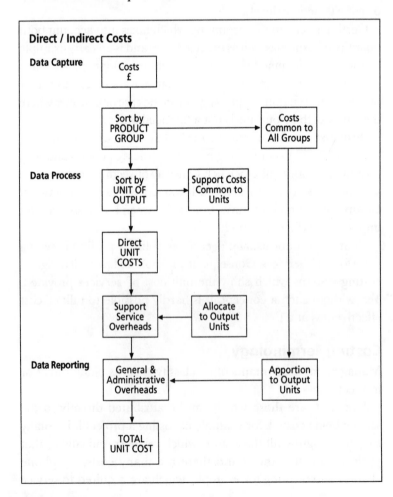

More useful for budgeting purposes is the classification of costs into those which are fixed, that is to say costs which remain the same whatever the volume of output, and those which are variable, that is to say costs which increase or decrease directly in proportion to volume.

Self Assessment Activity 5 (for answers see page 181)

An organisation for which you do voluntary work asks if it could use your car to visit a hostel 100 miles away. When you suggest this is rather a long way, the accountant says it is an emergency and in any case your car is not used enough – a car needs good mileage to give economic performance and running it an extra 200 miles will improve its running costs per mile. He demonstrates this with the following schedule which shows that costs per mile decrease as mileage increases:

Miles pa	5,000	15,000	25,000
Costs	£	£	£
Tax, Insce	750	750	750
Petrol, oil	1,000	3,000	5,000
Depreciation	2,500	3,500	4,500
Repairs	500	1,500	2,500
Total	**4,750**	**8,750**	**12,750**
Cost per mile	0.95	0.58	0.51

a) Are you convinced by this argument? – if not, why not?
b) Which costs are fixed and which are variable?
c) Budget for the costs at 30,000 miles pa.

If the total costs above are plotted on a graph against the mileage, then the line joining the costs will be straight line and where the line crosses the zero mileage perpendicular it will show the total fixed costs, that is the fixed costs and the fixed element of the semi-fixed costs. In the case in Self Assessment Activity 5 (£750 + £2,000 =) £2,750.

If you decided to charge for the use of your car, you could draw in the revenue line on your graph. Your income line would start at zero for zero miles. This is now a break-even chart because where the income line crosses the total cost line there will be neither surplus nor deficit. It shows the mileage at which income would exactly equal total costs and allows you to read off the expected surplus or deficit at mileages above or below the break-even point.

An understanding of the relationships between cost and volume is clearly important in budgeting and knowledge of break-even points is important, for example in circumstances where you need to fix prices so as to avoid loss.

It is useful in this area to appreciate the concept of contribution, the difference between the price charged for a product or service and the variable cost. For example if we had variable costs of 40p per mile and decided to charge 56p per mile this would give a contribution towards the fixed costs and surplus of 16p per mile.

To calculate the break-even point, divide the fixed costs by the contribution (in the example, fixed costs £2,750 divided by .16 gives a break-even of 17,187.5 miles – at that mileage there will be neither a surplus nor a deficit, which you can check arithmetically and against your break-even chart).

Self Assessment Activity 6 *(for answers see page 182)*

There is a policy that the canteen must break-even in any year. During last year the costs were as follows:

Variable cost per meal	food	45p
	fuel etc.	15p
Annual fixed costs	wages	£36,000
	overheads	£24,000
Average price per meal	72p	
Number of meals sold	700,000	
Canteen capacity	825,000	

It is estimated next year that the cost of food per meal will rise to 50p, fuel etc. to 16p, annual wages to £38,000 and overheads to £25,000. The catering manager needs to know how many meals must be sold to break-even. How can you calculate this and what solution might you recommend to deal with the problem disclosed?

In a situation where it is possible to place a value on the outputs, then it is also possible to calculate the contribution made by those outputs. Thus the contribution made by each meal in the box above (Self Assessment Activity 6) was 12p.

If there is a choice between different service outputs then priority should be given to the service which yields the greatest contribution in order to maximise the value added by the organisation. This rule does not apply when the resources are limited in such a way that demand for the services cannot be met and the limitation affects the different services unequally, in which case preference should be given to the service yielding the greatest contribution per unit of scarce resource.

Before leaving the subject of costs, it is worth sounding a cautionary note to remind ourselves that cost forecasts and budgets are an imperfect model of the future.

The classification of costs into fixed and variable is a convenient working framework in most cases but it cannot be used indiscriminately. Most costs are fixed in the short term and variable in the long term, so the definition of fixed/variable depends on the circumstances and, as we have seen, there is a large body of cost which falls somewhere in between as semi-fixed.

Moreover, costs vary for reasons other than output volume so that it may be necessary to identify a number of other relevant cost drivers in any case. And in a large organisation costs of one department are often passed on to another department.

Attempting to deal with all these complexities in a model of the organisation has become easier with the advent of personal computers and there are a number of activity based costing systems available for those organisations which need to establish complex cost estimating and monitoring procedures.

7. Budgets for Planning and Control

As a result of considering costing matters we have already been considering budgets in Self Assessment Activities 5 and 6 from the point of how to calculate the figures. But budgets are much more than an arithmetical exercise; they are a fundamental element of the two most important management functions of planning and control, and they are closely connected with the processes of decision making and the delegation of authority in an organisation.

To take a simple example of decision taking, when you set out on a journey you need to know where you are to start from and where you want to get to. Once these two things are known then you can decide how best to go from your present position to your destination. And the fourth most important process is action to translate your plans into reality. If after setting out you lose your way, you will need to go through the processes again until you succeed. These simplified steps apply to any decision taking process and they can be translated into charity management terms as follows:

1. Where are we?   Management accounts and

2. Where do we want to be?   Corporate plan and mission statement

3. How can we get there?   Action plans and budgets

4. Go   Proceed with the work of the organisation

Return to step 1 and repeat as necessary.

Steps 1, 2 and 3 of this cycle are the planning process, whereby we take stock of the situation, compare it with our goals, decide on a strategy for action and establish exactly how to proceed in the coming period; steps 3, 4 and 1 are the control process, whereby we take actions, compare the position with that which we intended to achieve, and take corrective action or amend our plans in the light of events as appropriate. Step 3 – the budget – is the pivot which connects the planning and control processes.

Mission statements

Of course, planning is more complex than the above simple description and usually starts with a vision for the future which can be usefully expressed formally as a mission statement for the organisation. This is a means whereby all concerned can ensure that they work together towards an agreed common end. Mission statements are particularly helpful in a voluntary body, where the absence of commercial customers and the profit motive can lead to a lack of goal congruence and an unclear focus on priorities.

The process of communicating and implementing goal congruence from the governing body down to operating managers is sometimes referred to as the cascade of objectives (*see chart opposite*).

The mission statement is necessarily a broad and unquantified statement, which needs to be subdivided into key activities and goals for planning purposes. The key strategic activities must then be planned in operation detail and in the short term and quantified by means of the budget. The budget is a central element for the subsequent assessment of performance, both for the organisation as a whole as well

The Objectives Cascade

- Vision
- Corporate Mission
- Corporate Values
- Strategic Objectives
- Critical Success Factors
- Key Corporate Goals
- Divisional / Departmental Objectives
- Action Plans
- Budgets
- Individual Objectives

subsequent assessment of performance, both for the organisation as a whole as well as for individual managers. Objectives at this level must be specific and quantified. They must be SMART – Specific, Measurable, Achievable, Relevant and Time-related.

The vision for the organisation, strategic direction and the setting of objectives is a top-down process which should take its authority and drive from the governing body. Once the budget preparation starts however, this process should begin with the operational managers who will in due course be responsible for implementing the agreed actions. Budget preparation is a bottom-up process which relies on input from those most closely concerned with operations and who will feed their requirements up for consideration and approval in the context of the agreed objectives.

Budgeting

It is convenient to base the budget on recent actual performance or on the previous year's budget as a starting point. However, this practice assumes that previous resource allocation provides a satisfactory model for the future – not necessarily a good assumption. A more rigorous approach, which requires every manager to justify his entire spending requests from scratch, is sometimes called 'zero base budgeting' or 'priority based budgeting'. (Readers wishing to explore this in more detail should refer to *Performance Measurement for Charities* published by ICSA Publishing 1995.)

The form of the budget is best seen as a large matrix with the departmental or responsibility analysis across the top (each column will have an organisation coding for identification) and the expense/income analysis down the left-hand side (each row having an accounts coding). When all the budget centres are combined, it is then possible to show how much of the total income/ expenditure is the responsibility of each budget centre manager, and what the total of each item of income/expenditure is overall.

For control purposes, the form of the budget must follow the accounting/reporting system so that actual can be compared with budget as the year progresses.

This analysis means that it is sometimes difficult in a large organisation to identify the cost of a service which is provided by many different departments. Activity-based costing systems are designed to allow this 'third' dimension to be tracked as well as the usual expense and responsibility dimensions. Charities are obliged to undertake some simple activity-based costing in order to comply with the Statement of Recommended Practice, Accounting by Charities, which requires charities to report expenditure under a functional classification (explained as the aggregation of costs in pursuit of a defined purpose – e.g. provision of services to elderly people or counselling – and is achieved by adding together all the costs – salaries, rents, depreciation, etc. – relating to that specific activity) to show separately:

• expenditure directly related to the objects of the charity
• expenditure in support of charitable activity
• expenditure on fundraising and publicity
• expenditure on administration
• any other expenditure.

Control implies a regular comparison between plan and actual, an explanation of differences and further action to bring the actual into line with intentions. The reporting of financial results should therefore be carried out formally on a monthly basis or perhaps quarterly in the case of smaller charities. Ideally the results will be presented alongside the comparative budget with variances identified and explained.

8. Capital Expenditure Decisions

By definition there is some expenditure, usually large amounts, which is expected to bring benefits to the organisation over a long period. Such expenditure (capital expenditure) will affect not simply the current budget but will remain effective over a number of future years. Accountants carry such expenditure forward in the balance sheet as fixed assets to be written off over the effective life of the asset by way of depreciation. The nature of this expenditure means that the use of resources is given up today in the expectation of future benefits. In a business, this type of expenditure is of strategic importance and must be justified by showing that the expenditure will produce a return to the investor greater than the cost of capital.

Such considerations do not apply with the same force in not-for-profit organisations. Even so, the issue of whether benefits available to future beneficiaries justifies the loss of benefits to present beneficiaries is a real one. The same issue also applies to the holding of reserves by a charity, which, like capital expenditure, implies that funds which could be used today are withheld for use sometime in the future.

Discounting

Corporate finance theory allows the comparison of current and future cash flows by discounting future cash at a rate equal to the average cost of capital. The discount rate is made up of three elements; a real rate required by a lender for giving up the use of his money (say 3%); an additional rate to compensate the lender for the effects of inflation on his money (say 4% at present but subject to variation from time to time and country to country). These two together make up the risk-free rate equivalent to the return on long term government stocks. The third element is a further addition to the risk-free rate of an amount to compensate the investor for the commercial risk – a further addition of, say, around 8% in the case of good quoted company shares but much more in the case of more risky businesses. This suggests a discount rate of around 15%, which means that a receipt of £1 in a year's time is worth only (1 / 1.15) 87p today, while the receipt of £1 in two years time would be worth only (1 / 1.15 / 1.15) 76p today.

Not-for-profit organisations are not in the business of trying to reward their owners with a profit commensurate to risk. As they may not have a quantifiable cost of capital, it would seem inappropriate for them to use a commercial rate such as that used above. However, some public sector operations are expected to generate a return to cover the cost of borrowing, and charities investing for the future should take into account the loss of interest which they could have earned from its investment – their opportunity cost of capital. In practice this is likely to be close to the risk-free rate – currently, say, the 7% quoted above.

This method of appraisal should be used to justify investment, or to compare alternatives, when outputs can be financially quantified (and it is sometimes possible to ascribe proxy financial values to charitable services which are not actually sold for value).

Care is required regarding the treatment of inflation. Don't forget that an inflation element is implicit in the discount rate and if included, it should be reflected also in the future cash flow calculations. Alternatively, provided inflation affects the cost of money and the future cash flow equally, it can be ignored from both figures. If it does not affect both borrowing cost and cash flows equally then it must be accounted for.

9. Value for Money

Most of this chapter has dealt with financial matters, although in a charitable organisation objectives are rarely financial in nature. Performance measurement in not-for-profit organisations is therefore much more problematic than in a commercial enterprise, where the return on capital employed is the single prime performance indicator.

Performance is too complex to be reduced to a single indicator, especially, in charities, to a financial indicator. The complex concept of value for money may be simplified by breaking it down into three aspects: economy, efficiency and effectiveness; where economy implies minimal expenditure consistent with the aims, efficiency implies the relationship of outputs to inputs or productivity, and effectiveness implies the relationship between outputs and aims.

These factors – the three E's – can be related to each other as the value for money diagram shown in *Chapter 4, page 152* also illustrates.

This analysis is useful because it allows non-financial inputs and outputs to be used as appropriate. Even in commercial businesses it is recognised that many performance indicators are not financial ones, but this is even more true of charities and public organisations whose purposes are philanthropic or social rather than simply economic.

Inputs

The value of expenditure is the main means of expressing inputs to an organisation. But physical measures are also useful and, where appropriate, systems to record quantities as well as values are required. Where resources are a limiting factor to the provision of services, perhaps bed space in a hostel or consultant time in a clinic for example, then recording the availability, cost and usage of that resource is especially important.

Inputs is the term used to denote the resources used in the production of outputs. Input measures may be total or partial; they must always be quantifiable and measurable. In identifying input units it will be necessary to define rules for measurement and it is also necessary to install procedures for measuring physical inputs, for example by counting, documenting, weighing, and so on. The detail required will depend on the significance of the inputs and the degree of control deemed appropriate.

The costing of services provided by charities is becoming of increasing importance, too, because of the changes in government support for charities, which put greater emphasis on service agreements and on contractual payment for services delivered rather than on grants.

Outputs

Outputs in charities are not so readily expressed in value terms as are the inputs. The services provided by charities are often provided to beneficiaries who are unable to pay an economic price for the services. Outputs can rarely be measured readily by means of money values and it is therefore especially important to install procedures to measure as closely as possible the physical outputs.

Fundraising is one of the few charitable activities where outputs, in the form of funds generated, can best be measured in money value terms (and even here caution is required since many years can elapse between efforts to attract legacy income and the actual receipt of legacies; legacy income is a measure of a charity's efforts several years ago but not necessarily of today's).

Where outputs are events which can be counted with a fair degree of certainty, the collection of output statistics is relatively easy, so a charity for helping children with no homes to find foster or adoptive parents will easily record the number of children linked to new parents. By analysing the figures to show how many children are linked within three/six/nine months of registration, the statistics give a more informative indication of the quality of the output. Moreover, since not all linkages are successful, it is also helpful to record the number of children who fail to remain with the foster/adopted parent and are re-registered; the number of such disruptions provides further evidence of the quality of the service.

Outputs should represent some delivery, service or result of special interest. It might be simply the number of clients seen, or the number of client diagnostic profiles completed without error, or number of clients well pleased with the service.

As in the case of inputs, outputs must be quantifiable and measurable. It is also common to define outputs in a qualitative way, such as completed without error or classified as well pleased – in other words outputs must be in accordance with agreed quality specifications.

Deciding which outputs are to be used in assessing efficiency and effectiveness is crucial to the performance measurement process.

Where outputs are not evidenced by events which can be counted, then other means of quantifying output must be devised. A charity formed to make authorities more aware of problems of drug dependency may use indirect measurement of outputs by counting the usage of its library or the pages of information issued but it may also need to carry out surveys from time to time in order to assess the quality of its output. But here it is useful to distinguish between outputs and outcomes.

Outcomes

We cannot always quantify outcomes in the short term or with precision nor do we need to try for operational performance measurement purposes since outcomes are by definition somewhat remote from operational activity. Operational activity is managed on the expectation that desirable outcomes will follow from the planned outputs. Thus a charity formed to protect endangered gorillas in Rwanda may properly consider outputs to be the number of ranger hours spent in patrolling the chosen area, or the number of poachers apprehended, or the number of traps destroyed. All of these outputs can be recorded and interpreted and all may be assumed to contribute to the desired outcome even if that outcome cannot itself be precisely quantified at any one time.

Strategic and operational performance review

Outcomes are at a higher, more strategic, level than outputs. They need to be reviewed, together with the assumptions which link outputs to outcomes, on a regular but long term basis as part of the strategic monitoring of performance. The fact that outcomes are remote and that it is often difficult to establish a cause and effect relationship between operations and outcomes is not any reason for failing to assess the outputs at the operational level. Indeed, it is only by measuring outputs that we can fully complete the task of measuring charities' performances. Some religious charities may be seeking outcomes which cannot be scientifically measured but they should do so by means of outputs which can be measured, perhaps in terms of parishioner visits, church members recruited, attendance at services or even cash offerings collected.

At an even higher level, the assumption that relief of poverty and the advancement of education are a good thing and deserving of support under charity law are rarely questioned since they have been considered self evident for several generations. The interface boundary, aspects of which politicians consider in most government terms of office.

The main point to make about collecting data on both inputs and outputs is that the data should provide information appropriate to the objectives of the activities of the charity. Information on one aspect of performance alone is of little help. Absolute figures rarely help in assessing performance. It is only when figures are used together as ratios or are compared with previous figures, or with figures from comparable organisations, that useful conclusions can be drawn.

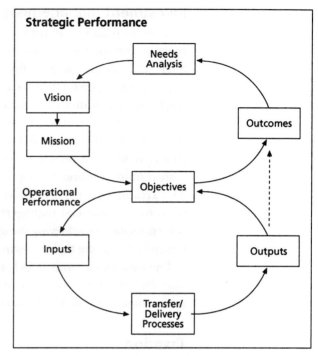

The chart illustrating strategic performance recognises the importance of vision, through the mission and values statement, in establishing aims and objectives. It also shows the importance of recognising and reviewing the needs of beneficiaries in informing the vision and the evaluation of feedback from results. Finally, it recognises that outcomes are sometimes rather remote from outputs but that outcomes are of prime importance in the evaluation of strategic performance.

These strategic and non-financial aspects of charity management are not, of course, by any means solely the concern of the financial manager. But he/she is closely involved in them and is well placed to quantify aspects of performance and to interpret them by way of meaningful ratios, indices and trends. Above all there needs to be close cooperation and good understanding between the chief finance officer and his or her colleagues.

10. Specialist Areas and Reporting Matters

In considering the financial management of charities it is impossible not to mention two rather specialist matters which have special relevance to charities.

Investment management

Investment is an important matter for those charities with large reserves and for those charities which have endowment funds. Such charities are likely to find that investments represent the largest single figure on their balance sheet and investment income will be a major source of income in any year.

Trustees' investment policy has up to now been severely restricted by the Trustee Investment Act of 1961 as a result of which many charity funds were unable to gain as much as they would have wished from investment in equities or from investment overseas. The Treasury is actively considering the repeal of the Act, which will provide financial managers with more opportunities and responsibilities for achieving the optimal balance between risk and return in managing their investment portfolios.

The Charity Commission's leaflet *Investment of Charitable Funds: Basic Principles* offers advice in this area and specialist professional advice should be taken if in any doubt.

Taxation

Taxation is another specialist matter affecting charities. In general, charities are exempt from income tax under s505 of the Taxes Act 1988 and from capital gains under s256 of the Chargeable Gains Act 1992.

Where a charity has trading subsidiaries it is common to transfer any profit away from the subsidiary into the charity by way of a profit-shedding covenant, thereby reducing or eliminating any liability for tax on profits.

In general, care must be taken to properly classify receipts on which tax may be recoverable to ensure that all tax recoverable is promptly claimed. There are specific reliefs which include, among others:

- covenanted donations
- gift aid relief for single gifts
- gifts free of capital gains tax
- gifts free of inheritance tax
- gifts from charitable trusts
- covenanted salaries

There is no general relief from VAT for charities although most charitable activities will be either exempt or outside the scope of the tax. However a charity may inadvertently make taxable supplies which could incur liabilities and penalties. Moreover, where a charity makes supplies which are exempt in addition to those which are taxable it may suffer a restriction on the input VAT which it has paid on supplies and could otherwise reclaim.

Needless to say these aspect of financial management are governed by complex statutory regulations and extra-statutory concessions which are liable to change from year to year. Specialist study or professional advice will be required to keep abreast of opportunities and threats in this field.

Reporting matters

The legal obligation to account for charity income and expenditure, and in particular to submit annual accounts in a prescribed format, are set out in Part VI of the Charities Act 1993 (*see Chapter 6*). Management reporting requirements are necessarily less prescriptive since they deal to a greater extent with matters of judgement and with details peculiar to an individual charity.

Good practice requires that financial management information should be available on a regular basis, as often as necessary for decision taking and at frequent regular intervals for monitoring purposes. For the smaller charity, quarterly reports may be sufficient but for larger charities monthly management accounts should be expected. Cash control is likely to require more frequent reporting, say on a daily basis, where receipts are substantial.

Where actual figures are reported they should be presented with the budget to which they relate to allow easy comparison. Material variances should be explained with a view to assisting management to take corrective action as appropriate.

Financial reports are rarely sufficient in themselves and should be accompanied by quantitative information wherever possible. This is especially important in the case of ouputs or services to beneficiaries, which are often not adequately measured by financial values. Most measures are relative and best expressed in comparison with others – by way of ratios (making use of comparisons implied by the value for money triangle), for example.

11. Self Assessment Activities – the answers

Self Assessment Activity 1

a) There is no right or wrong organisation chart which can be prescribed for all organisations but in a large organisation the chart might be in a form such as overleaf:

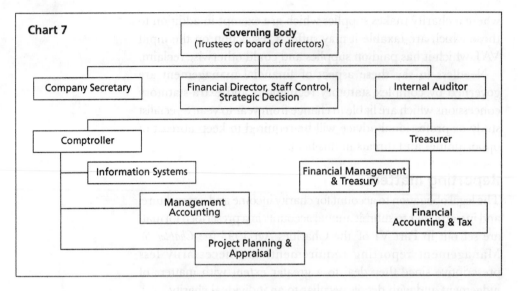

Chart 7

```
                          Governing Body
                    (Trustees or board of directors)

 Company Secretary    Financial Director, Staff Control,    Internal Auditor
                           Strategic Decision

     Comptroller                                              Treasurer

           Information Systems              Financial Management
                                                & Treasury

                  Management                          Financial
                  Accounting                     Accounting & Tax

              Project Planning &
                  Appraisal
```

The financial director may well combine his function with that of company secretary in a small organisation and indeed he often acquires a portfolio of general administrative functions which do not fit anywhere else.

In a larger organisation there is likely to be a separate IT manager with responsibility for systems maintenance and development. The internal audit function should report direct to the governing body so as to operate independently.

b) CIMA suggests that the Financial Management and Treasury function should combine four main roles:
   - plan and arrange finance
   - provide planning services
   - guide management decisions
   - analyse, report and interpret the organisation's performance to management.

This involves planning, monitoring and influencing movements in working capital and the management of short-term finance. In supporting operating managers it includes planning and arranging the financing of products, contributing to operating plans, appraising projects, and reporting on performance. At the strategic level it includes building strategic plans and contributing to the planning process and the control of strategic plans.

Self Assessment Activity 2

At which point on the working capital cycle is profit calculated?

The movements round the working capital cycle mean that as

value is passed there is a decrease in one value and an increase in the next. Thus as raw material is issued the value of the raw material stock goes down and the value of work in progress is increased by the same amount. This make audit and control easier than where value is not accounted for. However where property passes from the organisation to the customer, the cost of the goods or services sold should be less than the value for which they are sold. It is at this point, between finished goods/ services and customers/debtors, that profit/loss is calculated. Any profit is used to increase the value of the shareholders'/ owner's interest.

Why is profit different from cash?

In the long run profit is equal to cash. But in any accounting period there are likely to be major differences because of:

- differences in timing, items may appear in sales and cost of sales which have not yet been received or paid, and vice versa
- capital items affect cash but not profit, thus a loan repayment or a purchase of a new machine reduces cash but does not itself reduce profit. Conversely the depreciation of the machine will reduce profit but not affect the cash
- distributions or appropriations of profit may not change the profit itself but may affect the cash position.

What actions can be taken to improve profit?

There are essentially three ways to improve profit:

- charge higher prices and/or pay less for the cost of resources used. Either of these actions will increase the difference between the sales and cost of sales and improve the margin of profit on sales
- make the movement of value round the cycle pass more quickly. Even if the margin is the same or less, by selling more during the same period it may be possible by higher volume to increase the profit and the return on investment
- don't forget too, that the cycle is not a closed system. Losses can occur at every point; goods may be short delivered, stock can be misappropriated, debtors may fail to pay, and so on. Security is therefore important in maintaining profitable operations

In a business situation, financial management is heavily involved in balancing these three factors in order to maximise profitability and compete effectively in the market place.

How does this model differ from that in a charity?

The working capital cycle does not exist in not-for-profit activities because the customer does not pay a full commercial price for the services he receives. The competition to supply value in excess of cost in order to survive is largely absent. Similarly, the corporate finance cycle which rewards the owners for their risk by providing them with appropriate dividends or gains is also absent.

In a competitive market economy a company must be efficient in providing value to customers and investors if it is to survive. In a not-for-profit body the same direct imperative for efficiency does not apply. Installing internal arrangements to review efficiency is therefore important.

Self Assessment Activity 3

Forecasting methods are sometimes classified as:
- extrapolation, the projection of a previously identified trend
- leading indicator, where one series of statistics is closely followed by the series to be forecast
- model building, useful where there are a large number of complex inter-related factors
- scenario planning, to stimulate creative thinking about future developments under differing conditions
- delphi technique, an abstruse term for the common sense approach of seeking the views of all influential or well informed authorities.

Self Assessment Activity 4

You might reasonably guess that 1999 collections would be around £160,000. You would be more confident in your forecast if you had time to wait for audited figures for 1998 and naturally you would expect some background information about the area for which you were forecasting. Most important however is to have more detailed figures than yearly ones. Weekly, monthly or even quarterly would be better.

The monthly figures for 1997 and 1998 are produced below together with the moving annual totals. How does this affect your forecast?

Month	1997	1998	Cumulative 1998	MAT 1998
	£	£	£	£
January	11,586	12,528	12,528	150,969
February	11,387	11,404	23,932	150,986
March	12,065	14,145	38,077	153,066

April	14,589	16,633	54,710	155,110
May	13,943	14,990	69,700	156,157
June	12,622	13,335	83,035	156,870
July	11,991	12,885	95,920	157,764
August	10,456	11,024	106,944	158,332
September	11,995	10,954	117,898	157,291
October	11,784	12,300	130,198	157,807
November	12,024	11,182	141,380	156,965
December	15,585	14,602	155,982	155,982
	150,027	155,982		

It is clear from the moving annual total that the upward trend in collections was reversed in Summer 1998 and that, unless it is possible to change the situation, collections in 1999 will be substantially down on 1998.

Self Assessment Activity 5

a) The accountant should know better than to mix up fixed and variable costs in this way – unless it is a deliberate attempt to confuse the issue! When taking a decision on whether to use a service or not – or which level of service to use – any costs which are not affected by the decision (fixed costs) should be ignored; only those costs which change as a result of the decision (variable costs) are relevant. This an important principle, which is easy to see in this simple example but less easy to spot in more complex, real life decisions.

b) Licences and insurance are the same whatever the mileage and are fixed costs; petrol and oil and repairs vary directly with the mileage and are variable costs; depreciation does vary with mileage but not proportionately – doubling the mileage does not double the depreciation – hence depreciation may be classified as semi-fixed or semi-variable.

c) Once costs have been classified it becomes easy to budget costs at a new mileage:

Miles pa	5000	15000	25000	30000
Costs	£	£	£	£
Tax, Insce	750	750	750	750
Petrol, oil	1,000	3,000	5,000	6,000
Depreciation	2,500	3,500	4,500	5,000
Repairs	500	1,500	2,500	3,000
Total	4,750	8,750	12,750	14,750
Cost per mile	£0.95	£0.58	£0.51	£0.49

Self Assessment Activity 6

The old selling price will not give sufficient contribution to allow the canteen to break-even, even at full capacity utilisation. At the costs given it would be necessary to increase the capacity (unlikely in the short term) or to increase prices. Just as we can calculate a break-even from fixed costs, variable costs per meal and selling price per meal, we can also calculate a required selling price from an assumed break-even volume. In the revised budget below we assume a wish to break-even at 700,000 meals; this implies a contribution of $(63000/700000 =).09$, which with variable costs of .66 implies a selling price of £.75 or 75p per meal.

	Actual Last year £	Next year Budget £	A revised Budget £
Variable cost per meal			
food	0.45	0.50	0.50
fuel etc.	0.15	0.16	0.16
total	0.60	0.66	0.66
Selling price	0.72	0.72	0.75
Contribution	0.12	0.06	0.09
Annual fixed costs			
wages	36,000	38,000	38,000
overheads	24,000	25,000	25,000
total fixed costs	60,000	63,000	63,000
Number of meals	number	number	number
to break-even	500,000	1,050,000	700,000

Try another revised budget with a more prudent break-even assumption of 500,000 meals

About the author

David Wise is a chartered accountant and registered auditor as well as a practising chartered management accountant. He joined South Bank University in 1992 and was has been course director of the MSc in Charity Finance. He was awarded an MBA in 1993 and his book *Performance Measurement for Charities* was published in 1995 by ICSA Publishing.

CHARITY ACCOUNTING | 6

Neil Finlayson

1. Introduction

Aims and objectives

This chapter will help readers understand the principles of charity accounting, and current legal requirements. It will also discuss the practical benefits and uses of charity accounts.

By the end of the chapter the student will:
- appreciate the need for and importance of accurate accounts
- appreciate similarities and differences between commercial and charity accounting
- understand the difference between financial and management accounting
- understand charity accounts and the terminology used
- appreciate the principles of fund accounting
- understand the regulatory framework and audit requirements.

Further reading and learning opportunities are given at the end of the book.

This chapter is intended to assist both students and other interested readers to appreciate the uses to which charity accounts can be put and to understand the basis on which they are prepared.

Uses of charity accounts

If you are or want to become a trustee, chief executive, finance officer or fundraiser in a charity, a basic understanding of charity accounts is essential to your work. Charity accounts are also used and need to be understood by people working for local authorities, the government, and the Inland Revenue. In an ideal world, even the beneficiaries should be able to understand what is being done on their behalf.

New charity accounting regime

The Charities Acts of 1992 and 1993 were the first major legislation to affect charity accounting for over thirty years (*see Chapter 3*). They made significant changes to make the accounts of charities more understandable, comparable and useful in explaining what the charity concerned does.

The legislation was designed to make charities more publicly accountable and responsible, particularly through their published documents. However the changes will not just benefit the public – charities have many stakeholders, including their trustees, managers, volunteers, beneficiaries, individual, institutional and corporate donors. All will benefit from a better understanding of charity accounts. Well presented and thought out accounts will always assist a charity to get its message across, encourage new donors and volunteers, and focus public opinion on the needs of its beneficiaries, as well as fulfilling the charity's legal responsibilities.

The new accounting regime means that charities will no longer be constrained by unsuitable commercial accounts layouts or accounting policies which may be inappropriate.

The charity sector's own Guidelines

The charity sector now has its own internally-produced comprehensive guide on charity accounting in the form of the Statement of Recommended Practice or Charity SORP. However, on a practical level, it is realised that most charities are relatively small, with insufficient resources to implement all the recommendations in the SORP. Therefore, those unincorporated charities with income less than £100,000 are allowed more flexibility and the Charity Commission has issued guidelines to assist them. This means that even small and medium-sized charities can benefit from the new regime.

In conclusion

Remember: charity accounts should be seen primarily as a practical and useful tool for both understanding and explaining to others the activities of the charity. They should not just be a historic and costly document of little practical relevance to anyone.

2. The Importance of Accurate Accounts

Who needs charity accounts?

The Charities Act 1993 has introduced new legal requirements on the maintenance of accurate accounting records and the production of accounts. *These will be examined under the regulatory framework section, page 201.* But apart from the legal requirements, there are many other people who need, or have an interest in, accurate and understandable charity accounts.

It is a useful exercise to sit down and make a list of people who regularly ask you for your accounts.

To assist you, a number of interested parties or 'stakeholders' are listed below. Try to extend this list and make a note beside each party as to why they might want to see your accounts.

Stakeholder	Reason for interest	Implications
Trustees	1) *Understanding activities and their financial implications* 2) *Fulfilling legal responsibilities.*	
Paid Staff		
Volunteers		
Beneficiaries		
Donors, including grant making trusts		
Institutional and corporate funders		
Government departments		
Inland Revenue		
Rating Authorities		
Charity Commission		
The Press		
The Public		
....		
....		
....		
....		

As you can see, there is wide demand for a charity's accounts, which extends well beyond the pure legal requirements. Most of the people who might ask for them could also significantly assist the charity in one way or another, now and in the future. Well-presented, understandable and accurate accounts are a positive tool in promoting a charity's cause.

3. Commercial and Charity Accounting: The Difference

Motivation and purpose

Although the individual financial transactions are the same, the motivation and purpose of these two types of accounting are entirely different.

A commercial business raises capital which it uses to generate a surplus or profit. This is either distributed to those who contributed the capital, or retained in the business to generate more profit. There is normally a very strong link between cost and income. For instance, in a manufacturing company money is spent producing goods which are then sold. Because profit is the margin between these linked operations, the profit or bottom-line figure is of paramount importance.

A charity's purpose is to spend money on charitable objectives, rather than make a profit. There is often no direct relationship between income and expenditure. The raising of income comes first, and then expenditure decisions are taken: how much to spend, on what and when. The net surplus or deficit in any one year, the equivalent of the commercial firm's profit or loss, can be very misleading because there is not necessarily any match between income and expenditure in any particular period.

Lack of a single indicator of performance

Because there is no need to emphasise the bottom line figure as a single indicator of performance, the layout or format of charity accounts needs to be different from that of commercial accounts. The aim of the accounts is to show the movements on the charity's funds. They attempt to show in one statement how incoming resources have been used, and any changes in the net resources of the charity.

The users of charity accounts need to be able to assess what services the charity is providing and its ability to continue to provide them.

Hence the SORP calls for expenditure to be analysed according to function (for example 'Running Costs of Activity X', rather than just 'Rent and Rates', 'Telephone and Postage' etc) and for narrative descriptions of how the charity will fund its future plans and committments.

The other fundamental difference between commercial and charity accounting is the concept of fund accounting, which we will look at later.

4. Financial and Management Accounting: The Difference

Is the difference significant?

Both forms of accounting are similar, in the sense that they use the same financial transactions and information. For instance, if the charity pays rent of £500 per quarter, then £500 is entered in the accounting records each quarter. This basic financial transaction will be used for management and financial accounting. However, the difference between the types of accounting can be seen when one examines the purpose to which the information is put.

Management and financial accounting explained

Management accounting is all about the day to day operations and internal control of the charity's finances. Income and expenditure are controlled and monitored against a budget so that the management knows that they meet expectations and the charity has the cash to meet the expenditure. Alarm bells should ring, for instance, if £600 rent was paid in error or no payment was made in one quarter. Management would seek explanations for the variance and corrective action would be swiftly taken.

Financial accounting, which culminates in the production of annual financial accounts is about stewardship and external accountability. In the case of the rent paid, the annual accounts will record an annual charge of £2,000 (four times £500) and any unpaid rent at the balance sheet data will be recorded as a liability. The annual financial accounts show stakeholders how the charity has spent its money. They should be able to judge whether the money has been spent appropriately. For all but the smallest charities, the financial accounts will also be subject to an independent expert review, in the form of an independent examination or audit.

A useful analogy to help understand the difference between management and financial accounting is to compare it to running and maintaining a new car. Management accounting is concerned with day to day running and maintenance: filling up with petrol, checking the oil etc. Financial accounting is like an annual service where all the major changes in the year are examined, and corrected if necessary. The annual audit/independent examination is like the MOT, an independent one-off spot check to ensure everything is as it should be.

Other differences

Management accounting normally analyses income and expenses by type: e.g. rent, wages, insurance, because monitoring and control by type is relatively easy. However, analysis by type is not quite so useful in financial accounting, because stakeholders need to be able to assess whether money has been used appropriately. If donors have given money for medical relief in Africa, they will not be able to make such a judgement if the accounts show costs purely by type, such as salaries and rent. They need expenditure to be grouped under its functional nature or activity. For instance, an accounts heading for African medical aid, under which would appear the salary costs of doctors and nurses working in Africa and the rent for the hospital building.

This functional analysis is really only the grouping of income or costs under separate headings which reflect the actual activities of the charity. It should make the charity's financial transactions more understandable and therefore improve accountability to the stakeholders.

Unincorporated charities with income less than £100,000 per annum do not have to adopt this functional analysis, but are encouraged to do so, because sensible classification will obviously assist the reader to understand the activities of the charity better. It does not require expensive new accounting software. Expenses can be grouped at the end of the year, either manually or with the aid of a simple computer spreadsheet.

5. Charity Accounts and Terminology

The format of the accounts is set out in the Charities (Accounts and Reports) Regulations 1995 and explained in the Charities Statement of Recorded Practice (SORP).

The four components of charity accounts are:
a) a narrative statement or trustees annual report
b) a Statement of Financial Activities (SOFA) – formerly the Income and Expenditure Account. (This may be replaced by a simple receipts and payments account in the case of small charities.)
c) a statement of assets and liabilities or a balance sheet, which shows a snapshot of assets (what the charity owns) and liabilities (what the charity owes) at a particular date
d) supporting notes to the accounts which help explain and provide more detail in respect of the figures in the SOFA and balance sheet.

The Trustees' Annual Report

The contents of the annual report are strictly controlled by law. Section 45 of the Charities Act 1993 makes it quite clear that:
"The charity trustees of a charity should prepare in respect of each financial year of the charity an annual report containing:

a) *such a report by the trustees on the activities of the charity during that year, and*

b) *such other information relating to the charity or to its trustees or offices, as may be prescribed by regulations made by the Secretary of State".*

The Charities (Accounts and Reports) Regulations 1995 set out the requirements in relation to the annual report as follows.

"(a) In the case of any financial year of a charity in which neither its gross income nor its total expenditure exceeds £100,000, a brief summary of the main activities and achievements of the charity during the year;

(b) In the case of any financial year of a charity in which its gross income or total expenditure exceeds £100,000 a review of all activities including material transactions, significant developments, and achievements, of the charity during the year in relation to its objects, any significant changes in those activities during the year, any important events affecting those activities which have occurred since the end of the year and any likely future developments in those activities; and

(c) In either case, the report should be dated and signed by one or more of the charity trustees, each of whom has been authorised in accordance with the trust of the charity to do so."

The Charities SORP recommends an expansion of the formal narrative statement. This means that the Report should include information about the charity's objects, activities and achievements as well as a commentary on the financial position of the charity. This reinforces the importance of the Annual Accounts and Reports.

A checklist is provided in the SORP of the matters to be covered:
a) objectives, policies and organisation
b) developments, activities and achievements
c) financial activities and position
d) relationships with other bodies
e) funds held on behalf of others.

Either as part of the report or as a separate section in the report and accounts, there has to be a statement setting out the legal and administrative details (paragraph 27). These include such obvious things as the full name of the charity, a list of all the trustees and principal officers, the address of the registered office, the name and addresses of principal advisers, an indication of the nature of the governing instrument, details of specific restrictions and a summary of any specific investment powers.

For those charities which are incorporated, to avoid duplication the trustees/directors should ensure that their annual report as trustees includes all those matters which are required to be included in the statutory directors' report under company law.

Basis of preparation of SOFA

There are two main types of financial accounts: those prepared on a *receipts and payments basis* and those prepared on a *full accruals accounting basis*.

Accounts prepared on a receipts and payments basis are self-explanatory. The accounts show only the money actually received or spent in the period, with no timing adjustments. In particular, capital receipts and payments are recognised in full as income or charge in the period in which they occur.

The SOFA will still be split between income funds and capital funds and the income funds split between funds for general purposes and special trusts (restricted for a special purpose). The receipts and payments SOFA will be accompanied by a list of assets and liabilities.

Charities preparing accounts on a full accruals accounting basis (which is explained more fully below), will have a SOFA which takes account of timing differences and integrates with the balance sheet. This produces a fairer picture of the charity's financial transactions during the accounting period and the worth of the charity at the end of the period. For instance, if a charity pays its rent in advance on the last day of its accounting year, the receipts and payments basis would show the payment as a cost of the year in which it was paid. This can be misleading as the period to be covered by the payment is in fact the next year. Under full accruals accounting this would be adjusted by carrying forward the payment in the balance sheet as a prepayment, rather than charging it as a cost for the previous year.

Unincorporated charities with an income less than £100,000 have the choice of which basis to use. Charities formed as companies must use the full accruals accounting basis, no matter the level of income.

Change of basis

A charity may change the basis of its accounting system either because it has grown in size (to an income of over £100,000) or by the decision of the trustees. If this change is made, either to or from full accrual accounting, the corresponding amounts for the previous financial years should be restated on the basis of the new accounting policy.

Accruals Accounting

The concept of accruals is one of the four fundamental accounting concepts. It means that income is recognised in the accounts when earned, in the case of revenue, or when receivable, in the case of gifts, donations, bequests, grants etc., rather than when it is actually received. Expenditure is recognised when it is incurred, rather than when it is paid.

This introduces the concept of debtors and creditors into the accounts. For example where a covenant has been received from an individual and the tax repayment not received by the year end it would be accrued for or included as a debtor under accrual accounting. So if the covenant was a net £75, with tax to be recovered of £25, the figure shown in the annual accounts would be £100. On the receipts and payments basis the covenant it would be shown as a receipt of £75 and the additional £25 not accounted for until it was received.

Under accruals accounting, income matches expenditure so far as their relationship can be established or justifiably assumed. Both are included in the SOFA for the period to which they relate. However this assumes that the accruals concept is not inconsistent with the concept of prudence (or caution). If there is a conflict between accruals and prudence, then the concept of prudence will prevail.

Under accruals accounting it is recognised that fixed assets (computer equipment for example) will normally last for more than one year. Therefore to write them off in the year of purchase is not matching income and costs, because future periods will benefit from their use. The purchased fixed assets will therefore be included in the balance sheet and be written off or depreciated over their useful life. So the SOFA produced on an accruals basis will include a charge for depreciation which will not appear on a receipts and payments account.

Further Guidance from the Charity Commission

The Charity Commission has published two accounting guides:

Accounting for the Smaller Charity

This book does not assume any accountancy knowledge and skills on the part of the reader, only basic bookkeeping knowledge and some practical experience in business/charity administration. It is aimed at charities whose income is less than £100,000 who choose to work on a receipts and payments basis. It includes an example of the Charity Commission's standard accounts form which charities can use rather than design and construct their own.

Accruals Accounting for the Smaller Charity

This book assumes some prior knowledge. It expects the reader to be able to understand and prepare financial statements, such as a balance sheet and a statement of financial activities, from a trial balance of a nominal ledger with appropriate year-end adjustments to give a true and fair view of the transactions and events of the year and the financial position of the charity at the year end on the basis of the accounting policies adopted, the charity's circumstances and trustees' assumptions about future events and activities.

Statement of Assets and Liabilities or Balance Sheet

These statements show a 'snapshot' of assets (what the charity owns), creditors (what the charity owes) and funds (what resources the charity has available to use to meet its charitable objects) at a particular date. In the case of a balance sheet, this integrates or links with the SOFA prepared on the full accruals accounting basis. A specimen balance sheet is shown on *page 194*, and the terms used are explained *below*.

Fixed Assets

Fixed assets can be *tangible* or *non-tangible*. Examples of tangible fixed assets are land, freehold property, motor vehicles, furniture and equipment. Tangible fixed assets are usually shown in the balance sheet at what they cost or what they were valued at when they were acquired, less depreciation to date. Depreciation simply means writing off or spreading of the cost over the years in which the asset is expected to be used. (For example, the value of a car purchased for £8,000 and expected to last for four years would be shown in the accounts as £6,000 after one year, £4,000 after two years, etc.) Fixed assets can be revalued either upwards or downwards. Investments, including investment property, are included in the accounts at market value.

Investments

Investments are assets held for the income or capital gain that arises directly from them and not used in the charitable activities.

Some investments are held for the long term and are included under fixed assets; other are held for the short term and are included under current assets. Examples of investments include shares and property owned for investment purposes.

Current assets
Examples of current assets are cash and balances held in the bank, investments of a short term nature, stock, debts and other amounts owed to the charity.

Current liabilities
Creditors are the opposite of debtors. They represent a liability which has not yet been met. They are included in the accounts at their face value, that is the amount which will actually be paid to the creditor (the person or company who is owed money). They may include bank overdrafts or loans, trade creditors or amounts owed to suppliers, accruals, deferred income and provision.

Some of these terms may be unfamiliar. Accruals are expenses incurred during the period covered by the accounts which remain unpaid at the end of the period. Deferred income is income which has been received before the balance sheet date but relates to the following period and is carried forward. An example would be a government grant received shortly before the balance sheet date but intended to fund the charity's activities during its next financial year. Provision represents a charge made through the accounts for costs or expenditure which cannot be precisely calculated.

Net current assets
Net current assets are the current assets minus the current liabilities.

Liabilities – long term creditors
Some creditors fall due after one year. This means that there are contractual liabilities which are not payable within the next financial year. An example would the be the balance due on a long-term loan or mortgage.

Net assets
The net assets are calculated by deducting all the liabilities (current creditors and long-term creditors) from the total fixed and current assets.

Funds

The funds section of the balance sheet indicates how the net assets have been provided. They are divided into unrestricted funds, which include designated funds, and restricted funds, which include permanent endowment funds and money given for special appeals. Fund accounting is explained in detail in Section 5.

Notes to the accounts

These should help explain items in the accounts. They should include an explanation of the accounting policies under which the accounts have been drawn up as this will have determined the treatment of certain items: for instance, the rate at which assets are written off or depreciated, and why certain money has been treated as restricted.

An Example of a Balance Sheet

Balance sheet at....... (date)

	19X1		19X0	
	£'000	£'000	£'000	£'000
Fixed assets		1,800		2,000
Current assets	4,000		3,000	
Less: Creditors - amounts falling due with one year	(2,000)		(2,000)	
Net current assets		2,000		1,000
Sub total		3,800		3,000
Less: Creditors - amounts falling due after one year		(200)		(200)
Net assets		3,600		2,800
Funds				
Unrestricted funds:				
- Accumulated fund		2800		2300
- Designated fund		200		–
Restricted funds:		200		100
Permanent Endowment fund:		400		400
Total funds		3,600		2,800

Approved on behalf of the trustees on_____(date)

by_____(signature and position)

6. The Statement of Financial Activities (SOFA)

What is the purpose of SOFA?

The main purpose of the SOFA is to bring together all transactions in a single statement so as to present a complete picture which will give a true and fair view of the charity's financial activities during the year. It records all the charity's incoming resources and shows how they have been applied during the year. Essentially it combines an income and expenditure account with an analysis of the changes over the year in the different funds held by the charity. Care is needed to disclose all the transactions correctly in the restricted and unrestricted columns.

Columnar Format

The layout, with columns, is set out in the Regulations and must be followed. The minimum requirement will be a column for unrestricted funds, one for restricted funds and one for permanent endowments (if there are any). Fund accounting will be examined in the next section, *page 197*.

Grouping of Items by Activity

In future, income and expenditure will be grouped under standard headings such as fund raising and publicity. This will help make accounts more comparable. Functional classification of expenditure means that instead of disclosing expenditure by type such as rent, rates, light and heat, expenditure will be described by its nature such as fund raising, and direct charitable expenditure such as relief aid for Bosnia. This helps the reader understand what the charity is doing and how much it is spending on those activities. Charities with income less than £100,000 do not have to adopt the functional analysis but are encouraged to do so.

The following example illustrates the columnar format and the grouping of items by activity in a SOFA.

Help Charity

Statement of Financial Activities for the year ended 30th September 199X

	Unrestricted Funds £'000	Restricted Funds £'000	Total Funds 199X £'000
Incoming Resources			
Donations and gifts	250	100	350
Legacies	150	–	150
Local Authority contracts	50	–	50
Investment income - interest	22	10	32
Total Incoming Resources	472	110	582
Resources Expended			
Direct charitable expenditure			
Care for the elderly	200	50	250
Information and Education	100	–	100
	300	50	350
Fund-raising and publicity	50	50	100
Management and administration	100	50	150
Total Resources Expended	450	150	600

Often the accounting system records income and expenditure by type and not by the new functional classification. This should not be abandoned as it has its uses e.g. budgetary control and disclosure of certain items such as salaries which is still required in the notes to the account. Ways should be found to aggregate the information under the appropriate functional headings. This can be done manually or by using a standard computer spreadsheet.

Other Matters

The SOFA must include a statement of gains and losses, both realised and unrealised, on fixed assets and investments.

In rare cases a Summary Income and Expenditure Account is also required if there are movements on the permanent endowment fund, because the Companies Act will not allow capital to be included in the income statement.

7. Fund Accounting

The key concept behind charity accounting

Fund accounting comes into operation when funds are received and used for different purposes. Fund accounting appears in the Statement of Financial Activities (SOFA) with a separate column for each type of fund. It is enshrined in law by the Charities (Accounts and Reports) Regulations 1995, and explained in the charity SORP.

What are the different types of funds?

Permanent Endowment Funds

A fund where there is no power to convert the capital into income is known as a permanent endowment fund and must generally be held indefinitely. This concept of 'permanence' does not necessarily mean that the assets held in the endowment fund cannot be exchanged, nor does it mean that they are incapable of depreciation or loss. But it does mean that the permanent endowment fund cannot be used as if it were income.

Restricted Funds

Restricted funds are subject to specific trusts declared by the donor(s), or with their authority (for instance, through a public appeal). They can only be used for the purposes for which they are given. Restricted funds can be of two types: *restricted income funds* which must be spent to further some particular object of the charity; or *restricted capital funds*, where the assets must be invested or retained for actual use.

Unrestricted Funds

These are also sometimes known as *general funds*. They may be spent at the discretion of the trustees in furtherance of the objects of the charity.

Designated Funds

Where part of an unrestricted fund is earmarked for a particular project it may be described as designated as a separate fund. However that designation has an administrative purpose only and does not legally restrict the trustees' discretion to apply the fund. In other words, trustees will still have the right to use those funds in any way that furthers the objects of the charity.

Examples would be funds allocated for a new building, a staff redundancy contingency fund, or a programme guarantee fund established by a grant-making charity to ensure it can honour commitments it has made for future years.

The distinction between restricted and unrestricted funds is crucial. Misapplying restricted funds amounts to a breach of trust and could result in the trustees having personally to make good the misspent funds.

For this reason, it is recommended that assets and liabilities are analysed separately for restricted and general funds to ensure that each fund has adequate and appropriate assets. Such an analysis would normally be disclosed in the notes to the accounts.

The implications of fund accounting

Fund accounting is not new, stemming as it does from trust law, but in future will be highlighted by the layout of the accounts.

Many charities have failed to handle fund accounts correctly. A common mistake has been to treat interest on income earned on restricted funds as general fund income. Actually such income belongs to the restricted fund concerned and cannot be used for general fund purposes. However, this error has often been counter balanced by the fact that overheads have not been charged to restricted funds. The two factors may cancel each other out. In future the columnar format will make it more obvious whether income earned on restricted funds is being allocated correctly to those funds. The only exception to the rule about income earned on restricted funds, is the case of permanent endowments, where the income can normally be used for general fund purposes.

It may be possible for a small charity to have two bank accounts to keep restricted funds and unrestricted funds apart and so ensure that the interest is credited correctly, if it is concerned about this point.

The accounting system must also be able to earmark and/or identify individual types of income, match and allow the allocation of appropriate expenditure and identify the resulting fund balances individually. In most cases modification of the existing accounting system, or the use of a spreadsheet package, will be sufficient to cope with fund accounting requirements. It should be possible to avoid the cost of purchasing a new accounting system.

Action Point – what should I check?

1. All incoming funds must be categorised as restricted or unrestricted.
2. Interest on income earned on restricted funds must be allocated to the respective restricted fund.
3. Overheads should be charged to the appropriate fund.
4. Fund balances may need to be reallocated if this was not done correctly in the past.
5. It is not necessary or sensible to purchase a new accounting system to deal with these issues.

Fund accounting exercise

You are the finance director of a new charity and you are asked to prepare the accounts at the end of the first year ending 31st December 199X

During the year the charity received or spent the following income:

1. Received: £100,000 in respect of an appeal to fund the running of an orphanage in Romania. In respect of this project you have incurred the following costs:

Salaries	£2,000
Travel to site	£1,000
Licences, etc.	£5,000
	£8,000

2. Received: £50,000 in respect of a donation from a trust which has given you the money towards the cost of running advice shops for refugees. Of this sum £10,000 was spent by the period end.
3. General donations and covenanted income of £80,000 were received. From this the sum of £5,000 was spent on general charity expenditure on UK projects.
4. You incurred running costs as follows:

Fund-raising and publicity	£20,000
Management and administration	£30,000

5. Interest was earned on the unspent funds as follows:

Romania appeal	£5,000
Money from the Trust	£2,000
General donations	£3,000
	£10,000

You are required to prepare Statement of Financial Activities and Balance Sheet in accordance with the Charity SORP, with particular reference to fund accounting.

Statement of Financial Activities
For the year ended 31st December 199X

	Unrestricted Funds £'000	Restricted Funds £'000	Total £'000
Resources arising:			
Donations	80	150	230
Interest earned	3	7	10
	83	157	240
Resources used:			
Direct charitable expenditure:			
Orphanage in Romania	–	8	8
Advice shops for refugees	–	10	10
UK projects	5	–	5
	5	18	23
Other expenditure			
Fund-raising and publicity	20	–	20
Management and administration	30	–	30
	50	–	50
Resources used in year	55	18	73
Net incoming resources	28	139	167
Net movement of funds	28	139	167

Balance Sheet as at 31st December 199X

	£'000
Cash at bank and in hand	167
Funds:	
Restricted funds	139
General fund	28
	167

8. The Regulatory Framework and Audit Requirements

What is New?
The Charities (Accounts and Reports) Regulations 1995 were issued in October 1995 and apply for accounting years of charities commencing on or after 1 March 1996. So if your charity's year end is 31 December the first set of accounts to be produced which will have to comply will be those for the year ended 31 December 1997. The Regulations introduce the following:

Financial Thresholds:

Registered Charities	Annual Return	Basis of Accounts	External Scrutiny
Neither income nor expenditure over £10,000	Yes	Receipts and payments option	None
Income not over £100,000	Yes	Receipts and payments option	Independent examination
Neither income nor expenditure over £250,000 in this and both of the last two years	Yes	Accruals	Independent examination
Income or expenditure over £250,000 in this or either of previous two years	Yes	Accruals	Audit

The table covers only the new statutory obligations. It does not include other obligations imposed by governing documents and funding bodies. It is only valid for unincorporated charities and not for charitable companies accountable under the Companies Act 1985. It does not cover exempt or unregistered charities.

Those charities with an annual income of less than £10,000, i.e. those working under the light touch regime, need not submit a copy of their accounts (or report) to the Charity Commission unless they are specifically asked for them. All other registered charities must do so.

Charities covered by the light touch regime should prepare accounts and an annual report for their own purposes, so that these are available if required.

Charities whose income is less than £1,000 per annum are not required to register, provided they have no permanent endowment nor use or occupy land. Accounts will still need to be prepared but there is no requirement for audit or independent examination and no duty to submit accounts to the Charity Commission.

The Charity Statement of Recommended Practice (SORP)

The charity SORP sets out the principles and practices that should be followed when preparing the accounts and annual report. It compliments the regulations. The SORP represents best practice mainly for the bigger charities, though aspects of the SORP apply to all charities except where another specialist SORP applies (such as a housing association). Technically, it is only recommended practice, but the Charity Commissioners, *"expect the accounts of charities and their accounting practices to fully comply with the SORP... insofar as a charity diverges from SORP, the Commissioners expect the charity's accounts to clearly identify any divergence and to provide a full explanation. If no explanation is given, or the explanation is unsatisfactory, the Commissioners will raise the matter with the charity concerned and, if circumstances warrant it, institute an inquiry"*.

Smaller charities which follow the Charity Commission's guide *Accounting for the Smaller Charity* and *Accruals Accounting for the Smaller Charity* will only in addition need to refer to paragraphs 13-21 of the SORP.

Audit and Independent Examination

The Regulations introduced an audit for first time for many non-incorporated charities. The threshold of £250,000 income or expenditure was set as the level for audit for both incorporated and unincorporated charities. Below this level there are considerable inconsistencies in the treatment of incorporated or non-incorporated charities.

Annual Income Charity	Unincorporated		Incorporated	
	Audit	Independent examination	Audit	Audit exemption report
Less than £10,000	No	No	No	No
More than £10,000 to £90,000	No	**Yes**	No	No
More than £90,000 to £250,000	No	Yes	No	Yes
More than £250,00	Yes	No	Yes	No

The table *above* sets out the situation with the inconsistent problem area highlighted. Discussions are continuing between the Charity Commission, the Department of National Heritage and the Department of Trade & Industry to resolve this anomaly.

Audit requirements in the 1993 Act state that if a charity's gross income or total expenditure exceeds £250,000 in the relevant year or either of the two preceding years, then the accounts will have to be audited by a person who:

a) is an auditor, in accordance with Section 25 of the Companies Act 1989 is eligible for appointment as a company auditor or

b) is a member of a body for the time being specified in the regulations and is under the rules of that body eligible for appointment as auditor of the charity.

Guidance on charity audits

The Auditing Practices Board has issued a practice note for charity audit.

Limited Companies

The audit of limited companies is subject to a different set of regulations. In certain cases this requires a less rigorous standard of scrutiny than for an unincorporated charity. Incorporated charities with an income of less than £90,000 do not require any external examination at all and where the income is between

£90,000 and £250,000 they can provide unaudited accounts but they must provide an accountants' report.

Independent Examination

Charities Act 1993

This Act defined an independent examiner as *"an independent person who is reasonably believed by the trustees to have the requisite ability and practical experience to carry out a competent examination of the accounts."*

Regulations

Independent examination is of course a less onerous form of scrutiny than audit. The examiner is not required to form an opinion as to whether the accounts show a true and fair view but reports instead, based on examination carried out, whether specific matters have come to his or her attention.

The independent examiner is required to report on whether or not the examiner has reasonable cause to believe that accounts and records do not comply with the relevant legislation. The recommended reporting requirements are set higher than the compliance reports for companies under the deregulation regime.

Quiz

Questions

1. What is the main difference between commercial and charity accounting?
2. What is the key concept behind charity accounts?
3. What are the different types of charity fund?
4. If money is given in respect of an appeal for relief aid for Bosnia, is it restricted or unrestricted money?
5. What are the main components of a charity's accounts?
6. What are the two types/basis of preparation of the Statement of Financial Activities?
7. Can an incorporated charity (i.e. a charity formed as a company) ever prepare accounts on a receipts and payments basis?
8. At what level of income do all registered charities require an audit?

Answers

1. *The lack of a single indicator of performance or bottom line.*
2. *Fund accounting.*
3. *Permanent endowment; Restricted; Unrestricted; Designated*
4. *Restricted.*
5. *A trustees report; A Statement of Financial Activities; A Statement of Assets or Liabilities or Balance Sheet; Notes to the Accounts*
6. *Receipts and Payments; Full accruals basis*
7. *No.*
8. *£250,000.*

About the author

Neil Finlayson is Senior Manager with accountants Pannell Kerr Forster's charity unit. He regularly lectures and writes on matters relating to the sector and also lectures on the MSc Charity Finance course at South Bank University.

Acknowledgement

We gratefully acknowledge the contribution from Adrian Randall of Moores Rowland to this section.

STRATEGIC PLANNING : 7

Janet Cummins

1. Introduction

Aims and objectives

Strategic Planning is the creative process of deciding how to achieve your organisation's aims and objectives. As you work through the steps recommended here you will see that they are just a more formal way of organising a process with which you are already familiar in your everyday life.

By the time you have worked through this chapter and learned how to complete your plan for your organisation you will have a much clearer picture about:

- what your organisation does
- who benefits from it
- the worth or cost of its activities
- how you are going to achieve your objectives in the months and years ahead.

You will have made some hard choices about:

- what you are going to do and what you will not be able to do
- how you want to do it
- how to use your resources better
- how you will know when you have succeeded

You will have a model to follow for other planning in the future.

What is Strategic Planning?

Quite simply, it is the process of choosing objectives and working out how to achieve them - and we do it every day in our own lives. We call the process Strategic Planning when we apply it to organisations. It takes account of environmental factors which can be seen at this stage as likely to affect the organisation, and assesses the dangers too. Most importantly, the strategic planning process looks at the resources needed to achieve the objectives. Are they available? Are the objectives worth the cost of achieving them?

The second stage is more detailed planning, breaking down the objectives into smaller targets, deciding who will work on them and the timescale. The last stage is about monitoring progress, then reviewing and adjusting the plan in the light of that information. It is also worth reviewing the planning process. You may be able to do it better next time.

This simple guide gives you a framework to use for your strategic planning. But before we go into detail, it is worth looking at why a formal planning process is useful, the benefits to be gained, and some of the difficulties.

The benefits of strategic planning

The process of planning:

- establishes or confirms, the organisation's vision and clarifies its purpose.
- helps to identify key issues for the organisation
- provides a clear picture of the value of the organisation and its achievements
- encourages focus on outcomes and impact
- makes the best use of resources
- manages environmental changes
- organisational development and team building
- brings conflict into the open
- helps to identify problems and find solutions
- develops commitment to the organisation's objectives
- motivates staff and volunteers
- makes saying No! possible.

Some difficulties that may be encountered:

- planning takes time, which may be resented because it often has to be taken from an already overloaded timetable
- it may create tensions between "planners" and "doers"
- inability to separate planning objectives and the process of reaching them
- people may need time to learn the techniques used in planning
- many people find it difficult to think strategically (choosing what to do) as well as operationally (how to do it)
- planning challenges entrenched values, working practices and assumptions which can be very uncomfortable and indeed threatening.

Use the plan:

- to gain commitment and focus effort of trustees, staff and volunteers
- to make success recognisable
- for funders, current and potential
- for current and potential beneficiaries

3. Plan for Planning

Four steps for involving the whole organisation

1. Everyone in the organisation will have something valuable to contribute. However, it would be impossible to have everyone involved in every meeting. Choose a planning committee with some Trustees, the Chief Executive and some senior staff, some operational staff and some volunteers. Six to eight people is probably about right.

2. Establish how consultation with everyone else will be arranged. Make it clear from the beginning that all contributions are welcomed, though not every idea can be put into practice.

3. Decide the time scale of the planning process. With concentrated effort in a small organisation the planning described here can probably be done in 18 to 30 hours, plus time to gather information and to undertake consultation. Larger organisations will take longer. If too little time is allowed there will be a temptation to brush aside conflict in the interest of completing the timetable rather than resolving differences. If too long is allowed, everyone will get bored and commitment will be difficult to maintain.

4. Consider whether an outside consultant would help. Many organisations find it useful to have an impartial outsider to facilitate the process. Consultants can bring their experience of other organisations to bear on your situation. They can help you to get to the heart of the matter and can draw the sting of disagreement. Don't use them to do the work for you.

Plans for the future always create uncertainty and this makes people nervous about their own future. Take these concerns into account in devising your planning process and deal as honestly, openly and quickly as you can with everyone.

Agreeing the Plan

It is essential that the Board or Management Committee formally adopts the plan, and that everyone in the organisation knows where their work fits into it.

Review progress against the plan at each Management Committee or Board Meeting. Make it the first item on the agenda not only to consider progress against the targets set, but also to ask whether the plan itself is still useful. One way to do this is to review any variations from the plan that go outside agreed limits.

Some useful tips and planning tools:

- **Brainstorming** achieves more when people work alone first and then come together to share ideas. Do not allow criticism until all ideas have been gathered.
- **Gap Analysis** defines what you want to achieve, compares it with the present situation, and works out how you are going to fill the gap.
- **Charts** are better for giving the whole picture than a book, though you will want to produce a report as well. On the next page is a sample you could adapt for your own organisation. Other charts are shown at key points in the text to give you some ideas for your planning. Charts 2, 3, 6 and 7 can be linked to form an overall plan showing all departments and the elements of the plan. Consider writing the plan in pencil - with a rubber on the end!
- **Post-it notes** are very useful for gathering and arranging ideas. They have the great advantage that everyone can join in. Quieter or less confident people can contribute their ideas without being overwhelmed by more powerful voices.

Chart 1: Example			
Major Plan Elements	**Current Activities**		
Services/Activities			
Buildings			
Clients/Users			
Staff & Volunteers			
Communications			
Management Committee			
Organisation & Structure			
Finances: Income			
Costs			

3. An Eight Step Model Plan

1. Establish a clear, agreed understanding of the organisation's vision, its mission (what it does to achieve the vision), and the values which guide it.
2. Look out at the external environment as it affects your organisation – political, economic, social, technological trends and people's views of your organisation – and inwards at your organisation's structure, culture, philosophy and operations.
3. Identify the Strengths and Weakness of your organisation and the Opportunities and Threats, or Barriers, in the outside environment.
4. Define the financial and other resources which will be needed to achieve your ideas.
6 Determine Objectives within a time frame and how to measure success.
7 Set Targets to achieve the Objectives, including dates and who is responsible.
8 Monitor, Evaluate and Review.

It is important that planning does not take the place of action.

Vision, Values and Mission

Every organisation exists to make a difference in the world. Every plan starts with the organisation's vision of that difference. What difference do you want to see?

As individuals we each have our own set of values guiding us in how we live and act. These values develop over time in the light of our experience. Organisations also have values which guide their actions. People coming together as an organisation with a shared purpose to create a better world need to agree on the values which will underpin their organisation and the way it works. What are your organisation's values?

Strategic Planning is about turning dreams into reality; deciding how to make the vision happen in accordance with a set of values. An organisation's mission is what it actually does towards achieving its vision. To test whether you can tell people about your mission easily, clearly and quickly, try saying it in one breath!

Strategic decisions are about fundamental matters and choices about what will be done. For example, a group of people whose children are affected by the same disorder will need to decide:
• are we going to provide information about this disorder
• or pay for medical research

- or give support to families by paid staff or by volunteers
- or put our efforts into building up local self-help groups
- or do all these things?

Case Studies

When the Cystic Fibrosis Research Trust was set up in 1964, it started by focusing on research but later gathered together groups of parents who were supporting each other. Over the years it raised money to pay for research – some in laboratories to first find the scientific cause with the ultimate aim of a cure or eradicating the disorder, some in hospitals combining research with care for patients with CF. It provided information to parents of children with CF, and later to those whose children might have CF, and to doctors, nurses and other professionals. It began training volunteers to provide better support for parents and those with CF.

Arthritis Care takes another approach and concentrates on helping people live with arthritis and does not fund research.

Charity Projects was set up to raise funds for other charities and became a fundraising charity and a grant-giver. It chose the fundraising methods to use – Red Nose Day – and it chose which work to support.

Checklist
- ☐ What is your organisation's vision?
- ☐ What is your mission to achieve it - what are you going to do to bring that change about?
- ☐ List your own values.
- ☐ And those for your organisation.

4. SWOT Analysis

Gathering The Data: recognising *Strengths* and *Weaknesses*; identifying *Opportunities* and *Threats*.

All organisations exist within the world around them. The trustees, chief executive, staff and volunteers of an organisation must read the signs in its environment and adjust to achieve their objectives. As well as looking at the external environment, the planners must inspect the organisation and its operations in detail to assess their strengths and weaknesses.

This next phase of planning assesses the *Strengths* and *Weaknesses* of the organisation, and looks outward at the world to see what *Opportunities* there are for expansion or new ways of operating, and to identify the barriers or *Threats* that prevent you from doing what you want to do, or which make it more difficult. This is called a SWOT Analysis

Your aim to is to see what realistic possibilities there are for your organisation in the future, bearing all possible factors in mind. The dangers lie in chasing too many opportunities or in becoming downcast by the threats and barriers; over-valuing your strengths and underestimating your weaknesses - or indeed, vice versa.

Start by looking inward to assess your organisation's strengths and weaknesses. These questions will help:

- what do you expect your organisation to be doing?
- how well does your organisation's structure serve its purposes? (Trace the decision-making through the staff and committees.)
- are any decisions being taken twice, or being ratified by another group?
- how many committees are there?
- are they effective?
- is everyone – trustees, managers, staff and volunteers – clear about their roles and responsibilities?
- do you agree about your objectives?
- does everyone know what they are?

Look at your accounting, personnel, fundraising, investment management, operations, public relations, and at your facilities and buildings. What are your strengths? and where are your weaknesses? Choose the five most important of each. Record them on Chart 2 at the end of this chapter. Be honest about this assessment. Take care not to be too optimistic nor too pessimistic.

You will notice that, so far, not a word has been said about money – that second most important of resources (people come first!). Your financial situation, with its own strengths and weaknesses, opportunities and threats, is a crucial element of strategic planning. It is so important that you might care to consider it separately after you have looked at the environment around you. Analysis of your resources has a section to itself.

The next stage is to look at the world around your organisation. Use these STEPs to guide your thinking: Remember that you are looking for things which *affect your organisation.*

Social Trends

Consider matters such as the birth rate or numbers of older people in the population, changes in the way we live, Sunday trading, etc.

Technology

Can you use mobile phones, faxes, e-mail, Internet, cable TV and phone to do your job better? Can you distribute your Committee agenda and minutes by fax or e-mail overnight? Do you need to meet in person so often, or can you use video or telephone conferencing? Should you be getting ready to use the Internet? How long might it take until using the Internet became normal for your users? Can volunteers cope with the new technologies? Is it better to employ one person who can use them, or six volunteers who can only do a task in the traditional way?

Economic Trends

The economic state of the country as a whole affects all organisations. For example, movements in the Bank Rate will affect your organisation's investment income as well as the economic strength of your supporters. Look also at your local economy and the trends that might affect you. Growing or lessening prosperity in an area will affect all organisations, perhaps by creating more demand for services or help or reducing voluntary income. Local grant-givers may find applications for help rising.

Political, Legal, Fiscal Matters

Politics, both local and national, influence the environment in which charities and voluntary organisations of all sizes operate. Perhaps one of the most influential politically driven movements has been the introduction of the contract culture, where central and local government and health authorities contract with voluntary organisations among others to provide services, where before they may have given grants. What is likely to happen at your next local election? For example a local council may decide not to fund places at privately run or voluntary playgroups. This can spell the end of such organisations if their Management Committees have not thought about such a possibility and planned for it.

Every charity had to adjust its accounting practices as the Charity Acts regulations about accounts came into force. Many Acts of Parliament and EC Directives impinge upon charities and voluntary organisations. Are you sure you know which affect yours? Amendments to some laws and regulations, such as in the ways income support or housing benefit are calculated for example, can have an enormous effect on organisations, sometimes changing entirely the way an organisation works. Take account of fiscal changes announced in the Budget and throughout the year. For example, the budgets in November 1995 and 1996 reduced the basic rate of income tax. These changes came into effect in April the following year and affected charities' covenant and gift aid income, because the tax reclaimed from the Inland Revenue dropped. What effect is this having on your income and what will you do to make up the difference?

People's Views

Organisations use market research to find out what people think of them. You will need to know what the users of your products and services think of your organisation. If you have members you can use market research to find out what they think of you and whether they like the services you are offering. To find out, you will need to ask them. Some ways of doing this are:

- conducting a telephone survey
- bringing together small groups – known as Focus Groups – to discuss your services: you will need to facilitate the discussion to get the best from it
- sending out a questionnaire.

It is a good idea to combine these methods. Send a letter saying you will telephone, or send a questionnaire first and ask whether you can telephone to follow up and get more information. You can expect a higher response if you send a reply paid envelope. The Freepost service is the cheapest way to do this. Ask at your post office.

Other Organisations

What other organisations operate in the same area of work or locality as you? Are there overlaps (Threats), or possibilities for collaboration (Opportunities)?

Opportunities

What opportunities exist for new services, or new income, or new partnerships? You will be astonished how many you can find. Strategic Planning is about making choices from among possibilities.

Threats and Barriers

Look for the barriers or threats that make your work difficult, or impossible. And for those that might emerge if you were to take up some of the opportunities you have identified. Range widely to find as many as you can.

Chart 2: Strengths and Weaknesses

Major Plan Elements	Current Activities	Strengths	Weaknesses
Services/Activities			
Buildings			
Clients/Users			
Staff & Volunteers			
Communications			
Management Committee			
Organisation & Structure			
Finances: Income			
Costs			

Chart 3: Opportunities and Threats

Major Plan Elements	Opportunities	Threats or Barriers	Accepted
Services/Activities			
Buildings			
Clients/Users			
Staff & Volunteers			
Communications			
Management Committee			
Organisation & Structure			
Finances: Income			
Costs			

Case Study

The Trustees of an Under Fives Group became remote from the organisation and left all decision-making to the Management Committee which was in the main drawn from parents using the Centre and which changed year by year as the children moved on to school.

Many of the parents and carers had little experience in managing staff and running organisations. They had little time and expertise for fundraising so the organisation remained dependent upon grants from the local Council. The Council was balanced politically on a knife edge which brought different parties to power in quick succession, often only for a year or two. Each party had very different ideas about funding local voluntary organisations so the grant fluctuated.

The Management Committee failed to establish a firm financial base from diverse sources of funding and also failed to read the political situation and so to anticipate that their grant, and later their contract for providing services, would cease.

After several financial crises across the years, which involved making staff redundant, they were finally forced to hand the organisation over to a commercial enterprise.

Checklist

☐ List three principal social, economic, technological and political factors which will affect your organisation.
☐ List five strengths of your organisation, and three weaknesses.
☐ Think of three opportunities open to your organisation.
☐ What is the biggest threat you are currently facing?

2. Analysing and Using the Information Gathered

This section is about using all the information you have gathered. By the end of this exercise you will have:

• confirmed your Aims and Objectives
• decided which opportunities to pursue – developing current activities, adding new ones
• realised whether there are actions which you must take in the light of your investigations, for example upgrading a kitchen used for preparing food.

Doing a SWOT Analysis is fun. You can, and should, let your imagination run free in seeing opportunities. Now it is time for sober reflection. If you have been really honest in your inspection of your organisation it can be a salutary experience.

Are you still fulfilling your original aims?

You may find that your organisation has drifted or deliberately moved away from the activities it was originally set up to do. Are you still fulfilling your objectives in the best possible way? Would any of the opportunities identified, which seem so attractive, especially new sources of funds, pull your organisation away from its original path?

In an organisation which is growing and developing there is an uncomfortable period when the original organisation strains to accommodate new work. Does the new work fit the Aims and Objectives as defined in the constitution or trust deed? Should you change the organisation's objectives? Should you plan to spin off the new work into a separate entity?

These would be major strategic decisions, and exactly the sort of issue to prompt the need for some Strategic Planning and which it sets out to address. If you are in this sort of situation, pause for more thought, consultation and discussion. If necessary, consult an experienced charity solicitor who can help you to make an application to the Charity Commission to change the Aims and Objectives, or set up a new organisation.

Your Strengths and Weaknesses

Look closely at the Strengths and Weaknesses you identified and their effect in the different areas of your organisation's operations.

Some questions to ask yourselves:
- are you strong in areas which are peripheral to your main activities?
- are there weaknesses preventing the organisation from functioning as well as it might?
- what needs to be done to sort them out?

It may seem impossible to deal with a weakness without some investment. If this is not available, the plan then has to start with providing the necessary resources.

Opportunities

Only then can you turn your attention to the opportunities for expansion or development that you have identified. Assess each of your current activities for opportunities to develop. Do they draw on your strengths? Will an organisational weakness make any impossible? Should you cure the weakness in order to grasp the opportunity? Would any compromise the Values of the organisation? If so, what do you want to do about that?

Continue with opportunities for new activities, asking the same questions. Does an opportunity really fit in with the organisation's objectives? Does it fit with the culture - the way you do things. Beware bright ideas which involve changing the whole organisation's direction, or which go right against the established culture. Concentrate on opportunities which fit best with your Objectives and your culture.

Barriers

Have new barriers arisen which make your current activities more difficult? What barriers stand in the way of the new opportunities you have found? Can they be overcome?

Bring it All Together for Analysis

Finally, look at the opportunities for current and new activities, to find those:
• that fit best with your Values and Objectives, and
• do not have insuperable barriers.
Do any strengths and weaknesses make them more or less likely to succeed? Record your decision in the last column of Chart 3.

Finally, make a list of all the opportunities you rejected and in each case note why. This will be useful to explain the group's thinking to people who suggest ideas which you have already rejected and for future planning exercises.

At the end of the analysis you should know which activities you can develop or introduce against the lowest barriers, and which are impractical for one reason or another.

Unfortunately, this all sounds easier than it is. Human nature being what it is, there can be a tendency to overstate the opportunities and strengths, and indeed to see some barriers as opportunities, not recognising them for what they are. It is all too easy to get carried away on a tide of enthusiasm or to be unwilling to accept that there are weaknesses in the organisation. At the same time, guard against the reluctance to tackle anything new. Here an external facilitator may be very useful by helping to disentangle these factors, and to give an outsider's perspective.

Agreement with Results so far?

It is as well to pause here to confirm that you all agree about the results of this preliminary planning exercise. If you are not wholly in accord, have you at least agreed that you can live with your differences in going forward? This point in the planning process can be a watershed in an organisation's life and an appropriate time for individuals to reconsider their involvement.

5. Resources

At this point you need to look in detail at the implications of your planning. The two principal resources to consider are Finances and People. Accommodation may also be very important if you are intending to grow or develop, or if your lease may not be renewed or only at a much higher rent.

Financial Strategy

This is the time to assess your organisation's underlying financial health and to look at your Financial Strategy. Putting right any financial weakness or threat that you have identified becomes one of your objectives, in just the same way as addressing an organisational weakness became an objective. Chapter 1 of this book is on Fundraising, so I shall not go into detail except to say that it would be prudent at this point to do a Fundraising Audit. A SWOT Analysis for fundraising is an extremely useful exercise. It is carried out in exactly the same way as you have already done for the whole organisation, but concentrates on fundraising.

Financial Implications of Opportunities Identified

Now, go back to the opportunities you identified in the SWOT Analysis. You will need to cost them before you can make a sensible decision about whether they should become part of your work. As well as costing them, you need to assess what effect they would have on the financial health of your organisation. Will a project have to raise funds before it starts, or can you cover start-up costs? At what point will a project or area of work stand on its own feet financially?

Each activity or project 'costs' the organisation a share of the overheads, including the salaries of people such as the Chief Executive, accounts staff, fundraisers and others involved with all the organisation's work. The contribution each project's funding is able to make to central costs will have an impact on your planning.

Look at each opportunity in turn. You may find that a less favoured option will be easier to fund than the project you would really like to do. Many an organisation has been tempted away from its prime objectives simply because funding was available for something else. Should any opportunities be dropped for financial reasons? Do the financial implications change the order of preference?

People

The next resource to look at in detail is the staff, both paid and voluntary. This is the time to consider how new work might fit into everyone's workload. Workloads cannot be increased indefinitely.

Case Study

A Project Co-ordinator was appointed to develop some work that had been started on ways of dealing with conflict. She was given a free hand and found many opportunities, most of which she pursued with vigour until she almost became a victim of her own success.

She was pursuing new opportunities and managing the work she had started, writing up course material and reports for funders, running and developing a pool of trainers, and responding to ever-increasing interest in the work.

A review day with a consultant led to a redistribution of work to take advantage of the growing capabilities of a new member of staff and the appointment of more specialist staff for one day a week initially. The Management Committee made two strategic decisions:

- to engage a fundraiser to build firmer financial foundations
- that they would only take on work if it was fully funded.

Putting these good resolutions into practice proved difficult. Drawing up job descriptions and selecting outside specialists, etc. meant extra work. This is a problem which will be familiar to many people. It is sometimes almost more trouble to tackle the problems than to live with them!

Facilities

Consider your physical environment. Is lack of space a barrier? Or does spare space provide an opportunity? Consider 'hot desking' or 'teleworking' from home.

At last you are ready to decide exactly what are your objectives for the next three years and to put each into a time frame.

Chart 4: For Assessing Current Workload

Main Elements	Activities	Time Spent hours per week or %	Adjustments Agreed
Developing New Work	1 2 3 4		
Managing Existing Projects	1 2 3 4		
Public Relations	1 2 3		
Writing	1 2		
Fundraising			
Committee Work	1 Management Sub Committee 2 Board		

Chart 5: For Assessing Future Workload

Use this chart to review future work to which you are committed. You can also indicate how much work has been funded and whether more funds need to be raised.

Main Elements	Activities	Time	Year 1	Year 2	Year 3
Developing New Work	1 2 3 4				
Managing Existing Projects	1 2 3 4				
Public Relations	1 2 3				
Writing	1 2				
Fundraising Committee					
Work	1 Management Sub Committee 2 Board				

Checklist
☐ Assess your own workload.
☐ Would you have to make any changes to take on a new project?

6. Setting Your Objectives

Now you can decide exactly what you are going to do and the time frame within which you are working. Many organisations find that three years is as far ahead as they can look, but for others much longer is both necessary and appropriate. Decide now which is right for your organisation. The important thing is to look far enough ahead to get away from a hand-to-mouth existence, so that your organisation really does have a future.

In the course of your investigations you may have identified some matters to which you must attend, such as those demanded by the introduction of a new law, or saving a member of staff from burn-out caused by overload. Give them first priority so that they become objectives for the first year.

Next look at your current activities. Will they continue as they are or develop? Have you decided to wind up some? When will this happen?

What are your financial objectives for the first and later years? Do you need new resources for new projects, or to replace funding that is coming to an end?

Did you identify any organisational weaknesses to be remedied? What are the priorities?

If you found some real threats to current activities, decide now how to overcome them and when you need to act.

Once you have dealt with immediate threats and any structural problems, you can decide which opportunities to develop and when. Beware of trying to do too many things across too wide a range of activities.

Use Chart 6 at the end of this chapter to record your decisions.

Confirming Agreement

The overall direction of the organisation for the next few years has now been chosen and an outline plan made for the next three years. Before you do any more detailed work make sure through wide consultation that everyone really does agree to the plan. Token agreement or grudging acceptance is not nearly as effective as whole-hearted commitment, and impedes implementation. For really important matters, it is worth asking each member of the Board or Management Committee to confirm aloud their agreement to the action proposed and to record it.

Setting Targets

The next stage is to set targets for each element of the plan. They must be realistic, yet inspiring. Too high and they make success impossible and disempower people; too low, and you are not fulfilling the organisation's aims and objectives as well as possible. Negotiate them with those who understand the specific part of the work best.

There are several key elements:

- a quantitative target of what is to be achieved – so many people counselled; so many training courses run; so many newsletters produced
- the qualitative standard to be achieved
- the date by which the activity will be completed. For many activities, of course, there will be a series of dates, for preparation, introduction and implementation
- the person or people who will carry it out
- the budget for that activity.

Setting and agreeing these targets is absolutely vital to the success of the plan, and hence to the organisation's future. Failure to set targets and allocate responsibility for action is one of the main reasons why plans are not implemented.

Use Chart 7 to record your decisions. You may then find it useful to stick Charts 6 & 7 together.

7. The Business Plan

The Business Plan grows directly out of the Strategic Plan. It covers in more detail what will happen over the next year to bring the Strategic Plan to fruition. It starts with a statement of the organisation's mission, gives the background and history, the activities to achieve the mission and an analysis of the current environment. It goes on with the marketing strategy, the operational plans, including specific targets for the year, and the staffing required to implement them. The final section is the Financial Plan for the year.

Use the Business Plan to show your external audience your current standing and what you intend to do. Funders will often want to see it, particularly if they are making a substantial

Chart 6: Objectives			
Major Plan Elements	**Current Activities**	**3-5 Year Objectives**	**Year One Objectives**
Services/Activities			
Buildings			
Clients/Users			
Staff & Volunteers			
Communications			
Management Committee			
Organisation & Structure			
Finances: Income			
Costs			

Chart 7: Targets, Dates and Responsibilities			
Major Plan Elements	**Targets**	**Dates**	**Responsibility**
Services/Activities			
Buildings			
Clients/Users			
Staff & Volunteers			
Communications			
Management Committee			
Organisation & Structure			
Finances: Income			
Costs			

contribution to your organisation. If you need assistance from your bank during the year, for example to smooth the cash flow, or to support you while waiting for a late grant, it is the Business Plan that they will want to see. Its other main audience is the staff who need to see where they fit into the organisation's plans for the future.

Other chapters in this book cover the components of the Business Plan in more detail and there are plenty of additional books available which give model plans and advice and information about how to write Business Plans. After the Strategic Plan, which gives the broad view, the Business Plan is the most important guide to your organisation. It will be used by all sorts of people and other organisations to judge how effective and efficient your organisation is. Write it so that it is lively, interesting and informative.

8. Monitoring, Evaluation and Review

You will want to monitor and evaluate the success of the plan to achieve your objectives; and the quality and quantity of the activities your organisation undertakes. Both plan and activities should be regularly reviewed by the Board or Management Committee, and adjusted where necessary. Monitoring keeps track of what is happening and evaluation judges the value of the activity, the outcomes and their impact.

The whole trend towards evaluation by cost is shown in the changing patterns of support by bodies providing funds, whether from grant-making trusts and foundations, or authorities distributing public money. Service level agreements and contracts to provide services arise out of these ideas about cost and worth, and have been one of the greatest influences on the work of the voluntary sector in the past ten years. The requirements for reporting results are now very much more stringent.

Setting monitoring systems should therefore be an integral part of your planning. It is important to decide from the beginning how you are going to monitor and evaluate the work. It is much easier as an on-going process than trying to back-track later.

For some organisations, such as those running Advice Lines, monitoring raises issues about confidentiality which need to be resolved early. For others, the effects of their work may only be truly apparent years later. They will need to demonstrate considerable faith in the efficacy of their methods. It is important to negotiate and agree with funders what monitoring and evaluation they require, and to make provision for the costs of these processes when submitting applications or bids.

Monitoring and Evaluating your Activities

There are four elements to be monitored and evaluated: Inputs, Outputs, Outcomes and Impact. Easiest to measure are inputs and outputs relating to time spent, costs, people involved but they only give part of the picture and often the least significant part. Consider a training course. It is straightforward to count how many people came, how much they paid and how much the tutor, buildings etc., cost. But what were the outcomes for individual participants and how did the course make an impact on their professional development?

Monitoring and Evaluating your Plan

How will you judge success? Work out the key elements which have to be achieved for you to know you are being successful. They are known as Critical Success Factors. Agree the Performance Indicators you are going to use.

Review by Planning Team and Board or Management Committee

Having established how you will judge your plan, bring it on to the agenda of each Management Committee or Board Meeting, preferably at the beginning. It is an important agenda item and needs to be considered when everyone is fresh. In reviewing your plan regularly you will be able to see whether you are meeting your targets and whether any factors in the environment have changed which will affect your organisation.

Case Study

Within a few months of agreeing a strategic plan for development over three years, a Sports Club discovered that the local authority had won a grant from the Millennium Commission to develop a prestigious park for East London and that their building was in the middle of it. They found themselves being encouraged to form partnerships to bid for Sports Council grants and to join their development plan with those of other organisations.

Continuing Planning

As the first year progresses, detailed planning for the second year must begin in good time so that budgets and operational plans are ready when they are needed. It is a good idea to have a planning review once a year to confirm that aims and objectives are still right, to consider changes in the external environment and to look further into the future.

Publishing and Distribution

Your plan should be a working document. Decide how to make it known to everybody in the organisation. Some organisations display a chart, some publish a book. Who will you show it to outside the organisation? An overall view of your plan might be very useful to show to potential funders, to members, to those you want to influence. Lastly, consider how you will make sure the plan is used and does not just sit on the shelf. You will need to work out how to implement your plan.

Checklist

☐ What are your own objectives for the next year?
☐ How would you monitor your own work?
☐ What are your Critical Success Factors?

Finally

What could you use from this section straightaway in your own work?

9. Glossary

Critical Success Factor	Something that is vital to success
Culture	'The way we do things round here', the values, behaviour and attitudes of an organisation
Evaluation	Judging the worth or value of something
Gap Analysis	Looking in detail at the gap between where you are now and where you want to be, or where circumstances beyond your control will force you to be, in order to plan how to make up the difference.
Impact	Fundamental or broader change achieved
Input	Resources for an activity

Mission	What the organisation does towards its vision for the future; its 'business'
Monitoring	Collecting and analysing information
Objectives	Specific matters to be met
Outcome	Specific change achieved by action
Output	Results of action
Performance Indicators	Measurable factors which show performance
Scenario Planning	Imagining possible futures and working out what your organisation might do were they to happen
STEP	Acronym for Social, Technological, Economic, Political factors in the environment
SWOT	An acronym for Strengths and Weaknesses, Opportunities and Threats
Values	Underlying beliefs
Vision	The different world you want to achieve

About the author

Janet Cummins MBA, MICFM, draws on a wealth of personal experience. She has set up small local organisations and planned and run national and local projects and events. In 1993 she wrote her MBA dissertation on Strategic Planning for Charity Fund-raising.

MARKETING : 8

Moi Ali

1. Introduction

Marketing is a vast discipline and millions of words have been written on the subject. It would be difficult to cover everything in 20 volumes, let alone 20 pages. This chapter will look at:
- marketing – a definition
- your market – the factors that affect how you work
- a marketing strategy – how to develop one
- jargon – definitions of the key terms
- more about where to go and what to read if your appetite is whetted.

Having read this chapter you will:
- have a good understanding of what marketing is and why it is important for the voluntary sector
- know how to use marketing techniques such as incentives, endorsements and testimonials to your organisation's advantage
- be able to create a brand or a series of brands for your organisation and its products
- know how to commission an effective logo
- be able to produce a marketing strategy for your organisation
- know how to evaluate your marketing success.

2. What is Marketing?

'Marketing' is used in everyday speech as just another word for selling and promotion, activities which we hope will lead to sales. But you cannot have sales and promotion without something to sell or promote: a product or service. Even before you develop a product, you need to identify (usually by research) customers' needs and wants. Only then can you develop a product or service that can satisfy those needs. By first finding out what customers want, you avoid a mismatch between your service and their needs. That's what marketing is all about. Good marketing will help you to develop new services that are needed by the community you serve, and to attract the necessary funding to run them. Moreover, it will help you to plan according to real need, not gut feeling.

Marketing has been defined as getting the right product in the right place at the right price, and promoting it so everyone knows about it. In other words, marketing is about getting the right mix of Product, Price, Place and Promotion.

The Marketing Mix

The term 'marketing mix' refers to these four Ps – Product, Price, Place and Promotion.

Product

We tend to think of products as things – such as a packet of crisps. But this is too narrow – in voluntary sector marketing, your 'product' might be a service. Selling the product may involve an exchange of money. Or it could be that your product is a free service, such as counselling for refugees, an advice bureau, a hospice or a community arts project.

Price

If you are selling goods – for example second hand clothes, training manuals or cruelty-free produce – your products will have a price tag on them. It's different with services. Take a youth club cafe, for example. What's the price? Is it the £50,000 annual grant from the council or the 50p you charge for a sandwich? It's both. Youngsters visit the cafe to buy food and drink: you need to get the price right if you want to keep them coming. But you are also providing a drop-in service to local youth, paid for by the council. You need to price this service right, too, so the council feels it is getting good value for money. Even ideas have a price. If you believe that nobody should live in poverty in Britain, a cost will be attached to achieving this. The cost to the taxpayer would be enormous in terms of increasing welfare benefits etc. That is what is known as the 'impact cost'. To sell any product, the price must be right. For campaigning organisations and others selling ideas, your impact cost must be considered.

Place

Think of 'place' as the bridge connecting buyers and sellers. If you get your place right, you ensure that product and customer are brought together, thus creating an opportunity for a purchase. Traditionally 'place' refers to distribution – setting up a distribution system to get your baked beans from the factory to the shops. Tins of beans stacked in a factory are of no use to anyone – they need to be placed where they can be bought. 'Place' also has its use for service-providers. You need to consider how to get users to your service. Is your advice centre on a bus route, for example? Are collecting tins in the right places? Is there a distribution system to collect them or to put fundraising envelopes and leaflets through the right doors?

Promotion

This is the 'P' we most readily associate with marketing. There are lots of ways of promoting your service and your work. They include: advertising, annual reports, leaflets, brochures, posters, editorial coverage in newspapers, newsletters, direct mail, give-aways (pens, balloons etc.), bill boards and videos.

Marketing Mix Exercise

☐ What is your 'product'? (List all your products or services).
☐ What are your 'prices'? (It may be that the price depends on the customer – see above. Think about the various prices associated with your products and services and list them all.) If you are a campaigning organisation, you may need to consider the impact cost.
☐ What is your 'place'? How do you get your products/services to customers, or how do they get to you?
☐ How do you currently promote your organisation and its products and services? What techniques do you use? List them all.

What is marketing?

To summarise:
• marketing is not selling
• it is about being needs-led, not resource driven
• marketing is about listening to users and taking action on their views, thus providing the services that are required.

3. Seven Reasons Why You Need Marketing

1. Service-users are not in the privileged position of being able to shop around for the service that suits. So it is vital that you take time to find out exactly what your users require. Marketing techniques can help you find out what users want.
2. Where demand outstrips supply (e.g. for free counselling, Third World aid, a free crèche etc.) it is easy for voluntary organisations to deliver a second rate service. A marketing-led approach will ensure that you avoid this and strive for excellence.

3. Limited resources and tight budgets are common, and this can lead to charities developing services that meet the budget rather than satisfy the need. Marketing-led organisations do not fall into the trap of being resource-driven (though they have to work within their budgets).

4. To attract funding/donations, or to sell products/services, voluntary organisations have to compete with each other. The market is getting more competitive and only the strong will survive.

5. Contracts have to be negotiated with local authorities, health authorities and other voluntary organisations. Statutory bodies are changing their role from being providers to purchasers of services. The voluntary sector is now offering mainstream services that were previously provided by local and national government.

6. Much statutory funding which could be relied on over the years has dried up or is subject to immense competition. With more charities after less money, and with funders demanding 'value for money' and 'added value', a marketing approach cannot be avoided. An understanding of the market, and good products and services, can make the difference between survival and extinction.

7. HIV/AIDS, prostitution, drug misuse, gay issues – these are just a few of the 'unpopular' causes addressed by some voluntary organisations. Clever marketing can repackage the cause and make it more appealing or popular.

Why You Need Marketing: Exercise

☐ Why should your organisation take marketing seriously? List some reasons.

☐ How can you benefit from a marketing approach? (If you are having difficulty answering this, read the rest of this chapter and then return to this question.)

4. 'Customers'

Marketing puts customers' needs and wants at the centre. That's what many charities do anyway. In former days, service-users were expected to receive charity and be grateful. Benefactors and trustees knew best; it never occurred to anyone to ask what the user wanted. Today's voluntary sector listens to service-users and responds to their needs and wants. It also involves them in the development of services and gives them a voice and a role in decision-making. Why? Because it is good practice to run client-centred services.

So just as a holiday company finds out what holidays people want, and develops packages around meeting that desire, so a voluntary sector project for people with mental health problems should find out what they want and then meet the need. But there is a difference in the two approaches. In the case of the holiday company the 'service-users' (i.e. holiday-makers) are obviously also the customers. In the same way, users of the mental health scheme should be regarded as 'customers' or 'clients', even if they do not pay for the service. But so too should the funder, who parts with money to pay for the service. Your service-user and your service-funder are both customers. Without people to use your service, or without organisations to fund it, there would be no service. Your aim is to develop services that are needed by your target user group, as well as services that funders want to buy.

Different Customer Needs

A service-user might use a free alcohol counselling service because they have a drink problem and want help.

A health commission might contract a voluntary organisation to run the counselling service so it can meet its statutory healthcare objectives.

A whisky distiller might sponsor the service's annual report to reinforce its socially responsible image.

The user, the health commission and the whisky company are all customers, but their needs, wants and motivations are very different from each other. In other words, you do not have just one market, made up of one type of person.

Customer Identification Exercise

☐ List all of your customers/clients/user-groups.
☐ Now write down alongside each one what their individual needs, wants and expectations of you are.

Market Segmentation

Most markets are made up of sub-groups or segments. You need to spot the segments in your market and identify what makes one different and distinct from another, and to tailor your approach for these distinct markets. This is called market segmentation. Your market might be segmented:

• geographically (if you have clear regional differences, for example)

- demographically (sex, age, life cycle or family size)
- socio-economically (income, occupation, social class etc.)
- psychographically (in other words, according to the type of person who gives, their personality or lifestyle)
- behaviourally (how often they give/buy from you, what they look for from you).

Market Segmentation Exercise

☐ How is your market segmented?

☐ If you do not know, how do you propose to find out?

☐ How can you use your knowledge of how your market is segmented to the benefit of your organisation?

5. Your 'Product'

Even if you are involved in just one line of 'business', you will probably have a range of different products. By itemising each of your products, you can measure their effectiveness and performance, and develop separate promotional programmes. A charity for elderly people might have:

- residential homes
- a befriending and visiting service
- a day centre
- a meals on wheels service
- a publications division producing good practice guides for professionals who work with elderly people
- an information division producing advice for old people on how to guard against crime, keep warm in winter and keep fit in old age
- a training division running courses for professionals who work with older people
- a campaigning wing lobbying for improved rights for older people.

These are all distinct products, each requiring a very different marketing approach. That's why it is so important to make a list, so that you can see how diverse your work is, even if as an organisation you have a very integrated feel.

Product Recognition Exercise

☐ List all of your products/services.

☐ Do you currently treat each as a separate product?

☐ Is each one promoted, costed and evaluated separately?

☐ Do you run one product at a profit in order to subsidise a less profitable (or even loss-making) but nevertheless much-needed service?

☐ Are you clear that this is what you are doing?

Products Within a Product

Look at the exercise above. Imagine a charity with an information division as one of its services. Presumably this division will itself produce a range of products, such as:

- an advice hotline
- an over 60s diet and exercise pack
- a home security leaflet and video
- cut price home insulation products.

Now consider your own organisation. When listing your products, itemise the products produced by each of your services.

Incentives

You may want to use 'incentives' to help encourage take up of your product. An incentive is something additional to the product that is offered as an inducement. An environmental charity might offer a free address book made from recycled, chlorine-free paper to new members. If you are considering offering an incentive, ask yourself:

- what incentive?
- at what cost?
- is it appropriate?
- would it boost sales?
- by enough to cover the cost of the incentive?
- what is the evidence?

Bright Idea!

Be sure you will attract enough extra 'business' from an incentive. Offer an incentive to one group but not to another similar group. Measure take-up against the control group.

You might use incentives to:

- get people to buy from you rather than a competitor
- get people to respond: e.g. offer a free gift only if people join before a certain deadline
- get people to buy more of your product, e.g. offer an incentive for sales over a certain amount, to encourage people to buy more than they might otherwise do

Service organisations can also use incentives to advantage. For example, a drop-in centre for single parents might offer free children's activities or free refreshments as an inducement to get parents in.

Endorsements

You may be able to make effective use of endorsements to enhance your products. With an endorsement, you don't need to use a real person. For example, you could describe a dog food as the one that top breeders recommend. Is there any scope for you to use endorsements?

Testimonials

Testimonials quote someone's words. You don't need famous people: the words of ordinary people can be every bit as powerful. Perhaps you have service users or members who are willing to testify to how good you are.

Case Study

The Richmond Fellowship Scotland use testimonials from their residents. This one is taken from their annual report: "The Day Care Activities Scheme has made a great difference to my life. I was quite isolated before. I used to have nothing much in my life. The project has made me more confident... I used to be unable to mix with people very easily. I now feel that I have made relationships that I feel confident will last." This extract shows the power of testimonials. Get them working for you.

6. Your Market

There will be plenty of influences on your market, many of them beyond your control. Some will threaten; others will offer opportunities, as long as you have an eye on the market, are flexible and ready to adapt to changing environments and changing needs. Here are some of the uncontrollables you may face:

Technology

There are new technology implications for voluntary organisations, and not just because of the impact of new products (such as CD-ROMs) on how the office is run. There are potentially big implications for some services too. It may be, for example, that on-line shopping will create an opportunity for disabled people to shop from the comfort of their own home, thus making your Dial-A-Ride service redundant and causing you to rethink the needs of your customers. (Such a technological change could result in disabled people becoming socially isolated and more housebound than ever; research would uncover this and you could develop new services to address this problem.) We already have the technology to programme a computer to switch off lights, turn on the heating, close the curtains etc. This technology, put to use in the home of a physically disabled person, or someone with dementia, for example, could alter the way you support such people in their homes. It could also have major implications for your funding, if you are having to install expensive hardware.

Government policy and laws

The government's care in the community policy has meant the closure of many voluntary sector hospitals and other long-stay institutions for people with learning disabilities and mental health difficulties. It has also opened up new markets for housing providers to offer care. Government policy could have the effect of putting some voluntary organisations out of business, while at the same time boosting the work of others. Keeping a close eye on policy developments, and their potential impact on your organisation, is vital if you don't want to be left behind as your competitors move swiftly to adapt to change and to grasp emerging opportunities.

Legislation, too, can create new openings for charities. For example, if drugs were legalised, there might be a need for the establishment of services to respond to this move, perhaps by explaining the pros and cons of certain substances, and by providing public health information and training. If brothels were legalised, it might be necessary to set up health promotion and HIV awareness initiatives for prostitutes and clients.

When legislation was introduced to enable the government to launch a National Lottery, few charities anticipated the effect a lottery and instant scratch cards would have on their fundraising. They failed to take action to find other sources of finance in the period between lottery announcement and launch. Anticipating and monitoring change is an important part of marketing. If you wait until the impact of new legislation is felt before you act, you've waited too long.

Competitors' activities

The threat of new competition is always there. There are other organisations doing similar work, or who also specialise in your field. If one of them sets up a service in direct competition with yours, something that could happen at any time, your funding and service will be threatened. Increasingly, competition is coming from both the private and public sectors, as competitive tendering for services grows. You might find yourself competing with brand new competition from either of these sectors.

Culture and taste/trends

Trends can present charities and voluntary organisations with new marketing opportunities. Campaigning organisations can tap into the public's interest in a particular issue and meet their need to take some kind of action.

Successful marketing depends on knowing your market, having a clear picture of your competitors and what they are up to, and looking out for the uncontrollables. It also relies on your ability to respond to these uncontrollables by seizing opportunities and anticipating threats. Do all this and you will be better placed to cope with the difficulties the market place throws at you.

7. Image, Identity and Branding

'Branding' is the way goods from one producer or retailer are distinguished from those of another. It is a concept that is also relevant for voluntary organisations. It is a kind of shorthand: the name of your charity, product or service comes to represent a host of associations for your 'customers'. If they feel good about the Oxfam brand, they will be happy to support Oxfam in its many manifestations e.g. its shops, its publications, its campaigns, its mail order service.

Having established a brand, organisations do not have to start from scratch when launching a new product; new products will benefit from their relationship and association with the charity. Take the National Trust. It has launched a successful range of household paint in authentic 'period' colours. The paint's credibility is enhanced by its National Trust branding and associations. Customers have confidence in the paint because they have confidence in the Trust.

Creating a Brand

What goes into creating a brand? The ingredients are:
- the product or service – e.g. a community arts centre
- its name – e.g. Art for Art's Sake. (If it were called the Anytown Community Arts Urban Aid Project, it would have a very different image, even if its aims were the same.)
- the way it is advertised and promoted – e.g. features in the local press showing colourful paintings and beautiful sculptures

created by local people; a huge mural on an external wall depicting the range of activities that take place inside; cheerful leaflets designed and produced by people who use the Centre, and door dropped to local homes; an annual art exhibition
- its overall presentation – e.g. the way the leaflets look, the way the Centre is furnished and decorated, the way the project is promoted as 'the local choice'.

A successful brand must be strongly differentiated from those of competitors. A criticism of many of the cancer charities is that they do not have a strong enough identity of their own. They have failed to differentiate themselves from the others.

In traditional marketing a brand encompasses:
- physical attributes (such as, with perfume, its smell)
- aesthetic factors (the design of a scent bottle)
- rational elements (value for money, usefulness)
- emotional elements (in the case of expensive scent, it makes the wearer feel attractive or glamorous).

How can you translate the elements of branding to your own products? The emotional element is very relevant for many charities. People might buy your product for emotional reasons, and while other factors such as the value of your work, the probity of your organisation and so on are important factors, they do not outweigh the emotional feelings.

A strong brand is an asset. It cannot guarantee success, but it will tip the balance in your favour. Once it is developed, you need to work hard to maintain the brand value. If other charities start to copy what you do, you might find that you no longer stand out from the crowd. You must maintain your position as the biggest, the best, the smallest, the most caring, the most efficient, or whatever it is that you have built your brand around.

Product Names

Whether your product is the whole organisation, a particular campaign or appeal, or a service, it should have a name. That is part of its branding. Selecting the right name is vital. We take great care naming our children and pets. You should spend time selecting the right name for your product or service – one that is apt, concise and conveys the right image. The Coventry Charitable Trust for the Care and Support of Gentlemen of Limited Means might be descriptive, but it is hardly snappy and it sounds like something from Dickens.

Changing Name

Changing the name of your organisation is a big step, though it is a marketing decision you need to consider if your name is working against you. Names say a lot, and we base our assumptions on them, but the reality might be very different. That's not the point, however. If potential customers are switched off by the name, and it happens in sufficient numbers, you should be concerned. People might be supporting you in spite of the name, not because of it.

Case Study

....

The Spastics Society changed its name in 1994 to Scope. The term 'spastic' was, at the time the Spastics Society was founded, one that was applied to cerebral palsy sufferers. Now it has become a term of abuse, so a name change was inevitable. On the first anniversary of the name change, Scope had attracted nearly 40,000 new donors. It was also in talks with 25 potential corporate donors and sponsors, many of whom steered clear of the charity when it was called the Spastics Society. If they can do it, so can you!

....

The Charity as the Brand

Some companies have a clear corporate identity, and additionally they have a range of products each with their own branding. Others use their corporate brand to sell a range of other products, which may in themselves all be quite different. For example, the Sainsburys 'own brand' is used to sell everything from champagne to toilet rolls. The individual products are not given strong branding of their own; they sell by using the Sainsburys name. Sometimes a charity finds, like Sainsburys, that its brand is the organisation as a whole. The bits that make it up, or the services and products it provides, are not as distinctive as the organisation itself. For them, their own corporate identity is the brand. The branding and packaging of the whole organisation is what gives definition to the services provided by it. Its unique personality is what differentiates it from the many other charities working in the same field.

Branding Services

For service providers it is important to develop a perception in the market place of your individual personality which sets you apart from the competition. Visual identity combined with good quality of service can be the hallmarks that help you to differentiate what you provide from what is available elsewhere.

Repositioning the Brand

You might find yourself with a brand image that you do not want any longer. Third World charities used to promote themselves as aid agencies, fundraising to relieve the symptoms of poverty and disaster. This came to be regarded as paternalistic. Many decided to reposition and repackage themselves. Instead of images of starving children with swollen bellies, they used positive pictures. Instead of showing third world people as helpless victims they were presented as people who, with assistance in the form of money or expertise, could take control of their own destiny. Such charities found that their donor profile changed. Instead of attracting older and more affluent supporters, they now appealed more to younger people with an interest in politics and economics.

Visual Image

Just as we are often judged by how we look, your organisation will be judged on its letterhead, annual report, office and staff. The most obvious aspect of your visual identity will be your logo; other elements will stem from this. If you don't have a logo, or you are considering a new one, here's what you need to do.

Eight Steps to a New Logo

1. What do you want your logo to say about you (e.g. friendly, caring, efficient, concerned with animals, concerned with trees and the environment)? Write down or sketch your ideas for how this could be achieved.
2. Write any words or straplines (a brief statement or description of your work) that need to be included in the design.
3. Decide whether your logo will be a design or just a stylised version of your name (take advice from your designer).
4. Decide on how many and which colours.
5. Brief your designer about your work and your ideas for a logo.
6. Ask for a design that will also reproduce well in one colour and that will photocopy and fax clearly.
7. Ask to see the logo on letterheads, compliments slips etc. to get a proper feel for how it will look in use.
8. Select a design.

Bright Idea!

Your logo colours are known as your 'corporate colours'. Use them whenever possible to reinforce your visual identity. For example, if your colour is blue, use it for your interior colour scheme, choose blue flowers in reception and a blue front door. It helps make you more memorable, which is vital to effective promotion.

8. Developing a Marketing Strategy

To be effective at marketing you need to take a systematic and sustained approach. The marketing of your own organisation cannot be done in an ad hoc or casual way. Marketing is an integrated approach, a way of working, and it must be planned and carried out in an organised way. You must also keep your marketing under review, and evaluate success (and failure) as part of that review. To work in this kind of planned way you need to have a clear strategy – a marketing strategy.

There is no simple, off-the-shelf way of developing a marketing strategy. Marketing takes time and commitment. You will need to find an approach to developing a marketing strategy that suits your kind of organisation. Start with the four-stage approach set out below and amend it to your own situation.

1. Pull together a team of stakeholders – trustees, staff, volunteers etc. This is your marketing team and they will be responsible for shaping your marketing strategy. Each will have a different viewpoint, which is part of the strength of the group. Its many perspectives will ensure that ideas are questioned and challenged.

2. Carry out a review of where you are and what the current position is. To do this, get your marketing team to start by examining where your charity is now. This involves looking critically and objectively at how you operate, why you take the decisions you do, what influences your work. You need to look at your market, your products, your customers, and your promotional work. In short, you are aiming for a complete understanding of how you currently work and the factors in your operating environment that affect that work.

3. Now focus on where you want to go and on what sort of an organisation you would like to be in, say, five years' time. This is where your objectives come in. Draw up short-term (perhaps covering the following 12 months) and long-term (up to five years ahead) objectives. Your objectives should state very clearly what you hope to achieve.

4. Having done all this, you are ready to work on your strategy – in other words, on the details of how you will achieve your objectives. Look at your marketing mix. See how much time and effort needs to be put into modifying your products. How

much money can you afford for promoting them? Who are you promoting them to and how? Don't forget 'place' and 'price'. Consider all the elements of marketing and see how each one may have a role in helping you do what you do better.

Your Market

You operate within a market, and you need to understand that market if you are to be successful in it. In looking at your market you need to consider:
- the external variables over which you have no control (which political party is in power, locally or nationally, for example)
- the internal variables over which you have complete control (the set up/structure of your organisation, for example).

This will enable you to have a clear picture of the factors you can influence, and those which will inevitably limit you.

Carry out a 'SWOT analysis'. SWOT is an acronym which stands for:

Strengths: What are you good at as an organisation? What do you do better than others?

Weaknesses: What are you poor at? Where is there room for improvement?

Opportunities: What opportunities are there for you externally, either now or in the future?

Threats: What threats exist externally, now or in the future? Who are your competitors and what threats do they pose?

(For more details on SWOT analysis see Chapter 7, Strategic Planning.)

As part of your strategy you will need to make assumptions about the future market, including the actions of your competitors. You will need to be aware that you must build upon your strengths, strengthen your weak areas, take action to minimise threats and ensure that you grasp opportunities.

Your Customers

Start by listing who they are.
Next examine what they want from you.
Finally, take a realistic look at what you can offer.

Remember that meeting customer needs may involve changing your organisation so it is better suited to meeting those needs (i.e. altering internal variables) as well as recognising the constraints imposed by external variables over which you have no control, and working to provide the best that you can, given these factors.

You can only meet needs once you understand what those needs are. You will probably find in going back to basics – looking at what your customers actually need, as opposed to what you give them – that research may be required. You may want to ask your customers what they would like from you, what their needs and priorities are.

You must understand what is really important to your customers when they buy. For example, if your customers buy from your mail order catalogue because doing so fulfils an emotional need, you need to recognise this and reflect this need in the copy and design of your future catalogues. If they buy on price, perhaps a different approach is required.

Evaluation

You need to evaluate your work, and your marketing strategy should explain how this will be done. Traditional measures in business/commerce have included measurables such as:

- increased sales
- profits
- reduced costs
- advertising effectiveness.

Some of these are very useful to voluntary organisations, such as advertising effectiveness (it would be wrong of a charity to waste donors' money on ineffective advertising). Some are not. For voluntary organisations there is a whole set of other measures that are often a great deal more important than profit: for example, the social benefits of a service, the social need, the cost to society of not running the service etc.

Social Need: It might be very expensive to run a free condom service for prostitutes, and a commercial organisation interested only in profit would be unable to operate it if their bottom line is the balance sheet. However, the price of not running such a service might prove too costly in social terms, leading to the spread of HIV/AIDS among adults, the birth of HIV positive babies, and the transmission of sexual diseases.

Social benefits: The operation of a service to rehabilitate joy riders and to encourage them not to reoffend could be cost effective in terms of social benefit, but not by a strict financial yardstick.

9. Jargon Guide

There's enough jargon in marketing to fill a dictionary. Here are some of the main terms you might come across.

Cause-related Marketing

This is where a company develops a relationship with a 'cause' for mutual benefit. The company might gain publicity, goodwill, a useful database or a helpful association. In return the charity might get sponsorship, a donation or something else of value. Both sides gain.

USP

This stands for Unique Selling Point. It is what differentiates you from the others. For example, there might be hundreds of animal charities, but your USP is that you are the only one exclusively caring for abandoned or badly-treated reptiles. With no one else offering that service, you stand apart from the rest.

Donor Profile

A donor profile paints a picture of your typical supporter – e.g. young (18-30) Telegraph readers with no children, living in the Midlands/North of England and interested in the environment and politics.

Advertising Rate Card

Rate cards produced by newspapers and magazines set out what an advertisement costs according to its size, where it is in the publication etc.

Circulation

Circulation figures tell you how many people buy a particular publication and 'readership' figures tell you how many people read it. Readership figures are usually higher than circulation ones, as a publication will frequently be read by more than just the person who bought it.

Single Column Centimetre (scc)

This is the unit of vertical measurement that is used to measure the size of an advert and therefore its cost.

Active Customer/Member/Subscriber
Generally an active customer is one who has purchased from you, joined your organisation or sent for information from you within the last 12 months.

Co-op Mailings
Two or more non-competitive organisations come together and have their promotional material inserted into the one mailing, sharing the costs.

Cost Per Conversion
Add together all the costs of a direct mail campaign and divide by the number of orders received/donations made/subscriptions taken out. This is a good way of working out whether your campaign has been a success in terms of the response it has generated.

List Cleaning
Mailing lists need to be kept up to date. List cleaning involves correcting names and addresses, removing those who have moved away or those who have not responded to your mail within a designated period (e.g. after five mailings or within six months).

Piggy Backs
This is when you enclose literature in another organisation's mailing, for example by putting an insert into another charity's newsletter. This is a cheap way of doing a mailing. You can make money this way too, by offering a piggy back service in your own mailings.

News/Press Releases
These are stories written in newspaper style and issued by companies and organisations to the media in the hope of securing press or broadcast coverage for a story.

Photocalls
If an event has 'photo opportunity' potential, a photocall can be held. Invite newspaper photographers to attend at a certain time to take pictures.

About the author

Moi Ali has worked in public relations and marketing for over a decade, specialising in voluntary sector public relations. She runs her own consultancy in Edinburgh, The Pink Anglia Public Relations Company. She is author of the DIY Guide to Public Relations and the DIY Guide to Marketing for Charities, both published by the Directory of Social Change.

About the author

Mor All has worked in public relations and marketing for over a decade specialising in voluntary sector public relations. She runs her own consultancy in Edinburgh, The Pink Attelit Public Relations Company. She is author of the DIY Guide to Public Relations and the DIY Guide to Marketing for Charities, both published by the Directory of Social Change.

EMPLOYING STAFF : 9

John Burnell

1. Introduction

Aims and Objectives

It is unlikely that any trustee or senior manager reading this book will need reminding about the uniqueness of the voluntary sector in Britain. Already one of the largest in the western world, the sector looks set to grow even more significantly as charities take on more and more responsibility for what used to be provided by the local or central state.

The sector is changing rapidly. There is inevitably increasing professionalism, and in particular a concern with cost-effectiveness in managing charitable resources. Voluntary sector staff are increasingly from a wide range of backgrounds – from 1990 onwards, over 40% of Chief Executives and Finance Directors were appointed from outside the sector altogether, and very many of the new service providers are refugees from local government and the health service

This brings new challenges, particularly in the management of staff. Consider some of the facts:

- Over 30,000 charities, trusts, housing associations and other voluntary bodies employ staff in one capacity or another. There are probably more charity employees than there are civil servants – truly it is a third sector
- Of those 30,000, the very large majority employ only one or two staff. Those staff have most of the same rights as any employee in a multinational company – but trustees generally don't have access to the expertise to get the employment issues right
- Over 6,000 charities employ more than 5 staff – and well over a hundred have more than 1,000 employees, twice the size of an average district council. They are large bureaucracies in their own right – but with staff both utterly dedicated to the cause and in danger of being submerged by insensitive systems
- Charity workers are employees too. There is a high level of union organisation in many parts of the sector – MSF alone has some 20,000 members working in charities, some of them in very large branches, and Unison and other unions claim similar memberships

Trustees and executives need new skills, to enable them to ensure that their most precious asset, their staff and their volunteers, are used most effectively to provide a quality service for the benefit of their beneficiaries. Management and development of employees is a complex process, even when there are only a few of them. This chapter can only begin to scratch at the surface. But it should at least highlight the key issues, avert you from the real dangers, and tell you where you can go for more definitive advice. By the end of the chapter readers should have gained some knowledge of:

- the employment responsibilities of trustees and chief executives
- employment law, procedures and best practice
- effective recruitment and selection policies
- how to get the best out of staff
- how to cope when things go wrong – issues of redundancy, grievance etc.

2. The Responsibilities of Trustees and Chief Executives

What is employment?

This chapter will confine itself to the consideration of the employment of paid staff – although many of the points will apply to some extent to the deployment of volunteers, including trustees and committee members.

A contract of employment is generally said to exist if:

- a person agrees to undertake a range of tasks for an organisation
- that organisation agrees to make a payment to the person for doing so
- the person considers that this arrangement comprises her/his principal source of income from work.

If the last condition is not met, it is more likely to be a contract to provide services (such as the work done by an independent consultant), although you have to be careful not to fall foul of the tax regulations on this.

Once a contract exists, both parties are legally bound by it. The employee is obliged to undertake the duties set out and the employer is obliged to remunerate her/him for doing so. But employment contracts may not just contain anything the two parties want them to. There are some things that must be in them, some things that must not, and quite a few things that, whilst not spelt out, are presumed to be there.

The Duty of Care

Statutory obligations on both parties are discussed in the next section. There is, underpinning them all, a general duty between the employer and employee. On the employer's part, there is a duty to act reasonably and with care, for example to provide a safe working environment (whether under health and safety or common law). While from the employee, there is a general expectation of fidelity, that is, loyally to do anything reasonably required under the contract.

This duty of care is at the basis of all contracts, but is particularly important in employment matters, where we are talking about people's livelihoods, their future, the business of the employer and (particularly in the voluntary sector) a group of clients or customers who rely upon the employment relationship working properly for them to benefit.

The duty of care is not infinitely elastic. The emphasis is – as it is in all employment matters – on reasonableness, on the employer's part as to what they can require of the employee, on the latter's part in how demands and responses are made. The tests of reasonableness are grounded in a range of case law precedents, supported by statutory obligations, usually applied and interpreted by Industrial Tribunals.

Size isn't everything... but it helps

In considering reasonableness, the law says that account should be taken of the size and resources available, particularly to the employer. Where a large employer (say more that 50 staff) might be expected to have detailed employment procedures, one with just a handful of staff could offer the defence of a less formal approach being appropriate.

But that does not mean that you can get away with murder. Every employer has to observe the basics, and flagrant breaches of reasonableness will still be punished by the courts, no matter how limited the employer's resources may be. So the basic guideline has always to be:

Treat staff reasonably in a way that you would want to be treated if your roles were reversed.

That means being firm but fair, and it is a rule that can and should apply just as much to volunteers as it must apply to paid staff.

Who Carries the Can?

The responsibility for all actions rests with the employer as a corporate entity. A corporate entity can be as small as a charity with just one part-time employee, and throughout this chapter, the use of the word corporate will mean anything to do with your organisation as a whole, however big or small it may be. How you will carry out your corporate employer responsibilities will vary depending on the administrative arrangements in place, but in the voluntary sector, the trustees are normally ultimately liable for the actions of their employees.

Trustees may choose to delegate to a chief executive responsibility for most staffing matters. But the cost of any actions, right or wrong, still usually falls to the organisation, not the individual(s). The key points are:

- delegate only to people in whom you have confidence – but then don't meddle
- the more confidence you can demonstrate, the better motivated will they be
- if you are a trustee, only take action and make payments within your charitable objectives.

Even then, there are some things you can't delegate – ultimate responsibility for health and safety, for example. Sometimes it can be tough being an employer – so if in doubt, seek professional advice.

Checklist on Responsibilities

- ☐ Are you sure that you have got properly established contracts of employment with your staff, or are they sub-contractors?
- ☐ Are you aware of how to act reasonably as an employer, and do your staff understand their duty towards you?
- ☐ Do you have policies and procedures that are appropriate to the size of your organisation?
- ☐ Do you always seek to abide by the golden rule: "Treat staff reasonably in a way that you would want to be treated if your roles were reversed?"
- ☐ Are you clear about what you delegate to whom, and do you then make sure that you don't demotivate people by taking it back again?
- ☐ Do you know where to go for advice on personnel matters?

3. Laws, Procedures and Best Practice

What is Best Practice?

This is almost a philosophical question, so, in true pragmatic personnel style, will be skimmed over here. But in general terms, most voluntary sector managers would recognise the following elements as part of best practice in employment:

- Willing adherence to the current state of the mandatory law, both case and statute
- Willing embracing of optional elements of legal matters such as employment codes
- Commitment to staff involvement, consultation, empowerment and development
- Avoidance of unnecessarily low wage levels and unnecessarily onerous employment conditions
- Underpinning by a genuine acceptance of effective equal opportunities practices.

You need to know the basics of employment law if you are going to avoid the most obvious pitfalls. But there are many traps for both the unwary and the non-specialists, and it is very important, especially in matters of contracts, that you do get good advice either from lawyers or personnel specialists. What follows is a quick run through the most important parts, but only as a prelude to considering what you can do to ensure best practice, which in itself will help you get the best out of your staff.

Employment practice can perhaps be best described by:

- what you must do – the legal requirements on employers and employees alike; and
- what you could do – taking things as much further as is appropriate for your organisation.

Key Statutes

Employment law is very extensive, with many specialist and general books written on it, and, in the area of equal treatment and maternity in particular, it is becoming increasingly complex. The following are some of the key points you will need to know about, but if in any doubt, ask – it's much cheaper to pay to get it right now, than to be heavily penalised later.

Equal Pay Act 1970

The Act established the principle that people of different sexes doing the same job must be paid at the same rate. The principle has been extended by EC directive: work of equal value (not necessarily the same) must be remunerated the same. All this applies to non-wage conditions as well as to pay packets, e.g. working hours.

Employment Protection Act

(as amended in 1978 and subsequently) This Act established the right to complain to Industrial Tribunals of unfair dismissal. An employer's defence may be one of the following:

- employee misconduct
- employee incapability
- redundancy
- need to comply with the law
- some other substantial reason.

Not only must the reason for dismissal be fair, so also must the way it was carried out. The Act also introduced constructive dismissal.

Since 1978 there have been several subsequent amendments and a whole host of case law, but the principles remain the same.

Penalties can be high (basic award £6,000+, with unlimited compensatory awards).

Anti-discrimination Legislation

Sex Discrimination Act 1975 (subsequently amended), Race Relations Act 1976, Disability Discrimination Act 1995. All these Acts make it illegal to discriminate in employment (appointment, pay or how staff are treated) on grounds of gender (and related areas), race and disability.

Direct discrimination means open discrimination on the grounds of sex, race, disability or sexuality – such as refusing to appoint a woman to what traditionalists might still call "a man's job" – like in many parts of the building trade.

Indirect discrimination means making an unjustifiable requirement that one group is less able to meet than another, such as advanced literacy in English for a manual job, which many non-Europeans will not meet.

The presumption on disability is that the employer will make arrangements for a disabled worker to do the job, not exclude such workers because of impracticalities.

Positive action (helping disadvantaged groups to compete equally) is encouraged, positive discrimination (giving people jobs just because they are black/women/ disabled) is illegal.

Employment Rights Act 1996

(consolidating the Trade Union Reform and Employment Rights Act 1993)

This Act sets out the rights of nearly all employees to written Statements of Particulars of Contract of Employment within two months of starting, including:

- pay rates
- place of work
- details of continuous employment
- leave entitlement
- sick pay
- disciplinary and grievance processes
- pension rights.

The Act also incorporated EC maternity rights into British law and restated sliding scale entitlements to redundancy payments.

Health and Safety at Work Act 1974

This Act established joint employer and employee responsibility for safe working and general duty of care.

The ultimate responsibility for employee safety lies with the most senior levels in the organisation and cannot be delegated.

The Act forms the basis for a whole range of subsequent codes, EC directives and consolidating legislation controlling workplace environment, most notably:

- Control of Substances Hazardous to Health regulations (COSHH)
- Electrical Appliance Inspection regulations (EIR)
- VDU regulations
- General duty to conduct regular risk assessments.

Case Study
....

A small specialist advice centre set itself up as a workers' collective, supported by the Management Committee. Because of the heavy pressure and sensitive nature of the work, very generous service conditions were agreed, including:

- *ten weeks' holiday*
- *twelve months' sick pay*
- *sabbaticals every three years*

- *no changes to service conditions without full staff agreement.*

The service that was offered to clients was of a very high quality, but its scope and extent were limited by the views and availability of the staff. Pressure from funders meant that the Management Committee could no longer agree to these generous arrangements, but the collective nature of the organisation produced a stalemate in their attempts to shift the agenda.

With the assistance of external evaluation, the Management Committee developed and adopted a set of personnel principles and policies that, whilst recognising employees' previous conditions, placed emphasis far more on the delivery of quality services and rather less on employee rights. Key changes included:

- *enhancing the role of the co-ordinator to that of a full director*
- *introducing sickness control procedures that reflected good management practice and paid what the organisation could afford*
- *development and operation of comprehensive appraisal and support systems that related more to organisational objectives and less to personal development*
- *bringing leave and other conditions more closely in line with similar organisations.*

All the staff were asked for their commitment to the objectives of the organisation, and were told that without these changes, it would collapse. Those who were most opposed to the changes turned out to be those who were also the least willing to put the organisation first. They left with generous settlements.

The organisation learnt four key points:

1. *Staff involvement is critical to ensuring quality of service, but it is not the same as staff control.*
2. *Change can often best be effected with the assistance of an independent external assessment.*
3. *Unless staff sign up for the organisation's aims, they are not the best type of employee for the voluntary sector – narrow personal interests, however altruistic, are no substitute for real team work. It's worth paying them to go.*
4. *Service conditions in the voluntary sector do not have to be generous to attract the best staff – the cause does that, and the conditions need simply to be adequate to keep them there.*

....

Trades Unions

Most of the collective rights of unions, particularly in relation to industrial action, have been in effect abolished over the past seventeen years. The only significant area of collective statutory influence is in the joint management of health and safety. Unions retain their right to represent individual employees, and organisations may still choose to afford them collective negotiating or consultative rights.

Summary on the Law

Key areas of legislation cover:

- equal pay and equal rights
- protection against unfair dismissal
- anti-discrimination on grounds of race, sex or disability
- rights of individual employees
- shared responsibility for health and safety

Trade unions now have very limited collective powers.

There are very few specific obligations on employers to provide service conditions.

The whole system is underpinned by tests of reasonableness.

Some Pointers to Good Practice

Every employer will need to determine individually to what extent employment practices should go beyond the legal minimum. The following are food for thought, but can never expect to cover all the issues. You may well consider it worthwhile to develop an overall personnel policy strategy document, and incorporate all rights, obligations and procedures into a comprehensive Staff Handbook.

Pay and Associated Service Conditions

Have you got a pay structure that can justify differentials within it, for example through a job evaluation scheme? Do the differentials reflect the culture of the charity, particularly its public face – can you avoid accusations of "fat cat" charity director salaries?

Do you have established mechanisms for annual reviews and cost-of-living increases? Are these cross-referenced to other bodies in the voluntary sector?

Have you considered performance-related pay and all the associated issues of motivation, reward and potential divisiveness of a policy that could be seen as pitching workers against each other to earn different-sized shares of the cake?

Do you have a salary and benefits policy that aims, for example, to pay at the average level for appropriate comparators?

Do you have annual leave and sick pay arrangements that are both attractive and affordable?

Contracts of Employment

Do you issue Statements of Particulars on or before the first day of service to every employee?

Do you give full details in the statement, or do you rely on references to other documents such as a Staff Handbook?

Do you offer the basic minimum maternity leave and pay, or do you have local, enhanced arrangements, including paternity and carer leave?

Do you apply all conditions equally and pro rata to part time staff?

Do you have a pension scheme with an employer's contributory element?

Do you have a redundancy agreement that includes calculator enhancements, selection criteria and consultation arrangements?

Are you sure that you have an employer-employee contract, or could you be using self-employed sub-contractors?

If in doubt about whether your contracts meet the full requirements of the law, do you have the name of a good employment lawyer?

Disciplinary and Grievance Procedures

Do you have clearly set out processes that go from one stage to the next as issues become more serious?

Do your procedures allow for objective evaluation, independent adjudication and appeal at each stage?

Do you have a set of disciplinary rules and publicise them widely?

Do they reflect the kind of activities that your staff are likely to come up against when supporting your clients?

Do your procedures allow for representation and effective advice to be available?

Can your procedures cope with incapability as well as indiscipline?

Equal Opportunities

Do you check all your actions to ensure that you are avoiding illegal discrimination?

Have you extended the principles of your policy to cover ageism, sexuality and other areas of discrimination not covered by the law?

Health and Safety

Have you set up mechanisms to raise employees' awareness of safe working practices?

Have you carried out risk assessments, regular audits and safety inspections?

Is the reporting line for safety matters clearly spelt out and understood by everybody?

Managing the Process

One key to effective personnel management is to adopt a strategic approach, and ensure that, as far as the law (and best practice, if that is a choice) allows, every element of the employer/employee relationship fits within the strategy.

This is easier to do if you're starting from scratch – but in the voluntary sector, probably more than anywhere else, the more general experience is that a strategic approach to performance, including staff management, was not determined from the outset. Rather, a few like minded people got together to tackle a social problem, then they took on an administrator, then an assistant, and only then did they start thinking about their role as an employer. A case of "If I were you, I wouldn't start from here in the first place"!

Nevertheless, a strategic approach will pay dividends in the end, and will enable you to consolidate and manage if you've been going for some time, or think more clearly if you are just setting out. Even the most anarchic of situations can be managed with the right determination, as the case study above shows.

4. Effective Recruitment and Selection

Good staff make good charities. You may be lucky and keep them for years. More likely, you are going to have to replace people, and bring in new talent. It's vital you get it right.

Why make such an effort?

The wrong decision can result in:

- poor performance
- disruption and resentment in the workplace
- loss of income, efficiency and credibility
- expensive remedies through retraining, Industrial Tribunal judgements and the need to recruit all over again.

The real costs of recruitment can be as much as the equivalent of over six months of the appointee's salary – and that's a lot of tins to rattle. It makes sense to minimise the risk of getting the decision wrong. And that can best be done by closely examining what the job is really about, so that you know the kind of person you will need to fill it. Then you can plan the process carefully, using a range of selection techniques well beyond interviewing, combined as a recruitment assessment centre, including:

- presentations
- report writing
- in-tray exercises
- examinations
- simulation exercises
- group discussions
- evaluating references
- psychometrics
- as well as good old interviews, since everyone expects them.

Nobody expects you to do all of this all the time – the point is to choose what is appropriate to help you best measure what you really need in the successful candidate – getting to the heart of the person specification.

Where do you get your candidates?

There is a whole range of possibilities: word of mouth, contacts, personal recommendations, recruitment agencies and job centres, public advertisements, or headhunters – companies who identify potential candidates and approach them direct.

You will need to decide from the outset what is most appropriate – for the particular vacancy, for the style of your organisation, and in terms of what resources you can afford. For example, although recruitment agencies charge fees, they take much of the administrative burden away from hard-pressed managers. And although advertising is expensive, you will normally get more candidates to choose from.

The most important thing is that the process is fair, and is seen to be fair. However you go about it, can you be sure that everyone who might be qualified to do the job has had an equal chance of being considered. This can be particularly important in those charities that have higher profiles, particularly those that undertake a lot of campaigning.

So what's wrong with interviewing?

Nothing in itself, but poor interviewing will lead to poor recruitment decisions, and interviews alone are poor predictors of future job performance. They can however be improved:

- by focusing on the requirements of the post through thorough job analysis, looking at what the job is really about, how it is done, and what qualities candidates need to do it properly. This is normally expressed through the job description and person specification
- by ensuring that interviews are formalised and structured, avoiding first impressions, irrelevant assumptions and subconscious personal agendas
- by involving a panel of interviewers, who can then debate their impressions and retain the rigour of the results of job analysis.

These improvements need effective training, and the recognition that interviewing is only part of the selection process. In the short term that means greater effort and better planning of the whole of the recruitment process (not just a few interview questions thrown together at the last minute when the Panel can squeeze in a late afternoon meeting). But that planning will pay off because:

- it will offer a clearer operating framework for the appointing managers
- it will build on the work already done on job analysis, thus lending greater credibility to the process
- it will, with modification, provide a bank of information and exercises for future appointments
- it will, most importantly, improve the chances of a successful appointment. A day planning now can save months of agonising later.

An overview of selection techniques

Whichever methods you use, make sure that the process is effectively managed, particularly by giving appropriate weight to each element. Avoid falling into the trap of ignoring the results of the other elements in favour of traditional assessment in the interview stage.

Presentations

Asking candidates to make an oral presentation about a relevant topic can measure both their presentational and analytical skills. For example, if you are recruiting a fundraiser, ask them to look at your current income flows and devise a new fundraising strategy. Three possible approaches suggest themselves:

- give the candidates the subject well in advance
- give the candidates the subject on the day, with time to prepare
- give the candidates the subject and ask them to speak straight away.

Report Writing

If this is an important skill in the job, it can be a powerful measure of performance – provided that you are sure that it is the candidate's own work you are seeing. Be sure that you are clear whether you are considering writing skills, subject knowledge or both.

In-tray exercises

These present candidates with a range of tasks and documents relevant to the job, to tackle under controlled conditions. For example, for a chief executive, you might include items related to dealing with members, responding to trustee concerns, resolving staff issues and maintaining the public face of the charity (all before breakfast, of course!). Their purpose is twofold:

- to see how well candidates prioritise work
- to measure how well they do the work.

Examinations

Usually a pen and paper set of questions to test factual knowledge, as an alternative to asking direct technical questions in an interview.

Simulation exercises

An interpersonal exercise with a particular agenda and objectives, to observe how the candidates perform in a typical work situation such as a manager faced with an industrial relations issue between volunteer and paid staff in a charity shop.

Group discussions

Typically, all candidates are put together to deal with a particular problem, and are observed and evaluated doing so, such as a planning meeting on next year's appeal.

References

Another one of those things you feel you ought to do! Taking up references is fine for telling you how well someone has performed in the past, but the past may not relate to the requirements of the future. They are a useful check on other measures used by appointing managers, but no substitute for them.

Case Study

A long-established charity campaigning for social justice in an international context needed to recruit several new employees. Its young and enthusiastic staff group, conscious of their inner-city location, wanted to ensure that the workforce reflected the local community, which up to then it did not.

With three posts to fill, they decided to make sure that a black candidate was appointed to the secretarial vacancy, and to make the recruitment to the two campaigns officer posts open. Accordingly, they used their equal opportunities monitoring form to shortlist only non-Europeans, and a relatively inexperienced young woman was appointed after she and four others were interviewed. The other posts were both filled by white men.

It soon became apparent that the new secretary was unhappy in her post, and she was not able to relate well to overseas enquirers, of whom there were very many. After only four months she resigned, and during her exit interview, she explained that she had found out about the decision to appoint a black person, and had felt that hers was seen as no more than a tokenist appointment. There was no incentive to do well, and in any case, nobody had offered her training – they had assumed as a black person that she would be able to relate to other (overseas) black people.

After taking advice from outside, the charity learnt some important lessons:
- *it is illegal to recruit people because of the colour of their skin or other characteristic that defines their race, even if you are trying to redress an imbalance*
- *you need to be absolutely clear about what the job is about, and measure candidates for their potential to meet its requirements*
- *people who are not appointed on their own merits rarely succeed, and always need support.*

Next time round, they developed a clear person specification, identified a series of tests to measure the key criteria, and then targeted their recruitment drive at all local people. Their shortlist this time had black and white candidates on it, and the successful one was a black man with extensive secretarial experience in the third world. He is now doing very well, especially in handling overseas contacts. Confident that he won the job on merit, he is not afraid to ask for help in performing it better, and expects to stay there for several years. But they still had the expense of recruiting twice, when a clearer focus on the law and a better planned campaign would have saved money and effort in the long run.

Psychometrics

For recruitment purposes, these come in two forms:

- aptitude or ability tests, which measure current or potential skills levels
- personality profiling, which shows work styles and preferences, and will demonstrate how well candidates will fit in to the organisation.

Used properly, psychometric measures are very powerful predictors of future job performance – standing alone, perhaps four times as accurate as interviews, in combination with other measures related to the job, even better.

But the key is their proper use. Unless the person offering you support in this area has a licence from the British Psychological Society, you run a grave risk of being 'conned by cowboys', and the use of dud tests can be branded as unfair discrimination.

Ask about validation data and what strict conditions will be applied for their application. If in doubt about the answer, go to someone else who is more convincing.

But doesn't all this undermine equal opportunities?

Ten years ago, a lot of consultants made a lot of money convincing people that they had to improve interviewing skills and techniques to avoid discrimination. They were right. But now many of them are still arguing that good interviewing is the only way to select fairly, rather than being part of a broader approach to recruitment.

The wider the range of ways of testing against the job requirements, generally the more objective the process. And since equal opportunities is about outcomes, not processes, by constructing a careful recruitment assessment centre – particularly if you include validly chosen psychometric measures – you are far more likely to have the desired outcome of the best person being appointed to the job.

Recruitment and Selection Checklist

☐ Are you clear about the nature of the job you are recruiting to?

☐ Have you planned your recruitment campaign carefully?

☐ Have you decided whether and where to advertise, and whether to use outside help?

☐ How broad is your choice of selection techniques – have you gone beyond the standard interview process?

☐ Are you sure that all the selection methods you intend to use, particularly psychometrics, are valid?

☐ Have you ensured that your recruitment and selection process accord with best equal opportunities practice?

5. Getting the Best Out of Your Staff

So you've determined what your personnel policies are, established appropriate service conditions, and recruited good staff to meet your exacting requirements. It doesn't stop there. Every new employee starts with a flush of enthusiasm. It's your job to keep them that way – and nowhere is that more important than for trustees in their relationship with their chief executive. It's all about motivation and performance measurement.

Each individual employee will respond differently. But there are five general pointers that are worth basing your general approach on:

1. Praise produces better results than criticism.
2. Criticism when it's needed will work better coupled with ways of helping to secure improvement.
3. Targets give a sense of purpose, and targets linked to organisational objectives give a sense of identity.
4. People work at different speeds and to different abilities. Your job as a manager is to help them maximise their potential, not to set unachievable targets – constant failure is the worst demotivator.
5. Not everyone is as ambitious as you are – but if they are not ambitious at all, they are passengers you cannot afford. So give them incentives to succeed, not sanctions to fail.

The keys to successful management of staff are simple concepts, but they are the toughest to keep getting right: they are: Appraisal and Training & Development. Without them, your organisation will fail to react to change, be unaware of new opportunities, and will slowly grind to a halt and lose its identity and support.

Appraisal

Some staff are terrified of appraisal. That is because their manager sees it as a chance to have a go at them for their failures, and to sort out their pay. Managers like that give appraisal a bad name, and become self-defeating: the good staff drift away, and those that can't leave hang on and underachieve.

A good appraisal scheme:
- is an annual process, with regular intermediary meetings
- does not form part of regular management direction, but concentrates on global issues
- reviews past performance, highlighting successes and exploring reasons for non-achievement
- identifies the resources needed for future success – training, materials, staff – and how to secure and deploy them
- sets targets for performance for the next year – for the individual employee, but in full accord with the overall business and development plans of the organisation
- never produces surprises – both appraiser and appraisee will know what has happened, the point is to evaluate why
- does not determine pay, but rather influences overall performance. If you have performance-related pay, this should be dealt with as separate exercise against previously established criteria.

Case Study

A large social welfare organisation appointed as its Chief Executive a woman who was intellectually brilliant, with a total grasp of her subject. As a person, she was a brilliant public performer, but a bully, arrogant and often terrifying, and seemed incapable of winning respect or maintaining friendships. Her only approach to managing staff was to tell them how easy it was to do their jobs, she could do things in ten minutes (she probably could) so why couldn't they? Nevertheless, where it counted, in government circles, her autocratic approach ensured that she was the organisation, and the voice of the sector was heard loud and clear.

Perceiving performance-related pay and appraisal as being flavours of the month, she personally devised a scheme for evaluating the managers who reported to her, and told them that in the next month, their previous year's work would be measured against how well they had contributed to the corporate plan – which she too had written. Not *surprisingly, staff found the process very stressful, none of them matched her exacting (but previously unspecified) standards, and nobody got a decent pay rise. The old malaise of an extremely high casualty rate amongst staff reporting to her continued, and eventually the organisation lost all its most experienced staff apart from its chief executive. Then she had a heart attack.*

Too late, the trustees learnt that:
- *delegation does not mean ignoring what's going on – high staff turnover is always a matter for concern, and should be closely questioned*
- *target setting should be a realistic measurement of what staff can reasonably achieve – few people are perfect, but organisations work better if you recognise this*
- *staff work better, plan better and train better if they are praised for their achievements and helped to overcome their deficiencies; bullying has the opposite effect*
- *pennies saved through badly managed performance-related pay will often be outweighed by costs of demotivated and departing staff*
- *however brilliant, one person is not the whole organisation – which will collapse when that one person is removed.*

Run an appraisal system properly, and you will have well-motivated staff, signed up to your organisational objectives. Delegate as far as possible to them control over their own work lives, minimise interference (special note for Trustees – this particularly applies to you!) but rather set enabling frameworks, review regularly, and you will enrich your organisation through high levels of commitment and a flow of innovative ideas and actions.

Do the opposite and watch the organisation and its structures, sooner or later, crumble around you.

Training and Development

The world is constantly changing. Even in apparently steady-state jobs, there are new ways of doing things, and new expectations from customers. In the voluntary sector in particular, care standards are constantly under review, and unless staff are properly trained up, you will lose your competitive advantage.

But training is far more than just imparting new skills and knowledge. In the same way as the appraisal of individual employees is informed by how they meet their personal objectives, determined by the corporate plan, so also should plans for their development be relevant to organisational needs. Long gone are the days when staff went on a course because they felt it might be interesting, thought it might make them more marketable, or had a training budget to spend before the end of the year.

A good training and development plan:

- is the mechanism whereby staff are fully equipped to deliver the charity's objectives
- identifies current skill and experience shortages, and proposes ways of overcoming them
- relates to both individuals and groups of employees, and is culturally sensitive to the nature of the charity and how training is to be delivered
- recognises that employees have both short-term needs and long-term aspirations, and seeks to meet both within the constraints of available resources
- helps the charity plan for the future, by identifying what staffing requirements will be, and how far these can be developed in-house
- is flexible and regularly reviewed.

Motivation Checklist

- ☐ Are you positive in your praise and criticism towards staff, and do you set tough but attainable targets?
- ☐ Do you have an appraisal scheme that staff respond to positively rather than fear, and which offers positive feedback and shared objective setting?
- ☐ Can you separate decisions about appraisal and pay?
- ☐ Can you offer training that equips your staff to fulfil their roles in a changing world, within the context of the charity's own development needs?

6. But it Doesn't Always Go Right

So far, we have discussed what you need to do to get the best of out managing staff in a charity. Unfortunately (or perhaps fortunately), staff are human beings, with human failures. And organisations are made up of people, often working in changing and threatening environments. Things don't always run to plan. Demands on organisations, and the funds available to them, may change. Staff may no longer be able to provide the service that is required. Individuals may make misjudgments or misbehave.

These situations are always potentially fraught with tension; handling them well is tough. Good procedures help to take much of the sting out of them, and give the organisation a greater chance of coming out the other end in one piece. But handle them you must.

Redundancy

If the money isn't there (you've lost your Section 64 grant, your raffle has been undermined by the Lottery, or the NLCB has let you down), or the staff just don't have the skills to respond to new requirements, then redundancies may have to happen. It's nobody's fault, but it's still painful for everyone concerned, particularly for people who have given a large part of their working lives to the charity. Five key pointers to handling it properly are:

1. Consult early – staff may have good ideas on how to avoid the worst outcomes.
2. Try to retrain and redeploy wherever possible
3. Seek agreement on methods for selecting candidates for redundancy, and avoid systems that may be discriminatory.
4. Consider whether you can afford redundancy payments above the statutory obligations – but if there is no contractual right to enhanced payments, be careful how you use charitable funds.
5. Help staff to come to terms with their new situation, including perhaps offering outplacement counselling and career management support.

Capability

Sometimes the world moves on, and staff cannot move with it. The job they were employed to do has changed, and they cannot. Or their medical state may be preventing them from continuing to do a job well or at all.

- It's not their fault – but the charity still can't afford passengers. Try to find an acceptable settlement, including redundancy, early retirement or redeployment, with appropriate post-employment support like counselling and agreed references.
- Ensure that you have proper review procedures that give the employees a chance to put their point of view, and provide for an appeal against any termination of their contract.
- If the reason for incapability is connected with the employee's health, seek independent medical advice before proceeding – but the final decision is still yours.

Case Study

....

A small voluntary body of like-minded professionals decided to employ one of their number to organise a membership of several hundred into a more cohesive and campaigning force. Their chosen employee had strengths in administration, and established complex processes by which, over a period of nearly twenty years, members of the Management Committee felt increasingly imprisoned, whilst at the same time, all their ideas for a more outward looking body were ignored.

The Director clearly developed the view that he was the organisation, and that members of the Committee were a nuisance. Every time any of them tried to change things, a war of attrition followed, and they resigned to pursue their own interests rather than confront the great unpleasantness offered them by the Director. They got through seven Chairs in as many years.

Finally, the principal funder threatened to call a halt unless the performance of the organisation improved. The Committee, united by this threat, put together a clearer set of objectives and a business plan, in the face of opposition from the Director, who promptly went sick, claiming stress caused by his employers. Eventually, they decided that his presence could no longer be tolerated, and entered into negotiation on departure terms. A legally binding settlement was secured, but it was one that had to take into account very long service – nevertheless, with professional support effectively arguing the Director's deficiencies, the Committee were able to negotiate a relatively cheap way out. The organisation survived and thrived, the Director became unemployable; it was capable of change, he wasn't. They were all very much the wiser.

- *If you are a Trustee or a senior manager, it is your duty, however difficult and personally unpleasant, to confront problems when they arise – or you'll only make it more difficult for your successors, and less easy for the problem-maker to accept change.*
- *Proper guidance at an early stage on what is required will help employees achieve, and at worst will enable them to come to terms promptly with the fact that they may be in the wrong job.*
- *Employment protection legislation can be expensive to accommodate, and you should not do anything hasty that could jeopardise an employment contract – get professional assistance to secure your desired outcome.*

....

Misconduct

If an employee is doing what she or he shouldn't be doing, then you have an absolute duty to address the issue at the earliest opportunity. Failure to do so will mean that the charity will continue to suffer, and any later action may well be considered to be unfair. ("I didn't know I was doing wrong, you never told me when I did it before.")

Proper handling of employee misconduct is a complex matter, as many small employers, including in the voluntary sector, have learnt to their cost. Industrial Tribunal awards can be high, because they look not only at why you've sacked someone, but the circumstances and how you went about it.

Some pointers to avoiding the most obvious mistakes:
- have a clear set of disciplinary rules that set standards, ones that are understandable and relevant to your charity's objectives and operations
- publish clearly a fair disciplinary procedure that allows proper and objective assessment of allegations of misconduct and the right of both sides to have their say in accordance with the principles of natural justice
- make sure that everyone understands the process and is able to comply with its requirements, e.g. on the submission of documents or witnesses
- provide for an independent review of any decision through an appeal process
- remember that the prime purpose of a disciplinary procedure is to correct, not punish, so incorporate a series of incremental warnings with targets for improvement before finally dismissing anyone for failure to improve
- only sack staff for a first offence if their "crime" is so serious that they have broken all trust of their employer
- use as a measure of any disciplinary accusation whether, on the balance of probability (not beyond all reasonable doubt) the case is proven
- if in any doubt, seek professional advice – much cheaper now than at the Tribunal later.

Case Study
....

A major national dual purpose charity engaged in developing standards and securing trust funding to supplement local efforts appointed a new Chief Executive. Warned that she might be a bit of a loose canon, one of the Trustees was nominated to supervise her work, on behalf of the Trustee Board who were very keen to be kept informed in detail of all new initiatives and other major developments. Thinking that it was not the right way to deal with a person of such seniority, however, they excluded any reference to a disciplinary process in the contract, did not introduce performance targets, and relied on the good relationship with the nominated Trustee to see them through.

Whilst the Trustees felt that their new Chief Executive was good at leading the staff team, they were alarmed to learn that she was failing to keep them in touch with a range of actions that cost the charity money, including entering into partnership with a lottery operator who turned out to be bankrupt, failing to invoke legal break clauses on a merchandising operation that went very wrong, and misrepresenting the Trustees' views in an attempt to secure external funding. These concerns only came to light much later, when on several occasions the Trustees expressed their disquiet, but normally only orally.

After years of this, their patience finally snapped, and they told the Chief Executive that they had lost all confidence in her and that sooner or later she would have to go, asking her to name her terms. She promptly resigned and claimed constructive dismissal – by telling her that, she said, they had broken their relationship of trust, making it impossible for her to remain. She won, and the charity learnt some painful and expensive lessons:

- *hoping to act in an informal and friendly way is no substitute for having good procedures. Their existence, if properly handled, is the sign of professionalism, not heavyhandedness*
- *if someone has got to go, make it as easy as possible for them to do so, including offering support to come to terms with their own shortcomings*
- *all employees, even Chief Executives, have a right to a proper disciplinary process. If one had been invoked earlier, many of the problems might have been avoided*
- *proper records of performance based on realistic targets will provide the effective basis for organisational success and satisfactory disciplinary outcomes. Their absence enables poor performers to offer the excuse that they didn't know they were getting it wrong, and feign surprise when confronted too late with their shortcomings*
- *however good an employee may be, if she does something really bad in another area, that still has to be addressed. Failure to deal with poor performance early on makes it much more difficult to confront the issue later.*

If you really have got it wrong up to now, you either have to start again, or buy your way out of trouble, as this charity eventually did. Either way, it costs a lot in time and effort. Unfortunately, new Trustees and managers inherit the shortcomings of their predecessors.

Absence

Some staff take more time off than others, and everyone is ill at some time in their working lives. That is inevitable; the issue for employers – particularly for voluntary sector employers who have to account for every penny of charitable funds – is to minimise absence whilst not appearing to be too harsh. Deliberate absenteeism is misconduct, and should be treated under your disciplinary procedures. Excessive sickness absence can be either a matter of incapability or indiscipline, and you need to decide which it is and therefore how to handle it.

- If an employee is genuinely ill, and their absence is affecting your operations, get medical advice on the prognosis and particularly how long before you can expect them back at work.
- If absence for the anticipated time is unacceptable – this is more likely to be the case for key employees – then a dismissal with notice will probably be fair, if it is handled properly under your incapability procedures, appropriately amended to suit the circumstances.
- If you have a sick pay scheme, you do not normally have to allow an employee to exhaust their entitlement before they are dismissed, particularly if the prognosis is that they will never be fit to work again – but beware of appearing too harsh.
- Ensure that the medical advice you get is independent – the job of the employee's GP is to look after their interests, not yours.
- If you are concerned that sickness absence is not entirely genuine, or if patterns to it start to emerge, then again it is worthwhile getting medical advice. Either the employee will be shown to have a real problem, in which case it can be addressed; or it will become clear that the sick pay scheme is being abused, which can be dealt with as a disciplinary matter, with warnings and procedural controls like requiring medical certificates for every day of absence.

Grievances

Employers have a duty to manage difficult staff situations. Employees have an equal right to complain about how they are being treated. Make sure that you have a system to allow them to air their grievances that is based on the same objective principles as a good disciplinary procedure.

Dealing with the Difficult Bits – Summary

- Be sure to have fair selection arrangements for redundancy, and involve the people affected.
- If people can't do their job, it's not usually their fault, so handle cases of incapability sensitively and fairly but firmly.
- Be sure that you have a clear set of disciplinary rules.
- Introduce disciplinary procedures that are fair, effective and properly used. It's cheaper and better to get it right now than pay up at the Tribunal later.
- Always act promptly and firmly on absenteeism, but be sensitive in cases of real need.
- Offer your staff fair grievance procedures, and treat them with the same respect that you expect for your disciplinary processes.

About the author

John Burnell FIPD has worked as a general manager and a specialist in the public and voluntary sectors. He runs his own consultancy, Personnel Solutions, is a senior consultant with Charity Appointments and a director of Spencer Charles Public Sector Career Management. He is the author of a text-book for non-specialists in the voluntary sector, *Managing People in Charities* ICSA, 1997.

ORGANISING VOLUNTEERS : 10

Justin Davis Smith

1. Introduction

Aims and Objectives

Over 23 million people volunteer in the United Kingdom each year – some 10 million every week, and yet some organisations are suffering from problems of recruitment and retention. This chapter examines the key factors which go into making a successful volunteering programme and provides practical guidance on how organisations can get the most out of their volunteers and ensure that their volunteers have a worthwhile and stimulating experience.

Successful involvement of volunteers depends upon a clarity of purpose and a positive commitment to volunteering that runs throughout the organisation, from the board of trustees, through senior management to the paid staff. It involves the organisation paying serious attention to the individual needs of the volunteers and to providing a supportive environment in which volunteers can flourish and develop.

For some organisations this commitment has led to the development of a formal volunteering policy, which lays down the reciprocal rights and responsibilities of the organisation and the volunteer, in terms of training, support, level of commitment and standards of behaviour. However, this needs to be tackled sensitively. There is a danger of overformalising volunteering and of stifling the flexibility and informality which lies at the heart of many successful volunteer programmes.

What follows is an attempt to help organisations which involve volunteers (or are considering involving volunteers) make sense of the rapid changes taking place in their world, and position themselves so they can not only survive but prosper.

By the end of the chapter, readers should have achieved the following learning outcomes:

- an understanding of how to establish a volunteering policy which answers the questions:

  Why involve volunteers?

  What do we want them to do?
- the most effective methods of recruitment

- whether and how to select volunteers
- the training, support and supervision of volunteers
- the retention of volunteers.

Key points are summarised in a checklist at the end of each section.

2. Establishing a Volunteering Policy

Who volunteers?

Involving volunteers has never been an easy task; in fact it has often been suggested that managing volunteers is harder than managing paid staff because of the absence of the wage link. After all, if volunteers are unhappy or dissatisfied with their work there is nothing to stop them from turning their backs on the organisation and walking away. Today the task of involving volunteers is becoming harder still. The old certainties around definitions and boundaries are being replaced by greater fluidity and imprecision, and volunteers themselves are demanding a better deal and a greater say in the framing of their activities.

The trend towards involving more volunteers is by no means universal. Many organisations have experienced a decline in volunteers over the past 10 to 15 years, particularly the more traditional welfare agencies which have tended to rely on a certain type of volunteer that no longer exists, or at least is disappearing fast. The Red Cross, for example, has admitted to losing 40% of its volunteers over the past decade, and it is by no means alone.

The Challenge for Organisations

But this shift, although difficult for the organisations which are losing out, should not be seen as a problem. Increased competition for volunteers should keep organisations on their toes and lead them to pay more attention to the needs of their volunteers. Those organisations which recruit and hold on to their volunteers will be those that give their volunteers the best deal – a not unwelcome development

Repeated surveys have found that certain groups are under-represented in terms of their involvement in formal voluntary work – the unemployed; the young; the retired; the disabled and those from black and ethnic minority communities. But with the decline of the 'traditional' volunteer, the pressure will be on organisations to pull in those who have been excluded in the past. And this pressure will be increased by other long-term societal trends taking place – like the move towards early retirement and increased life expectancy which will open up a huge new pool of potential volunteers among healthy active 'third-agers'.

The Why Question

Before embarking on the process of recruiting volunteers an organisation should ask itself the important question: 'Why are we doing this?'. Without a positive answer (which goes beyond the simple negative ' we can't afford paid staff') the likelihood of a successful volunteer programme is greatly reduced.

There is, of course, no set answer to the question; volunteering can and does serve a number of different functions and different organisations will respond to this question in different ways. For some organisations the prime reason for involving volunteers is to help the organisation fulfil its function and carry out its work; for others the involvement of volunteers is almost an end in itself, with the emphasis being placed on the value of volunteering to the individual volunteer. The important thing is for organisations to answer this question for themselves.

Too often organisations drift into involving volunteers without any idea as to why, beyond a vague feeling that volunteers are useful and perhaps the only way in which the organisation can afford to carry out or expand its work. It is often in such cases that trouble occurs, as paid staff (and volunteers) come to fear that volunteers are being used only to save money or substitute for paid employees.

But there are many positive reasons why an organisation should seek to involve volunteers. They include the fact that:

- volunteers can help with the delivery of the organisation's core services
- volunteers can provide the 'image' and 'legitimacy' for the organisation, particularly helpful in its request to the public for money
- volunteers can bring a diversity of skills, talents expertise and experience to the organisation, and a different perspective to that of paid staff
- volunteers can provide community outreach and access – acting as door-openers and power-brokers
- volunteers can provide an element of passion and enthusiasm sometimes absent from the workplace
- volunteers can be innovative and risk-takers as their livelihoods don't depend on the next promotion
- volunteers can provide continuity during times of high staff turnover

Whatever the reason or combination of reasons, the important point is that the organisation has thought about why it wishes to involve volunteers rather than rushing headlong into an ill-thought-out recruitment drive.

An Example

The Royal Society for The Protection of Birds answers the question of why involve volunteers in the following way:

"Ask anyone why we should involve volunteers and nine times out of ten the answer will be to save money. Volunteers are excellent value for money, but there are other good reasons for working with them too:

- they increase our capacity for work – we can get more done and concentrate on priority work
- they help us to cope with peaks and troughs in the workload
- they are an excellent way of getting RSPB messages into the community
- in some circumstances, they are more credible than staff – staff are paid to promote the Society – the message can be a lot more powerful coming from a volunteer
- they give us access to new skills that we could not afford to employ
- they strengthen our political clout
- they keep us in touch with grass roots feelings and perceptions
- they can focus their time and energy on one specific task without distraction.

(Source: *RSPB Working with Volunteers: A Handbook for RSPB Staff*)

Informing the Mission

It is not sufficient for an organisation to have thought through the issue of why it wants to involve volunteers; its thinking needs to be translated into a concrete set of aims or principles. Many organisations have begun to develop Mission Statements as a means of codifying their objectives and values. Some refer to the role of volunteers as a way of emphasising the importance of volunteering to the mission of the organisation.

An Example

A good example of a Mission Statement which elevates volunteering to a core principle is that provided by the American Red Cross. It states:

"The Mission of the American Red Cross is to improve the

quality of human life; to enhance self-reliance and to help people avoid, prepare for, and cope with emergencies. It does this through services that are governed and directed by volunteers and are consistent with its congressional charter and the principles of the International Red Cross.

Principles of the International Red Cross:
- Humanity
- Impartiality
- Neutrality
- Independence
- Voluntary Service
- Unity
- Universality."

This is both a clear statement of the overall purpose of the Red Cross and the principles which underpin its work, and of the central position identified for volunteering. The Mission Statement makes it clear that the services to be provided will be 'governed and directed' by volunteers. Volunteering is not seen as an add-on extra, a peripheral element tacked onto the core work of the agency, but rather it is firmly located as a guiding principle underpinning the work of the Red Cross.
(Source: *The American Red Cross, Volunteer 2000 Study*)

Such a strong assertion of the primacy of the voluntary ethic in the Mission Statement leaves no doubt as to the commitment of the agency to the involvement and development of volunteering.

Conflicting aims?

Some of the problems which arise over the involvement of volunteers are due to a conflict of aims within the organisation. Is the agency about delivering a service or is it about involving volunteers? Some organisations like Volunteer Bureaux might argue that their primary aim is to look after the interests of the volunteer; others would argue that the involvement of volunteers is secondary to the main purpose of the organisation. Both are legitimate aims and both are consistent with good volunteering. The important point is not whether the involvement of volunteers is the main purpose of the agency or the means by which it will achieve its goals; but that the organisation is clear about the role of volunteering and that it clarifies and codifies this role through such mediums as a Mission Statement.

An Example

"The American Red Cross while stating that voluntary service is a key principle of its work, nevertheless is in no doubt that the involvement of volunteers is not a goal in itself but is secondary to the main purpose of the organisation. It explains: Volunteers are secondary only to the mission of the American Red Cross. It is a well understood principle that voluntarism for its own sake is not what the organisation is about. The organisation does not exist to provide opportunities for volunteer involvement, but rather volunteer participation is valued because it helps the Red Cross to accomplish its mission and reach out to provide services in the most cost-effective and compassionate manner possible".

(Source: *The American Red Cross, Volunteer 2000 Study*)

Translating Mission into Policy

With support for the principle of volunteering firmly established within the organisation's key statement of aims, it is now possible to produce more detailed guidance on how the organisation should best seek to introduce volunteers into its work.

For most organisations the most appropriate next step is to produce a written Volunteering Policy, to explain the principles underpinning the involvement of volunteers and give guidance on the practical issues of recruitment, support and management.

The Policy will be directed both at the organisation and at the volunteer; it will provide details of what the volunteer can expect from the organisation but also what the organisation can expect from the volunteer.

As with Mission Statements, a successful Volunteering Policy will be produced after full consultation with interested parties, including management, paid staff, trustees and volunteers.

An Example

A good example is provided by the Gloucestershire Wildlife Trust. In its Volunteering Policy it sets out very clearly the principles which underlie its involvement of volunteers, as follows:

"The Gloucestershire Wildlife Trust is an organisation governed and primarily staffed by volunteers. One of the central roles of salaried staff is to support volunteer involvement by creating an environment in which the contribution of volunteers can be maximised and appreciated. This can be achieved by:

• creating an image of the Trust which is inclusive rather than exclusive

• encouraging existing staff and volunteers to be open and

welcoming to new volunteers
- ensuring that barriers to involvement are recognised, and where possible removed (e.g. payment of expenses, provision of transport etc.)
- valuing volunteers, regardless of the type of service or level of commitment
- implementing the Trust's equal opportunities policy at all levels."

(Source: *Gloucestershire Wildlife Trust Volunteering Policy*)

Resourcing Volunteering: Six Costs

In order to implement the Volunteering Policy resources will need to be set aside. Volunteering is not cost free. Of course volunteers bring added value to an organisation, and can be a cost effective way of delivering services, but there is a need to recognise that there are costs involved in bringing a volunteering dimension to an organisation's work. These include:

1. recruitment costs
2. costs for expenses
3. training costs
4. management support costs
5. insurance costs
6. office based costs – a desk to work at, a computer to use.

A Volunteer Co-ordinator

Some organisations show their commitment to volunteering by employing a member of staff with specific responsibility for volunteering. The staff member may be full-time or part-time or indeed unpaid, and will be expected to take on a wide range of tasks, including setting up and managing the volunteering programme and advocating on behalf of volunteers within the organisation.

Katharine Noyes Campbell and Susan Ellis in *The Help I Don't Have Enough Time Guide to Volunteer Management*, have summarised the key functions of the volunteer manager as follows:

- programme planning and administration – including assessment of organisation and client needs for assistance; setting up programme; advocating for volunteers; managing budget
- recruitment and public relations – including planning recruitment strategies and developing recruitment materials
- interviewing and screening
- orientation and training
- supervision

- motivation and recognition
- programme evaluation
- record keeping and reporting.

Once an organisation is clear about the purpose for involving volunteers, has drawn up a Volunteering Policy, and has identified a budget to support the work, it can begin the search for new recruits.

Checklist 1: Establishing a Volunteering Policy

☐ Establish why it is that you want to involve volunteers in the work of your organisation.

☐ Emphasise the positive reasons, which will help overcome any suspicion that volunteers are only being used to save money.

☐ Draw up a Mission Statement outlining the organisation's key aims and values and ensure that reference is made to the role to be played by volunteers.

☐ Develop a Volunteering Policy in consultation with staff, volunteers and trustees and include within it details both of what the volunteer can expect from the organisation and what the organisation can expect from the volunteer.

☐ Ensure that sufficient resources are available to support the involvement of volunteers and to pay for such essentials as expenses and training.

☐ Identify one member of staff (paid or unpaid) who will have lead responsibility for developing volunteering in the organisation and advocating on behalf of volunteers.

☐ Ensure that all staff are 'volunteer-educated' and encouraged to look for opportunities of involving volunteers in their work.

3. Recruitment

The laws of Supply and Demand

Statistics tell us that the numbers of people volunteering in the UK have increased over the past 10 to 15 years. Yet despite this welcome trend it is apparent that many organisations are not able to recruit sufficient numbers of volunteers to meet their needs. Whilst talk of a recruitment crisis may be premature, it is nevertheless the case that a number (perhaps an increasing number) of organisations are finding it more and more difficult to attract new volunteers.

A full discussion of this issue is beyond the scope of this chapter. Nevertheless it is helpful to have some idea of the factors which are contributing to the recruitment difficulties. One way to look at the issue is through the well-established concepts of supply and demand. Put very simply, what appears to be happening is that the demand for volunteers is outstripping the supply, leaving a shortfall of volunteers amongst some agencies. This qualification is important, because it is not the case that all organisations are experiencing such difficulties. On the contrary some agencies, operating in particularly popular fields, such as the environment, have noted a volunteering boom in recent years. This in itself raises important issues of organisational appeal which will be discussed more fully below.

The key challenge for organisations is to develop a recruitment policy that will help ensure that it is successful in attracting its share of volunteers.

The Motivation of Volunteers

In drawing up a recruitment strategy it is important to have an understanding of why people get involved in voluntary work – to be aware of the individual motivations that lead people to give up their spare time. Only with such an understanding is it possible to frame a recruitment message that will strike a chord with a prospective volunteer.

Much has been written about volunteer motivations, most of it from an American perspective. What all the studies agree on is that people's motivations to volunteer are mixed, encompassing both altruistic motivations – a desire to help people in need, to serve the community; and self-interested motivations – a desire to meet people, learn new skills, do something enjoyable.

An Example

For example a national survey of volunteering carried out in 1991 by The Volunteer Centre in the UK (now the National Centre for Volunteering) came up with the following list of motivating factors:

Reason for Volunteering	% of respondents
Connected with own needs/interests	39
Connected with needs/interests of family or friends	43
Connected with paid work	11
To meet a need in the community	26
To improve things/help people	39
To meet people/make friends	25
Someone asked me to help	51

I offered to help	49
I started the group	5
I had time to spare	28
I'm good at it	18
Give me a chance to learn new skills	11

Looking at this list we can see both the wide mix of motives there are for volunteering and the broad split that exists between altruistic and self-interested reasons. So, for example, four out of ten volunteers cited the meeting of their own needs or interests as a prime motivator to volunteer, while a similar number cited the desire to improve things and help people. A quarter of respondents said they volunteered for social reasons – to meet people and make friends; while a similar figure said their prime motivation was to meet a need in the community.

(Source: *The 1991 National Survey of Voluntary Activity in the UK*)

Six main motivations

Two American psychologists, Clary and Snyder have come up with a useful list of six main motivations to volunteer:

1. *values* – for some people volunteering serves the function of enabling them to act on deeply held beliefs about the importance of helping others
2. *understanding* – for others, volunteering serves an understanding function by satisfying the desire to understand the people whom one serves, the organisation for which one volunteers, or oneself
3. *career* – for some people volunteering enables people to learn new skills which may help them with finding a job or developing their career
4. *social* – for some volunteering is about social contacts and meeting people
5. *esteem* – volunteering may help raise a person's self esteem by making them feel better about themselves
6. *protective* – volunteering may help an individual to escape from negative feelings of guilt or loneliness.

But whatever theories we look at, the key findings to note are that people volunteer for a variety of reasons which include self-interest reasons quite as much as altruism.

Implications for Recruitment

The implications of these findings for recruitment are very clear. If an organisation is to attract volunteers then it needs to frame an appeal which takes account of the personal needs and altruistic motivations of individuals. In other words, the successful organisation is likely to be the one that spells out in its advertising literature the benefits likely to accrue to the individual volunteer as well as the contribution the volunteer can make to the organisation and the community at large.

Horses for Courses

What is the best way to recruit volunteers? McCurley and Lynch in *Essential Volunteer Management*, published by the Directory of Social Change, suggest three main approaches, depending on the requirements of the organisation. All have advantages and drawbacks.

1. Warm Body Recruitment – appropriate when the organisation is seeking large numbers of volunteers for tasks that are not highly skilled or can be picked up quickly, such as envelope stuffing. The advantage of this approach is that the net can be cast wide, using simple, cheap recruitment methods such as leaflet drops, posters, adverts on radio etc.

2. Targeted Recruitment – clearly if particular skills are required then the scatter gun approach will not be the right one. Not only might the organisation not get the volunteers they need but they might get lots of unsuitable ones who will need to be turned away. If specialist skills are required, the organisation will require a more targeted approach. They may choose to go to their local Volunteer Bureaux for assistance, place an advert in the specialist press, or approach a company to see if they have a volunteer or secondee who might be able to help.

3. Concentric Circle Approach – the third broad approach to recruitment is the least proactive and draws on the fact that word of mouth is the most effective means of allowing volunteers to spread the word. The advantage is cheapness and effectiveness; the disadvantage is the lack of targeting and the fact that such an approach may work against the organisation's efforts to broaden the base of its volunteers, as people will tend to recruit those from similar backgrounds to themselves.

Projecting a Positive Message

Whatever method chosen for recruiting volunteers it is important that an upbeat message is given. With 170,000 plus charities in existence, several hundred thousand non-registered voluntary groups, and thousands of volunteering opportunities in the public sector, the competition for volunteers is fierce. Volunteers have a choice and will exercise it, both over which organisation to join and whether to stay once they have started. The issue of retention will be considered below, but first organisations have to appeal to people to put themselves forward.

Elements of the Message

McCurley and Lynch argue that a successful recruitment message will have four elements to it:

- Statement of Need – why is the volunteer activity important; what need is going to be met. This, they say, is often missing from the recruitment message.
- Nature of the Task – what will the volunteer be asked to do; how will the task help meet the need identified above.
- Dealing with Concerns – some volunteers have fears that there will be too much responsibility placed upon them or not enough; that they will be expected to work evenings or at weekends.
- Benefits – what the volunteer will get out of the experience and what can be expected in terms of expenses, support and training.

Organisations which construct their recruitment appeal in this way will at the very least put themselves in the running for attracting the attention of the would-be volunteers.

Equal Opportunities

Data shows that not all people find it easy to break into volunteering. Those least likely to volunteer include the young, the old, the unemployed, the disabled and people from black and ethnic minority communities.

Why should organisations be interested in questions of equal opportunities? Well for one thing because it is important for the image and effectiveness of the organisation that the community is broadly reflected in the composition of its volunteer force; and for another because organisations need to fish from a potentially larger pool.

Because of the informal nature of volunteering and the fact that much anti-discrimination legislation does not apply to volunteers, equal opportunities issues are often ignored. This is a shame because it means many good people are lost to the organisation.

A starting point for organisations interested in addressing issues of inequality in access to volunteering is to develop an equal opportunities policy, or ensure that the existing policy covers the issue of volunteering. However, as with the development of a Mission Statement, more is needed than a simple expression of intent not to discriminate. There is a need to translate the policy into practical steps to bring it about. These will include:

- thinking about where advertisements are placed. Making sure, for example, that the minority ethnic press is used.
- thinking more generally about the organisation's literature. Does it need to be in languages other than English? What about the stories and pictures represented, are they reflective of the population as a whole? David Obaze (Manager of the Resource Unit for Black Volunteering) has argued that the term volunteering may be off-putting to some black people and suggests use of the term 'helping' instead in recruitment literature.
- removing age bars. Some organisations impose retirement ages on volunteers of 60 or 65. Others impose age bars at the younger age range, and don't allow people under 18 to volunteer. There may be certain types of volunteering that are not appropriate for young people but blanket age barriers send out the wrong message to young and older people about their worth and their ability to make a contribution.
- making sure that expenses are offered so that people from low incomes or without paid work are not prevented from volunteering.
- conducting outreach work – using black people to recruit black people; young people to recruit young people etc.

An Example

A new study carried out by The National Centre for Volunteering, *A Route to Opportunity*, looks at the strategies organisations have adopted in trying to recruit volunteers from five groups traditionally under-represented in formal volunteering: younger people, older people, unemployed people, disabled people and people from black and ethnic minority communities.

The study found that those organisations which had been successful in opening up volunteering to new groups had adopted a range of approaches, including:

- making sure they paid out of pocket expenses
- offering a variety of different types of volunteering opportunities requiring various levels of skill and commitment
- organising transport where necessary
- ensuring that buildings had full disabled access
- making it clear in recruitment literature that volunteering is open to all
- targeting recruitment campaigns at the specific group they want to recruit

- adopting non-rejection policies for people who want to volunteer
- employing a diverse paid staff group, thereby illustrating to potential volunteers that the organisation is committed to equal opportunities
- providing appropriate training and support.

Checklist 2: Recruitment

☐ Draw up a recruitment strategy that takes into account the needs of the organisation and the motivations of people to volunteer.

☐ Project an up-beat, positive message in the recruitment literature which emphasises what's in it for the volunteer as well as for the organisation.

☐ Choose a recruitment method appropriate for the organisation's needs.

☐ Be aware of equal opportunities considerations and take active steps to ensure that certain groups of people aren't excluded because of the recruitment methods adopted.

☐ Remember that while word-of-mouth is the most effective recruitment method, it may serve to reinforce existing inequalities in representation.

☐ Take positive steps to recruit people from groups currently under-represented in volunteering, such as the young, the disabled, the unemployed and those from black and ethnic minority communities.

4. Selection and Placement

To select or not to select

If the recruitment campaign has been successful, a number of people may consider coming forward to volunteer. The next task faced by the organisation is how to deal with the enquirers. Should they accept everyone who expresses an interest in volunteering or embark upon some sort of selection process? If the latter what criteria should be used to select and reject volunteers?

This is one of the most difficult tasks of the whole volunteering process. It involves the organisation engaging in the complex task of balancing the needs of the agency with the needs of the volunteer; and it may involve dealing with the sensitive task of having to tell someone that they are not suitable for a particular volunteering opportunity.

Three approaches to selection

There are three broad approaches:

1. The non-rejection approach
2. The straight forward recruitment approach
3. The matching approach

All of these approaches have merit and are appropriate for different organisations in different settings. There is no right way. Organisations need to think through the issues and adopt the approach which is right for them.

Non-Rejection Policy

For some organisations the idea of rejecting a volunteer is anathema. All people have something to offer and it is the responsibility of the organisation to find something suitable for that individual to do. Organisations which run a non-rejection policy start from a strong value base that emphasises the importance of volunteering for the individual rather than the needs of the organisation. Such a policy is clearly not easy to implement but where successful sends a very strong message about the intrinsic right of each individual to volunteer.

Recruitment Approach

At the other end of the spectrum to the non-rejection approach lies what can best be described as the workplace model of selection. This model mirrors the approach taken in the recruitment of paid staff, where the organisation decides what tasks are required to be undertaken within the organisation on a voluntary basis and sets out to find a suitable person to fill the vacancy. The tools used are the standard ones used in selecting for paid staff, namely job descriptions, person specifications and interviews. (*See Chapter 9.*) Organisations which adopt this model argue that it is essential to get the best people to best serve the interests of the organisation and its clients. The needs or interests of the volunteer are seen as of secondary importance.

Matching Approach

There is a third or middle way between non-rejection and the workplace model, which can be described as the matching approach. The rationale behind this approach is an acceptance that the needs and interests of the volunteer and the organisation may differ; but that if the volunteer placement is to work it is essential to try and achieve a balance or a match between them.

The Matching Approach to selection differs in several important respects to the workplace model. Rather than have firm job descriptions and person specifications, the organisation will have a portfolio of different tasks that it requires to be carried out. These may be combined in any number of ways. Instead of using a predetermined job description as the basis of selecting a suitable candidate, the organisation will use the interview as a means of ascertaining the skills, interests, and preferences of the individual and will then seek to build up an individually tailored opportunity from the list of tasks required that most closely matches the needs of the individual. At this stage it is likely that a job description or description of tasks will be drawn up setting out the key tasks to be carried out by the volunteer.

Of course the reality is never so clear cut, and there is likely to be an overlap of approaches by most organisations, although the non-rejection policy remains very much a minority approach.

The Interview

Unless an organisation is operating a non-rejecting policy, it will be necessary to arrange for some form of selection meeting. Even for those with a non-rejection policy it will still be necessary to discuss with the applicant the most appropriate type of volunteering for them within the organisation.

If the selection approach has been adopted, the interview will be broadly similar to that which would be used to look for a paid worker; with the emphasis on trying to find out whether the applicant is suitable for the work. If the matching approach has been favoured it will be more informal than this; with the emphasis on trying to see if the volunteer is appropriate for any of the range of tasks on offer within the agency.

Some commentators have argued that too heavy a reliance on the structures and language of the workplace can be off-putting to prospective volunteers. To this end some organisations prefer the term meeting to interview and talk of task descriptions rather than job descriptions.

Eight steps to a successful selection meeting

Mark Rankin in *Managing Volunteers: A Handbook for Volunteer Organisers* has identified eight steps to be followed in a successful selecting meeting:

1. help volunteers feel at ease – choose right location etc.
2. talk about range of opportunities on offer
3. invite volunteers to talk about why they want to volunteer and what they want to do

4. look for possible match between the two
5. feed back positive information to the volunteer and discuss how they can best be involved
6. clarify any problems
7. communicate the outcome of the discussion
8. if selected make clear the rights and responsibilities of the volunteer.

Interview Skills

Rankin lists the skills needed for a successful interviewer as:

- re-phrasing and summarising
- empathising
- giving feedback
- listening
- questioning.

Taking up References?

Another thorny issue is the question of references. Should they be taken up as matter of course? Some volunteer managers say yes, others see the practice as cumbersome and bureaucratic and argue that they should be taken up only for particularly sensitive posts. If it is decided to take up references then it is essential to communicate to the volunteer the purpose of the exercise, to get their permission, and to give reassurance that the information will be treated in confidence. Again it may be that talk of references is not the right language for volunteering and that asking a prospective volunteer for the name of someone who can vouch for them might be more appropriate and less intimidating.

Police Checks

One particularly sensitive issue is the practice of checking up on the criminal background of prospective volunteers who apply for work with vulnerable clients, particularly young children. Some argue that it is an essential check for organisations to take and that they would be vulnerable to accusations of negligence if they failed to take every precaution possible to check the background of their volunteers.

Others argue that it is an infringement of civil liberties, and that in any case a criminal record is a very poor predictor of future criminal behaviour. Much better than running a police check they say is to ensure that proper support systems are in place and that no volunteer is placed in positions of unsupervised access to vulnerable clients without proper checks and balances being built into the system. Protecting clients, the argument goes, is all about good practice not about arbitrary screening for criminal records.

Currently the legislation does not allow for the routine screening of prospective volunteers although the practice clearly still goes on in some instances.

But things are set to change. In November 1996 the government introduced a new Police Bill to the House of Lords containing provisions for the setting up of a self-financing Criminal Records Agency to provide wider access to criminal records checks on people applying for both paid and unpaid work in the child care field.

There was opposition from voluntary groups who claimed that the cost to the individual (or to the organisation if they chose to shield the individual from the charge) would have a disastrous effect on volunteer recruitment. The Scout Association, for example, estimated that the checks would add £500,000 a year to its recruitment costs. Although there is no statutory obligation on organisations to carry out a check under the new provisions, it is widely felt that organisations will be forced into making them to prevent laying themselves open to the charge that they are failing in their duty of care.

In response to these concerns the National Centre for Volunteering drafted an amendment, which was tabled by Lords Dubs and Weatheril, which would exempt volunteers or their organisations from the cost of making the check. The amendment was passed in the Lords but at the time of writing the government has refused to back down and is continuing to push the Bill through Parliament.

Rejecting Volunteers

As we have already heard some organisations operate a non-rejection policy and make it a matter of principle not to turn away any offer of help but to find a volunteer placement for all applicants, whatever their skills and capabilities. For others this is not deemed feasible and organisations will not be able to take on all those who apply.

In such instances the organisation needs to deal very sensitively with the applicant. It is important to try and not reject out of hand. For someone who has made the effort to offer their services on a voluntary basis it can be very hurtful to be told they are not required. It may put them off volunteering for good and may discourage friends and associates from putting themselves forward for rejection. It may be that the individual, while not suited for the post they applied for, may be able to do something else of value in the organisation. If there is really nothing for them then the organisation should try and direct them to an alternative agency which may be able to offer them something or to the local Volunteer Bureau, which will be able to advise them on something more suitable.

Checklist 3: Selection and Placement

☐ Decide whether you are going to accept all applicants or make a selection of some kind.

☐ Try to match up the interests and skills of the prospective volunteer with the activities required by the organisation.

☐ If selecting, make sure the process is not too formal and off-putting to the volunteer applicant.

☐ If the nature of the volunteer activity requires a check to be carried out on the applicant's criminal background then handle this process sensitively and remember that a criminal record by itself should not be used to exclude someone from volunteering.

☐ If it is not possible to place an individual within your organisation try to refer them on to another agency which might be able to offer them something.

5. Training, Support and Supervision

Induction

All new volunteers will require an element of training. Even volunteers who have been appointed because they have the requisite skills to do the task will require an introduction to the organisation and the activity they are being asked to do. McCurley and Lynch in *Essential Volunteer Management* have distinguished between three types of induction:

- cause induction – an introduction to the work of the organisation. What its purpose is, perhaps explained in an annual report or introductory meeting for new volunteers
- system induction – introduction to the organisational systems – the facilities and structure of the agency
- social induction – introduction to staff, trustees and to other volunteers.

Induction can be via a one to one meeting, or a general meeting for all new volunteers, and is best accompanied by a written introductory pack of materials, which might include copies of the Mission Statement and the Volunteering Policy.

Training

For many volunteers some degree of training in the actual task will also be required.

Some volunteers find training off-putting, even threatening. For some it is the language rather than the concept itself which is the problem, bringing back memories of unsatisfying educational experiences; hence some organisations prefer terms like preparation which is felt to be more informal and less rigid. But whatever it is called it is important that the volunteers have the right skills to do the job properly and also that volunteers are offered the opportunity to grow and develop in their work.

There are at least two different types of training: formal training needed for some complex tasks, often very intensive and detailed. e.g. training for councillors, advice workers and Aids Buddies. It may take place either in-house or externally to the organisation; and less formal coaching or on the job training in basic tasks, like answering the phone or operating the photocopier. No matter how it is delivered, training can serve the following functions:

- enable volunteers to do their tasks more efficiently and effectively
- make volunteers feel their work is being taken seriously by the organisation, and is not just a marginal activity
- provide job satisfaction for the volunteer; offering help with personal development and career progression
- provide a benefit to volunteers – training may be used by the organisation as a means of rewarding their volunteers and thanking them. Examples might include CV preparation and public speaking courses
- provide a link to some recognised qualification such as an NVQ.

The Supportive Environment

Alongside training, support is essential to help ensure that volunteers can perform to the best of their abilities and also to ensure they are gaining satisfaction from their experience; an unhappy volunteer will not hang around. Rankin in *Managing Volunteers* has identified seven broad categories of support for volunteers:

- giving advice
- giving information
- direct action

- training
- systems change
- personal support
- facilitating mutual support
- supervisory support.

At the core of the issue is the need to create a supportive environment; a climate that allows volunteers to ask for help. Support needs to be made easily accessible and volunteers need to know who they can go to when they require support. The support needs of volunteers will change over time, so the organisation needs to constantly review its procedures.

An Example

A good example of a statement of support is provided by the Gloucestershire Wildlife Trust. Its Volunteering Policy states:

"New and existing volunteers need to know what is expected of them, to whom they are accountable, and who is responsible for supporting them. Support for volunteers should take place on both a personal and practical level, including:

- the opportunity for contact and discussion with a Volunteers' Coordinator
- the provision of necessary tools and equipment
- the keeping of an accurate database of volunteers' records
- the encouragement of volunteers to claim out-of-pocket expenses
- ensuring that volunteers are aware of health and safety procedures and requirements
- regularly thanking volunteers and seeking opportunities to provide encouragement and feedback
- giving volunteers the opportunity for periodic reviews to consider their option to reduce or develop their current commitment to the work of the Trust, to identifying future development or training requirements, and to comment upon any support, training and supervision they are currently receiving
- the provision of insurance cover as appropriate
- the acceptance that different volunteers are able to offer different levels of time commitment, and that this may change for individual volunteers from time to time
- supporting volunteers in their decisions to say "no" when necessary, and encouraging others to take on more challenging roles when they are willing and ready to do so."

Rights and Responsibilities

Many organisations have chosen to look at the issue of support in terms of the rights the volunteer can expect from an organisation but also the responsibilities the volunteer owes to the organisation.

An Example

The RSPB has produced a summary statement of the rights and responsibilities of its volunteers, as follows:

A Volunteer has the right to:
- a good understanding of what the RSPB is and does
- know what they are expected to do
- know who they are answerable to
- be part of a team and included in appropriate meetings and social events
- appropriate training
- know who they can talk to (other than their manager) if there are problems or difficulties
- be properly valued – and thanked
- receive regular and constructive feedback
- be trusted (with confidential information if necessary)
- have safe working conditions
- have adequate insurance cover
- be taken seriously by paid colleagues
- not to be out of pocket
- be consulted
- say no.

Volunteers have the responsibility to:
- be reliable
- tell their manager if they are not available or running late
- respect confidentiality
- carry out the agreed project
- give constructive feedback if appropriate
- be accountable and to accept constructive comment
- take part in relevant training
- ask for support if it is needed.

(Source: RSPB, *Working with Volunteers: A Handbook for RSPB Staff*)

Problem Solving

It would be nice to think that if an organisation followed all the procedures laid down in this chapter then it would encounter no problems in its involvement of volunteers. But of course reality is not like that and almost inevitably, despite the best of intentions and the most well thought out systems, problems will on occasions arise. Some organisations have adopted formal grievance and disciplinary procedures to deal with volunteer difficulties; others have developed less formal mechanisms for resolving disputes.

Whatever systems are put in place the best advice that can be given is that organisations should plan in advance and avoid being caught on the hop. A rushed policy is almost always a bad policy.

The Legal Status of Volunteers

In recent years concern has been expressed about the legal status of volunteers and the implications this might have for organisations which involve them. The issue has come to the fore following recent Industrial Tribunal rulings where it was held that just because an individual was a volunteer did not necessarily mean that they were not an 'employee' and thus covered by employment legislation relating to such things as unfair dismissal and sex and racial discrimination. In coming to a view on whether an individual was an employee the Tribunal held that they would need to consider whether there was a contract between the organisation and the volunteer and the degree of the formality of the relationship. Of course it might well be argued that volunteers should have the same 'employment' protection as paid staff, but the wider implications of this trend could be far reaching in the extreme not only in terms of resources (how could this be afforded?) but in undermining the fundamental distinctiveness of volunteering.

In practical terms it means organisations need to think carefully about the nature of any agreement they ask volunteers to sign which might suggest some form of contractural relationship, and the types of management systems put in place for volunteers. Concern has been expressed about the trend in recent years towards treating volunteers in exactly the same way as paid employees, with the sole exception of payment, with volunteers subject to the same management instruments of job descriptions, annual appraisals, and grievance and disciplinary procedures. Such an approach it has been claimed fails to take account of the distinctive nature of volunteer motivation and may serve to put people off from getting involved. Question marks over legal status provide added weight to the argument that organisations should not copy management systems in place for paid staff but should develop specific systems appropriate to the needs of volunteers, along the lines outlined in this publication.

Checklist 4: Training, Support and Supervision

☐ Ensure that all volunteers are given a basic introduction to the work of the agency and to their own volunteer task.

☐ Review the training needs of volunteers on a regular basis and develop a programme of delivering the training required.

☐ Ensure that a wide range of supportive mechanisms are in place for volunteers, ranging from individual supervision to mutually supportive volunteer groups.

☐ Set up procedures for dealing with any difficulties should they arise.

6. Retention

Keeping Volunteers Motivated

Recruitment is of obvious concern. But so too retention. The key to holding on to volunteers is keeping them motivated, and central to being able to do this is recognising that motivations may change over time. Paul Ilsley in *Enhancing the Volunteer Experience* offers the following list for keeping volunteers motivated:

- allow volunteers to participate in problem solving and significant decision making
- assign volunteers to tasks and roles that fit their individual needs and interests
- give volunteers work that offers opportunities for both personal development and meaningful service
- soon after volunteers join the organisation, work out explicit agreements that specify a feasible commitment of time and other resources and allow for personal variations in time, energy, and interest.
- provide on the job experiences that include constant opportunities both for reflective study and evaluation and for joint planning and design of organisational service goals and action.
- provide a job structure that allows for individual advancement through a series of steps that leads to higher levels of responsibility, skill and influence
- develop channels for supportive feedback from clients, co-workers, and managers or leaders and for recognition of volunteers by the organisation and the community
- encourage meaningful learning activities both inside and outside the organisation.

The Importance of Recognition

Central to keeping volunteers motivated is providing recognition of their achievements. The *1991 National Survey of Voluntary Activity* found that whilst the vast majority of volunteers felt they were doing a worthwhile job, a significant proportion (36%) felt that their efforts were not valued by the organisation. Clearly an organisation which appreciates its volunteers is likely to be one which holds on to its volunteers.

Recognition can take on a variety of forms – from the informal 'thank you' and occasional social occasion, to the more formal certificate of achievement or 'long-service' medal. Whatever form is chosen, McCurley and Lynch suggest that certain rules need to be followed. Recognition they say should be:

- honest
- given to the person, not to the work
- appropriate to the achievement
- consistent
- timely
- individualised as much as possible.

Exploring the Reasons for Leaving

No matter how successful an organisation is in motivating its volunteers and providing a climate conducive to a satisfying volunteering experience, there will be occasions when a volunteer decides to leave. This may have nothing to do with the failings of the organisation; in fact it may be a sign of success – the volunteer may have gone on to get paid employment. Or it may simply be due to changed individual circumstances – the volunteer may have moved home or job and be no longer available for voluntary work.

Whatever the reason it is important for the organisation to find out. It may be that the volunteer was unhappy with their experience and that they have some useful feedback to give to the organisation about how things could be improved in the future. To this end it is suggested that each volunteer should be invited to take part in a leaving interview or discussion, either with their manager or with some other relevant person within the organisation.

Checklist 5: Retention

☐ Pay attention to the importance of keeping volunteers motivated. Remember if they are not happy they will leave.

☐ Ensure that volunteers feel valued by the organisation and not taken for granted.

☐ Think about different ways of rewarding volunteers – a certificate of achievement or a volunteer party are examples.
☐ Talk to volunteers when they leave to find out if there are any improvements which can be made to the volunteering programme.

About the author

Dr. Justin Davis Smith is head of research at the National Centre for Volunteering. His publications include Volunteering and Society, NCVO Publications, 1992, and An Introduction to the Voluntary Sector, Routledge 1995.

TRUSTEES AND GOVERNANCE

11

Jenny Harrow

1. Introduction

Aims and objectives

The aims of this chapter are to describe and analyse the multi-faceted roles performed by charity trustees, to identify the opportunities and tensions experienced in those roles and to develop the view of the 'trustee as decision-maker' in the charity context.

Its objectives are to extend and enhance the user's knowledge of trustees' roles and responsibilities and to stimulate ideas about the demands accompanying those roles, through the presentation of a variety of 'live' issues and situations facing trustees.

The chapter identifies and expands on the nature of the role of trustees in charities and presents charity trustees' activities as focusing on a series of decisions:

- to come in to the charity's work
- to stay and learn about the charity
- to try to contribute effectively to the charity's work and guide its future.

It is expected that readers will have learned by means of this chapter:

- the nature of the role of trustees in charities
- the key elements associated with trustee decision-making
- the relevant questions for trustees to ask, as the basis of their decision-making
- the changing contexts in which charity trustees 'decide'
- the advantages and limitations of using 'checklist style' approaches, in assessing the nature of the trustee role
- through case studies, something of the range of opportunities and dilemmas facing trustees in the decision-making process in charities.

2. What is a Charity Trustee?

Charities in England and Wales are governed by trustees, who are unpaid volunteers responsible, individually and as a group, for their charity's activities, direction, and good name. They are required to control the charity and to ensure that the objectives for which the charity was formed are met, subject to a legal operating framework. They are, crucially, unable to benefit from their position.

The term 'trusteeship' implies integrity, stability, ability and willingness to act consistently in the best interests of the charity's recipients. The implications for the personal characteristics of trustees are daunting. Trustees seem to need to be:

- generous and resource-rich (in time and facilities, if not cash)
- able to interpret and act on the ideas of others
- capable of reaching judgements that can be looked at openly
- innovative on behalf of and committed to their charity.

As a special kind of volunteer, charity trustees hold their position individually but are normally required to work collectively in a trustee group. Being good at working with others – a skill which many of us take a lifetime to begin to learn – is yet another core requirement for the charity trustee.

Governance

Charity trustees are in charge in the sense of directing the charity's activities and deciding the fundamentals of its progress. This is increasingly called the system of governance in charities. This term means the structures which a charity uses for those directions and decisions to occur – committee systems, patterns of delegation, types of internal controls and so on. You may think that to talk about governance is to make a trustee role sound too grand, or that it implies elections (which may be the case in some charities) or that it suggests a more powerful image than the charitable reality. But it is helpful in conveying the real role of the trustees – to direct, to plan ahead, to energise – without taking on the small detail of the charity's work or its day to day operational managerial decisions.

In addition, a charity may seek a patron (often titled or royal, in Britain) to be a figurehead and act as the ultimate supporter of a charity. An alternative title is that of president. Presidents or patrons are not members of the board of trustees and have none of the responsibilities of trustees, even though their position in a charity's hierarchy seems to imply that they are the ultimate authority. Some patrons may be very passive in their involvement; others very pro-active.

Where trustees decide to seek a patron, it is worthwhile making an attempt to assess the pros and cons of such a designation. Some charities find that the time spent in liaison with their patron has a greater resource implication than the rewards provided by that patron. Since patrons are not answerable for the charity in the way trustees are, it is also possible they may be outspoken in public, in a way trustees would not wish and could not control. As with trustees, fixed term appointments of patrons may be desirable.

The role of trustees

Charity trustees are leaders, whose primary purpose is to develop and help deliver the charity's mission and purpose, taking the initiative to generate new ideas and sustain those which are tried and tested, and pro-actively develop the charity's strategy. In smaller charities, the strategic and operational issues are closely intertwined, however; and in larger charities, some trustees may be more inclined to become involved in the day to day activities of the charity, i.e. the operational concerns. Nevertheless, to borrow from the political world, 'charity trustees should be steering not rowing...'.

As the key players in the governance of charities, trustees face a raft of bodies and groups, which will require them to explain what they have done and will be doing in various ways. The stakeholders with an interest in trustee behaviour and performance include:

- the Charity Commission
- donors
- other volunteers
- fellow trustees
- founders
- paid staff
- local / national media
- funders – trusts, public bodies
- other charities
- beneficiaries
- the general public.

The trustee as 'saint'.....

Facing multiple stakeholders, bringing in a range of personal abilities and interpersonal skills, and motivated by ideas of gain for others, seems to suggest that the ideal charity trustee is a saint. Many of the attempts to set out what charity trustees should be, which prescribe rather than describe, present an aura of saintliness about this role, implying that trustees should have minimal personal egos.

This approach is not entirely helpful. It is important to be realistic about what can be offered and achieved by charity trustees; and not to work towards such a model of trusteeship that few can aspire to.

It is worth considering whether, in order to lead and inspire charities, some trustees need to be less than 'comfortable' people. Some may even be – and need to be – 'difficult'.

Some questions for reflection

- What has been your image of the 'typical' charity trustee?
- To whom do you think trustees should be primarily accountable – the wider public interest, the charity's users, the charity's funders, the publicly-established charity regulators?
- How important do you consider 'staying power' among trustees to be?
- If you know people who are charity trustees, what do they think about their role – is it onerous, fulfilling, exasperating?

3. Charity Trusteeship as a Series of Decisions

As individuals, trustees decide:

- to come in to the charity's work
- to stay and learn about the charity
- to try to contribute effectively to the charity's work and guide its future (including the decision to leave the charity; or take on other trusteeships).

Even though these decisions take place in the collective environment (i.e. with other trustees) they must be made individually, with caution, realism and reflection, as well as with enthusiasm and energy. Charity trustees are also learning individuals: they may be fast or slow learners, retentive or forgetful, open about learning needs or closed to learning 'new tricks'. Whatever their learning profile, there has to be a case for their 'growing into' a trustee role; although both trustee and charity may be impatient about the time this takes. The learning involved is likely to be lifelong.

Thinking about charity trusteeship as a series of decisions may also help to put the role in perspective. A major paradox of charity trusteeship is that many charities see their trustees as a major organisational resource with a high commitment level, just at the time when many trustees need to put increased effort into sustaining their paid careers and/or responding to the needs of families and friends.

The decision to come in to the charity's work

Although the increasing external emphasis on trusteeship concerns liability, few potential trustees tend to ask the direct question "what are my liabilities?" Some would see this as churlish since it is, after all, for charity. A tiny minority of trustees will be founding trustees – those who have worked hard to gain charitable status for their organisation – but the majority of trustees seem to be those who have been invited to take on the role.

The invitation

If you are receiving – or making – the invitation, the following questions and some of the possible answers are critical:

Why have I been asked?
- to fulfil an identifiable role (e.g. raise profile, handle money)
- to be polite/friendly/flattering ("you're such a kind person, you were the obvious choice...")
- to represent an important but otherwise detached organisation with which we're connected ("it just happened to be you...")
- to bring in 'new ideas', 'new blood' (high expectations, though uncertain how all this will be achieved)
- to provide status and / or money (a local or national 'notable')
- and/or you're available... (living locally, between jobs, retired, finished a stint on something else...)
- and/or you are a good friend/ professional ally of the committee chair, treasurer or senior staff member...

Any combination of these answers, or unconnected others, may explain the invitation – if in fact it has ever been thought through in this way. There are no wholly 'right' and 'wrong' reasons. Even the most sloppy rationale sometimes produces excellent trustees. However, getting a picture of the reality behind the invitation is important, as the base for these initial and subsequent decisions.

Is there a better way for inviting potential trustees? As an invitee or inviter, you may want to reflect on whether:
- an informal or formal invitation is preferable
- a brief profile of the charity is provided or the invitee is left to reach their own picture of what goes on
- a specific brief has been drawn up, for which the invitee is particularly fitted – i.e. a charity trustee job description.

If the answer to the third point is 'yes', this may be done systematically and in line with personnel practice in large organisations – but with the accompanying warning. If you devise a 'person specification' and go further, adding the equivalent of a 'job description', you need to know also what to do when:

- the person 'spec' cannot be fitted – partially or fully
- the invitee cheerfully accepts the invitation and turns out not to have the expected skills and qualities
- the specification is more than well-filled but the role turns out not to be one that the charity needed.

The mere existence of a job description for a trustee – as with many of those relating to paid work – is no guarantee either that what is sought will be delivered, or that the organisation knows and understands what it wants and needs.

There are a growing number of advocates of such job descriptions for trustees. Some include additional advice, such as do not draw these up in isolation from the existing trustees, do take account of the critical dimension of the relations between trustees and paid staff (if any) and ensure that the job description does not overlap with but complements the work of the charity's senior managers. To this, we would add the importance of injecting a note of realism. Charity trustees should not be expected to be – and should not cast themselves in – the role of Wonderwoman or Superman. They are properly non executives, and their roles, if set out in detail, should reflect this.

Advertising for trustees

The invitation may, more rarely, have been an open invitation – that is, the charity has advertised for trustees, or approached a charity appointments company which offers the equivalent to executive search. This is a small but growing practice. Would-be trustees must decide for themselves what such an advertisement signifies. There are contrasting views about this practice. In advertising for trustees, is the charity unable to attract trustees in the normal way, ready to take anyone, or possibly an organisation with waning support or other major problems? Or is it very open and clear about what it wants, with a structured approach to meeting its specific needs and with major future opportunities?

It is reasonable to suppose that most charities' positions lie well towards the positive end of the spectrum. The advertisements will tend to set out the particular and special attributes of a charity, as its 'unique selling point'. Whether or not it is planned to use such overt recruitment methods, existing trustees may also benefit from drawing up their own real job descriptions and reaching a shared view of what is and what is not needed on the trustee group

Cynicism versus enjoyment

Going through such an exercise may produce evidence among trustees of forward thinking and planning, excitement and recognition of potential new directions or complacency, or perhaps disappointment, frustration and anxiety. It would be strange not to encounter a degree of cynicism among the members of any organisation as to its running and its abilities. That cynicism may be of value as a means of checking a tendency towards an inflated organisational ego. Charities are as prey to this as other organisations; perhaps more so, given the unique value of much of their work. However, too much cynicism, however measured, may damage trustees' working relations and check the enthusiasm of newcomers.

As a trustee, there is also the possibility of actually enjoying what you are doing. None of the growing number of valuable guides to acting as a charity trustee have so far been entitled 'enjoying charity trusteeship'. This is a pity, and the emphasis on trustee liability in particular seems to preclude this. But this may be missing a vital ingredient.

Charity trusteeship ought not be presented as a penance, but as enjoyable. Trustees cannot benefit materially from their role. What they can (and should) have is a 'moral income' from their work – enjoyment, derived from valued and valuable work. To enjoy their role, trustees need to have an innate sympathy for or interest in the core field of the charity they have chosen – or which has chosen them, a capacity for working jointly with others and the time available to meet the charity's needs.

Judging the time demands of trusteeship for any one charity is complex and dependent in part on individual trustees' background knowledge, existing abilities and skills, personality traits and working preferences. 'Guesstimates' may need to be made among existing trustees – some of whom may downplay (or inflate) their time-commitment – and trustees should be encouraged to add their own hours of contribution to those of other volunteers and helpers, as part of the moral income which the charity receives.

Some questions for reflection

- How do you respond to any request to undertake voluntary work?
- Should being a trustee be thought of as just another kind of volunteering, or is it something special?
- What impression do you get of charities which advertise for trustees?
- What personal qualities would you rank as the most important for charity trustee work?

The decision to stay and learn about the charity

Once a trustee, what sustains the initial interest, what questions are helpful to ask, and what kinds of answers are being sought by trustees? As with many other individual decisions, some will have a quick response, others will suspend judgement for far longer. The organisational culture of the charity (i.e. 'how we do things around here'), will help determine how incoming trustees are handled.

Meetings

The characteristic trustee activity is in formal meetings — committee or board meetings, accompanied by papers, agendas, and minutes, and thus the incomer's first questions will tend to be "who are all these people? what is going on? who is going to explain things to me and when?".

The case is increasingly made for an induction process for new trustees. This follows logically from the development of trustee job descriptions, but requires decision-making from within the charity as to what this includes. It may range from a formal induction pack to a social meeting among trustees, to introduce the incomer before the work starts. A full approach would include:

- an information pack giving the background to the charity's core activities and aims, as recorded by the charity (reports, financial statements, as set against its statement of objectives)
- some documentary material or commentary showing 'how others see us'. In larger charities this is more easily done, for example through press reports on and attitudes to its work; but many smaller charities will have the equivalent (e.g. correspondence from donors, recipients or related charities) which provide a view of its external profile
- a formal organisational chart showing the decision-making structures of the charity, its committee(s), membership and working lines between trustees and paid staff. The organisational

'picture' is one of the best means of assessing the nature of organisational culture in any given setting. In small charities, where structures are minimal or lacking (e.g. no paid staff) this needs also to be set out.

• an identification of the two or three major policy decisions which have affected the charity over the past two years.

This last aspect is clearly subjective and differences of opinion, among trustees or between trustees and staff, may themselves be revealing. Examples may range from large issues such as a merger proposal, to the apparently small, such as whether to prosecute disadvantaged individuals who have made false claims on the charity's resources. Where no questions have come to the fore, the incoming trustee might question the extent to which this shows welcome stability or a dogmatic view of what is happening in the charity.

Observe and absorb

What is important is that such an induction process should offer the incoming trustee the chance to ask for clarification. It has been known for existing trustees to use a new trustee's lack of knowledge to better inform themselves!

The newcomer should therefore observe and absorb what is going on. Part of that observation needs to be focused around the ways in which the charity's trustees work as a group; since it is as a group, rather than as individuals that trustees' behaviour is judged. No single trustee has more authority than another; although human nature suggests that the key postholders – chair, treasurer, etc. – are deferred to. But all trustees need to know that their individual views have a right to be heard, although their decision-making is collective.

The questioning trustee may sound ideal for helping charities review their work, but for existing trustees, a newcomer may be seen as unsettling, destabilising, or worse, as a threat to their work. As a rule of thumb, any early invitation (e.g. to join the finance committee) should be avoided until some of that 'observation' and 'absorption' has taken place.

In particular, much of the emphasis on learning for the new trustee is about 'internal' knowledge – what is happening as the charity sees it. It is then possible to neglect the external dimension – how the charity is seen in its external environment. This monitoring of the charity's external standing is an important role for all trustees and gains an extra dimension when a new trustee joins.

Trustee competence

Incoming trustees' self-perceptions range across a competence spectrum. At one end, there may be those trustees who are concerned that they cannot do their job; whilst at the other end, there may be those trustees who feel that they already know everything they need to know.

A trustee's location on that spectrum may vary from meeting to meeting. Encouraging a sense of detachment may help. In fact, all trustees may find it helpful, from time to time, to step back and observe their working processes. But the trustee-as-observer is not intended to remain the trustee-as-spectator; the observer must become a participant!

Shifting between uncertainty and certainty may be stressful in performing any role, and particularly when this role is to be acted out on behalf of others. Accepting the likelihood of 'trustee stress' may also be important – on the one hand, not feeling intimidated into taking things on and on the other hand, not feeling guilty because there are areas which remain unclear. A matrix of trustee perceptions, in relation to degree of involvement and contentment with their role and function may be depicted as follows:

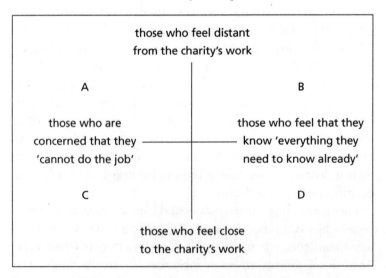

Trustees in this matrix could be described generally as:

A types: may find little reward in their role but may not express their feelings and stay on, loyally

B types: may tend to see themselves as 'specialists', called in from time to time, yet they are still full members of the trustee group

C types: may compensate for their uncertainties by involvement in grass roots day-to-day issues

D types: may run the risk of freezing others out, deliberately or
            not.

This may also be useful where two trustees are willing to 'pair'
and to locate each other – honestly – on the matrix. A trustee's
own perceptions may well contrast with those of fellow trustees.

'Mixing competencies' – a balanced trustee group

Much advisory literature on charity best practice stresses the
importance of having a 'balanced' group of trustees, that is, a
well-assorted mix of skills, abilities and backgrounds to give a
pluralist perspective on the charity's work and direction. This
sounds an obviously good idea – but precisely what that mix
should be for each charity, and how to achieve it, is much more
problematic. Always thinking that there could be a better group
of trustees round the corner could stimulate a trustee group into
a lively search for new blood – or it could simply be another
element in the over-idealism discussed earlier, as well as being
unnecessarily critical of those who do stay on as trustees. It is
also possible, though, that many groups work better when they
are of a like mind – that is a fairly coherent group, with a shared
identity.

An incoming trustee should be able to ask – or soon discover –
whether he/she has been invited to: supplement and further
support the existing skills and knowledge of the trustee group;
complement those skills, by bringing in new area(s) of expertise;
or to counterbalance the existing ideas and approaches of the
other trustees.

If a trustee is being brought in to challenge prevailing views, or
to be a (necessarily) disruptive influence, what counts as being
'competent' will be very different to those situations where a trustee
is joining kindred spirits. As a like-minded trustee, areas of
competence are likely to include a combination of practical
understandings and personal qualities – for example:
- knowledge of key areas relating to the charity's situation – e.g.
  fundraising, public relations, investment management
- ability to work co-operatively whilst thinking independently
- skills of leadership (local/national), and creativity.

In a more counterbalancing role, those competencies may include:
- knowledge of what 'the competition' is doing, identifying areas
  not yet taken on board, e.g. internal audit practices

- ability to challenge working practices or systems authoritatively, but also
- skills of leadership and creativity.

Some questions for reflection

- What would be your attitude towards being offered 'trustee training'?
- How would you assess your existing skills when working co-operatively in a busy group, with other busy people? How might these be adapted or strengthened in a trustee capacity?
- What is likely to be the impact on a charity of a trustee's adopting a standback attitude towards its work or alternatively becoming closely involved on almost every issue?
- How useful might job descriptions be for charity trustees, when they are often not that useful in the world of paid work?

The decision to try to contribute effectively

It is an irony of the charity world that a trustee who is taking on too much, and giving too much attention to detail, can be ineffective in their governance role. Yet identifying or even checking such over-commitment is itself complex, given that the role is voluntary.

No-one can stop a trustee from delving as deeply as they wish into a charity's work, asking a myriad questions and participating in all aspects of its organisational life. Other volunteers and some charity staff may also welcome this. Deciding what counts as 'effective trusteeship' is therefore not easy. There are no legally set performance indicators for measuring the contributions of trustees, individually or collectively. As governors in the beneficiaries' and the public's interests, trustees must oversee:

- *the charity's inputs* – the resources of various forms which it commits to its work
- *the charity's processes* – through which its activities and commitments occur
- *the charity's outputs* – the end results of those activities and commitments for a variety of stakeholders
- *the outcomes of the charity's work* – the ways in which, and the extent to which these meet the objectives for which the charity has been established and the goals which it has set.

Self-assessment

Any self-assessment by a trustee as to their effectiveness should begin with a re-assessment of their range of motivations for joining. What did they intend to accomplish and what style of involvement did they plan to offer and feel would be best used?

This is not to argue that new trustees might have in mind some kind of personal 'first hundred days', for the accomplishment of aims, or the introduction of ideas. The identification of a fixed point, fairly early on in a new trustee's career, for a review may help to avoid 'new trustee drift'. Once that 'first review' is conducted, a more regular reflection could usefully concentrate on a review of the extent to which trustees:

- deliver the charity's integrity – its promises, the openness with which it conducts its business, its managerial and employment practices
- ensure the charity's efficiency – knowing its resources and monitoring their use, to achieve given ends
- participate in the development of the charity's strategy to best progress its aims.

An alternative approach is for trustees – new to or familiar with the charity – to ask regularly a single. core, question – but to be prepared to reflect as honestly as possible over the answer, and to record those answers over time. The single question is *"what are the things which we have to do well?"*.

To avoid an unrealistic response (i.e. 'everything'), a charity may find that over time, different concerns come to the fore, for example: sustaining a reputation as a good employer, recruiting a different membership/supporter group, or reinterpreting a role for changing times (most commonly associated with charity name changes).

As an important variant on this, trustees may also find it useful to ask, "what have we done well?"

Gaining and reflecting on answers to this question may not only provide learning points for the future, but enable trustees to give proper credit for what has been achieved and to understand how this was done. Giving praise as an activity is often omitted from formal analyses of trustees' roles; and it is possible that the concentration on 'onwards and upwards' improvement in charities will omit this important aspect. Although this should not be confused with trustees' being self-congratulatory or complacent, it nevertheless has an important place – for the trustees themselves, as well as for the charity's staff, donors and recipients.

The trustee as strategist

To accept a governance role is to accept responsibility for the charity's overall purposes, its developing vision for the expression of those purposes, and the planning processes which are adopted for reaching these desired ends. Although many larger charities employ senior managers to promote and enhance this longer-term perspective, it is still the trustees' responsibility to further strategic activity.

There is no model template for trustee/staff relations. Ideas about partnership sound attractive but are hard to pin down. It is the trustees' responsibility to identify those areas in which they have primacy in decision-making. In exploring trustee/manager relations in any charity, central questions for the trustee – and senior manager(s) – include:

- how is 'planning' understood in this charity and is it a valued activity?
- who plans strategy in this charity, for what purposes and why? what resources are given to this activity?
- what are the charity's working strategic planning documents, and what is their status and impact?
- who evaluates strategy making and results in the charity, against what criteria and with what results?

The easy answer – that trustees and managers divide, respectively, into strategists and operational activists – is not easy at all. The case that managers are primarily concerned with operational issues can become complex, especially in small charities where the strategy/operations divide seems minimal. Further, many trustees learn best from operational involvement.

It can be very revealing for the charity's staff and trustees to undertake the same exercise separately and jointly, by asking what counts as 'strategy' and what counts as 'operations' in this charity. The results may prompt the need for clarification of roles. This may be critical, where for example, the job/role descriptions of trustees have been developed in isolation from those of senior managers.

Allowing for the problems of interpreting what is meant by 'weak' and 'strong' trustees and managers, a matrix showing the weak-strong continuum for both looks like this:

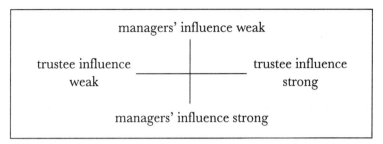

Locating yourself as a charity trustee or as a charity manager at some point within the quadrants of this matrix may be a useful exercise for personal reflection but not necessarily one done in the open and shared – at least not initially.

The position on the matrix for any given charity may vary from issue to issue. The conclusions to be drawn by using this matrix as a basis for thinking about the charity will need careful interpretation. Charities where both trustees and managers are relatively 'weak' (though perhaps apparently secure in their resource base or sphere of work) may be more common than we think, given the tendency to claim dynamism, energy and innovation as hallmarks of the charity world. However, it is also likely that many charities will exhibit signs of both trustees and managers being 'strong'. To operate in the charity sector – whether for moral or other reward, or both – is demanding. Stories of charity success (by volunteer or paid leaders) tend to focus on people who are energetic, demanding, innovative, challenging and therefore ultimately, quite likely to be 'difficult' people.

A working relationship

Where trustees and charity managers have what they understand to be a good working relationship, this may not necessarily be easy to define. 'Partnership', for example, which sounds so attractive, can be very uncertain. Ultimately, it is the charity trustees who have to be satisfied with their managers' performance – and not vice versa – and the size of the charity as well as the nature of its work will be a key factor here. It may be especially important for the relations between staff and trustees not to be characterised by only one working relationship, i.e. that between the trustees' chair and the chief executive. Although this is clearly a key combination, it is vital for all trustees to have a channel of communication with staff. If much of the major decision-making is done primarily by a few people, that process should be kept formally under review

Training for trustees?

The 'effectiveness' of the trustees will be affected by external factors over which they have little control – e.g. changes in regulations, charitable 'scandals' which impact upon them regardless of their involvement, and the rise of new charitable competitors. It is often these factors which open up a knowledge gap for trustees, between what they know and what they ought to know. Further, for trustees to be able to act effectively, existing skills and knowledge may need support, further definition, or even replacement, implying the need for charities to develop or at least reflect on a training strategy. An obvious area for injecting a training approach might be that which focused on relations between trustees and managers. Another might be a course on 'working with difficult people'.

Should charities therefore automatically provide training for trustees – in the sense of the provision of deliberately structured experiences to enable learning to take place? Good practice in larger charities seems to incorporate training in set areas (e.g. financial management, investment appraisal, conduct of meetings) as a matter of course, but ironically these may be the very charities where many trustees are already trained – in the sense that they come with pre-existing skills in such key areas. Nor should we assume that in smaller charities, the training need is greatest. It may be far easier to disguise in larger charities, where a few especially able trustees dominate the rest.

Training is designed to be a process whereby people develop; and it may be that to talk about trustee development rather than training is preferable. The following points need to be borne in mind by the individual trustee:

- *don't* ask for training in a blanket fashion – this could turn into a never-ending activity
- *don't* ask for training unless you are prepared to accept the demands which it places on you
- *do* ask for training which contributes to group as well as individual trustee performance
- *do* ask for training that has clear price tags attached (whether for the charity or for the individual – cost, time foregone and so on)
- *do* ask for training that mirrors the priorities of the charity
- *do* ask for training which has an inbuilt evaluation process, in which you can have a say on its relevance and efficacy.

Training – of trustees and/or charity staffs – is not a goal in its own right (even if it becomes a learned skill that you can then take elsewhere). It is an activity aimed at leading to better quality decision-making. All cases for training should be measured against what it can to do to enhance the chances of that taking place.

The trustee as donor?

One element of measuring the effectiveness of a charity is the extent to which it is receiving sustained financial support. Although many hard-up charities may be most effective in their work, the practical interest which charities can command and retain, can be seen, however crudely, as an effectiveness measure. This is the near-equivalent to the financial 'bottom line' in private firms.

So what should be a trustee's giving role? The reticence in British charities' literature about this is not found in America, where trustees may be sought whose personal qualifications include 'affluence'. Thus some may be expected to give as part of their trustee commitment. A trustee therefore needs to ask:
• am I expected to donate and if so how much, and how?
• if not, why not? If I do not give, why should others?
• is this charity working on a 'donor substitute' model, i.e. my time/expertise as a money alternative?

Trustees are entitled to seek clarification from the charity on their practice of paying trustees' expenses. Many charity trustees will not be and have never been in a position to donate on a considerable scale; and others may find their personal circumstances changing during trusteeship. Although not entitled to be paid for their trustee 'work', reimbursement of trustees' expenses is allowable; and it is important that the process by which this is done is made very clear to any newcomer. Thus, any new trustee on a constrained budget should be able to understand the charity's approach in an open fashion. It is not sufficient for such a trustee to be told not to worry only to find that no system is in place for dealing with expenses, or that she or he is routinely the only member of a trustee board claiming expenses, and is thus made to feel uncomfortable.

The decision to leave the charity; or take on other trusteeships

Where charities have a rolling programme of trustee entry and departure (i.e. time limited trusteeships), this may not be a matter of individual choice. An incoming trustee may be more willing to serve:
• if the commitment has a 'sell by' date

- if fellow trustee composition will gradually change over time
- if the forward planning approach which this pattern offers is likely to be mirrored elsewhere in the organisation.

However, rotating trusteeships may create problems, including:
- organisational 'subterfuge' to keep 'the best' on
- a very limited screening of incomers, because they won't be around that long
- a real organisational learning loss, unless learning transfers can be accomplished, when the excellent trustees complete their term of office.
- a less-than-involved performance by those trustees coming to the end of their involvement.

The trustee who resigns – whether 'before time' or as a non-time limited trustee – will need to advise the charity formally in writing, and seek confirmation of its receipt, if appropriate, from the Charity Commissioners, when an annual report is next due. Job/role descriptions for trustees may clarify an individual's personal decision to resign; they also provide a firm basis for a resignation request from the trustees as whole to one of their number. In whatever circumstance resignation occurs, an exit interview, conducted by a fellow trustee, and reported back, may have organisational learning potential; as well as being a cathartic experience for the outgoing trustee.

Taking on other trusteeships may reflect an individual's change of interest, greater availability, or greater 'marketability' as a trustee. But in the increasingly complex charity world, where competition (for example for public service contracts) is a growing experience, trustees may need to consider whether they are facing conflicts of interest if they take on several trusteeships.

In considering trustee departure, as well as joining a charity, this discussion has assumed that trustees will be prepared to ask questions; and that they will follow up the answers they receive. It is also possible that trustees will choose not to do this. In situations where charities are in difficulties, and where charity trustees are not prepared (or not able) to exert their authority over a charity's affairs, they may be required to step down. A recent Charity Commission annual report (1995) describes such a situation, where a receiver and a new manager were appointed by the Commission, and an entirely new group of trustees subsequently brought in. This development is rare, but highlights the point that trustees may not avoid their responsibilities indefinitely.

Asking questions and the use of 'checklists'

This section has encouraged trustees to query, question and continually probe within their charities – because in the last resort it is the trustees who say 'yes' or 'no' to ideas, schemes and plans. No participant in governance can be secure by saying "I didn't know".

Even so, trustees may recognise the need to be wary of 'over-asking' – especially where to do so may seem unkind, adversarial or even hyper-critical in an organisation where, against the odds, staff and trustees have been doing their best. Framing the questions correctly and offering help, given the personalities and context, is a matter of skill and judgement which no checklist can ensure.

Again, waiting for the answers – which may not be immediate – is also important. Where the quality of the answer leaves the trustee in continuing doubt, the case may be made for a range of alternative next steps, including:

- independent review (e.g. by consultants),
- internal review (for example through internal audit procedures)
- external professional advice (always important for trustees to take – and to be seen to be doing so),
- informal comparisons with other charities (through personal contacts, networking)
- formal comparisons which other charities, developing into a benchmarking process.

The judgements which trustees then have to make, individually and jointly, become critical and are not amenable to checklist style thinking.

Checklists in many spheres help to demystify and even popularise tasks, increase basic knowledge quickly by suggesting the boundaries and coverage of a particular topic, and add to our thinking capacities, once the inevitable gaps have been spotted. Their use – unchecked – may create problems of providing false senses of security and a belief that the users are in effect, in control.

Charity trusteeship is inherently an insecure, albeit rewarding, exhilarating, and demanding form of voluntary service. Charities by their nature may contain both pockets of innovation and pockets of inertia; both evidence of sophisticated strategy development and lucky muddling through. Charity trustees' performance in that demanding role has to be a voluntary one; one in which they necessarily receive authority to govern their charity, take responsibility for their decision-making which is the hallmark and rationale of government and accept external and internal accountabilities for those decisions.

5. Working with Trustees – Case Studies

1. The decision to come in to the charity's work

A group of trustees run an exercise among themselves to write an advertisement for a new trustee, before deciding whether to go ahead with this approach. They have no facilitator to help them, and are self-directed. "Just say what you really think" is the only direct advice which is given by the chair. Descriptions, without author's names attached, are written on flip-charts and posted up; the trustees walk around, looking at them. The majority are a mixture of the bland, the positive and the self congratulatory. – ("we aim to help children in all walks of life.... we know we can change people's lives.... this big-hearted charity...."). One stands out:

"Wanted: a volunteer committee member, ready to behave as if they are being paid the earth; totally flexible lifestyle to allow for unsystematic and overly-demanding call on time; patience to stand fools gladly; creative – but willing to hand over good ideas to less competent others who will take the credit; professional – but always ready to defer to others less knowledgeable but more 'keen'. You need to be: calm and reflective – to help survive in and make sense of the operating style which staff thrive on; have direct knowledge of key planning areas – financial, personnel, legal, – but deployed sensitively so as not to draw attention to the knowledge/skills deficit elsewhere in the charity; have excellent networking skills and organisational contacts – to get friends to fork out regularly or do something for nothing."

The charity's chair – who has not written the 'advertisement' – now has to cope with this.

- Does the chair close the meeting with general thanks and a promise to come back "when we have digested this"?
- What effects might the rogue advertisement have on other trustees?
- Was this a cry for help, a tongue-in-cheek opportunity to complain and get it over with, a fundamental source of evidence that much is seriously wrong, or a wind-up?

- Should the trustee in question be expected to resign, encouraged to resign, or asked to resign; or offered a platform for putting things right or achieving 'turnaround' (i.e. more work!)?
- What should be the stances of key trustees?
- Can and should this be shared with salaried staff? Is it too late to call in a facilitator – or even mediator? How can best use be made of this outpouring and whose responsibility is it to set this going?

2. The decision to stay and learn about the charity

A reputable and 'traditional' philanthropic type of charity is growing in awareness of the extent to which it is facing competition from donors and falling income, just at the point at which the demands for its help are reaching unmanageable proportions. It is well known throughout the sector, and its name appears in all the handbooks and guides to grant-making bodies and used by social workers and other advice workers. It has a good reputation for responding quickly to requests for help and generally has a good relationship with public service organisations. Its relations with some fellow charities are on occasion rather less cordial, when those charities seek its specialist knowledge and publish that information in their newsletters as reflecting their own expertise.

Amongst the small trustee group, the majority have a strong collective memory about the founding of the charity by an independent-minded and high achieving individual. "What the founder would have wanted" is a regular point for reviewing the charity's work. This secures the charity's continuing independence rather than closer working (or exploration of merger options) with other charities; and encourages trustees to give the same degree of effort to their work as did the founder.

To enhance the internal professionalism of the charity, a full time director is recruited, with an extensive and well-known reputation for practitioner skills in the relevant field. This director comes from the sphere which makes regular use of the charity; and thus is also aware of its external image. After several years of enthusiastic and competent handling of the growth in demand for the charity's help, the director is becoming convinced that the charity should change its name – and the helpful but inevitably rather patronising picture of its work which goes with it. This view is listened to with interest by the trustees, who do not regard a name change as a useful development but rather a distraction from the current work. However, the director's previously successful work in getting media appeal slots seems to be beginning to wane; and after a particular disappointment and refusal from a TV programme, the question of the name change is now back on the agenda. Although the newer trustees accept and back the case for change, the majority are still unconvinced; arguing that their best donors "know who we are and understand our work". Discussion is amicable, perhaps to the point of hiding the feelings of those proponents of change.

- What are the advantages and disadvantages of trustees' harking back to and revering the strong views of the founder (as they recall/interpret them)?
- How might the charity's director now progress this area further (e.g. develop/commission other logos/possible titles for the trustees to see)? Should this 'second review' be the end of the matter?
- Are there other levers that can be used; and how should the 'pro' trustees use them?
- What can be learned from the decisions and experiences of those charities 'rebadging' to become more modern and to better explain their role?

3. The decision to contribute effectively to the charity's work

A charity providing social, community and financial support for women from ethnic minorities who experience host language difficulties but who wish to develop their employment potential is becoming well-known locally. Following its undoubted success in attracting funding from a private European grant-making body, it becomes the local Mayor's 'designated charity' for a year. Its trustees are predominantly women (including those speaking for minority women's needs and aspirations), with a sprinkling of representatives who are nominated councillors.

The trustees have so far managed the charity themselves without full time paid help – the 'Euro-coup' was the brainchild of a high flying trustee with appropriate contacts who was between assignments as a management consultant, and has now left the area and the charity. The part-time appointment of a manager is made and greatly welcomed by the trustees. The position of the Mayor's designated charity is set to bring in further funding; and the publicity which this produces creates in turn, further requests for the charity to set up new support groups in the area.

Considerable proceeds from civic functions begin to come in and the trustees and their part-time manager face increasingly complex decisions regarding their financial affairs. In the short term, given the energy and popularity of the mayor, they may even end the year with some reserves. New funding sources are also being explored, including those within the European Community; and an increase in the complexity of the organisation seems clear. The Mayor takes – not surprisingly – a close interest in progress; and strongly advises the trustees to "get some finance training very fast". It turns out that the Mayor has been lobbied in this by councillors who attend meetings intermittently, and who are concerned about what they see as a lack of financial expertise. When the Mayor's office produces the offer of some free finance training under the auspices of a large locally-based company, for both the trustees and the part time organiser, it is an offer which seems too good to refuse. It is also virtually impossible to decline.

The short training programme is a near disaster. Six evening sessions are presented by staff members of the firm who change every week, patronise the trustees and their paid staff member, convey the complexity of such items as cost and profit centres, financial budgeting and so on, in such detail and at such a pace that the trainees are soon lost. The tutors are unable to take into account different learning needs and paces in their small group. Although professional staff, they are themselves volunteers and seem to mean well. No evaluation – formal or informal – is set up. The trustee chair is therefore at a loss for words when she next sees the Mayor, who exclaims "well, now you're trained, you must feel so much more confident".

- Where should financial training figure as a training priority for trustees?
- Is self training an option?
- Should trustees and staff be trained together?
- When and how should generous offers of training help be accepted and refused?

Comment

Each of these case studies emphasises the alternative directions in which trustees are able to go and the multiple choices which face them. To suggest that there is no completely right answer is reasonable, given that some of the contextual detail is lacking but each of these, with the inevitability of hindsight, indicate some general learning points. These include:

Case study 1

- the questions which arise about the real objectives of the exercise; and the reasons why the trustees were to be on their own for the exercise.

- bringing in a facilitator/expert may sometimes send the wrong signals – that conflict is expected, that trustees "are not to be trusted" – and can be costly. Nor would it necessarily defuse this situation. In the absence of such an expert, the chair is in charge.

- greater time spent introducing the rationale for the exercise – and flagging up that it may or may not work – would help accommodate both this hyper-critical response and the positive and cheerful ones, which may be in danger of being neglected.

- many organisations tend to look for the bad news first – is this really 'bad'?

- a communications issue has arisen here – but can the unthinkable be thought? Why not advertise like this in modified form – a new form of realism? (which has been used in some public service job advertising).

Case study 2

- historical roots of charities do matter – but how to celebrate these to gain greater achievements is a complex question.

- reliance on collective memory can be risky and unproductive; but the chances are that the really dynamic (i.e. difficult) charity founders would be likely to challenge any interpretations of their views!

- changing names of 'products' – or relaunching existing brands in new colours or with new designs – can send mixed messages in any organisational world, charity, public or private. The trustees are entitled to be cautious if they see that their constituencies for funds would be put off by such change; but they are in danger of complacency unless they have tested this to be the case.

- a fuller scale external environmental review of the charity's position (of which a name change may be a core but not only part) is called for.

- learning from another organisation's experiences is always a sound idea in principle but difficult to achieve in practice – especially when these types of experiences may be painful, the results uncertain and the charity doing it is under pressure – don't rely on being given too many insider learning points for nothing.

Case study 3

- charities experiencing a sudden influx of funds and thus growth may expect some sort of time lag between their financial planning sophistication and their financial state. They may need to choose an approach to handle this which will conform with their major donors' demands. A professional appointment, to advise trustees, is ideal – as long as the advice is tailored to the trustees' objectives. Training the trustees is an admirable goal but is unlikely to be effective quickly – even if the training content itself is appropriate.
- any debates about trustee training need to take into account the trustee profile that is being sought – frightening away would be trustees because they lack expertise can be counterproductive – but training that is too complex, or, perhaps worse, too basic, can lead to further trustee disenchantment.
- training – what it is designed to do, not only now but in the future – needs to be a focus of discussion and agreement; and any training opportunity requires built in evaluation which is communicated to the relevant audiences and acted upon.
- a charity of any size may experience instances of misplaced generosity; and will need to assess the effects; charities do not have to be endlessly thankful and they are entitled to say what they do not want as well as what they do. In this case, joint ownership of the training offered ("so that we can sit down together and see where we have got") would have been ideal but seems to have been difficult to achieve.

Keeping contacts with the firm and the results will have to be set against the impact on trustees who may have experienced difficulties. Explaining the problem to the Mayor may help – but perhaps after the funds have rolled in? A more complex alternative is to 'enrol' a concerned councillor' trustee as training adviser; in which case the agendas of all parties need to be clear.

6. Glossary

benchmarking	the activity of making comparisons with any aspect of an organisation's' approach, practice and outcomes with those equivalent in an organisation, or organisations, held to be leaders in the sector.
charity trustee	any member of a management committee, charity board, or council member, who voluntarily accepts unpaid responsibility for

planning, directing and guiding a charity's work; and who is answerable within a public regulatory framework for the performance of those responsibilities.

governance
the system or patterns of decision-making and control within a charity, through which a charity's activities are planned, promoted, delivered and audited

internal audit
mechanisms for regular and systematic understanding and assessment of organisation efficiency and probity, operating independently within the organisation and reporting to key decision-makers

patron
(optional) figurehead of the charity, lending their personal characteristics to the charity's work – their high profile, valuable contacts and/or social standing; their respected expertise; not a charity trustee and varying in degree of association and practical impact.

About the author

Dr. Jenny Harrow is director of the Doctoral Programme at South Bank University's Business School and head of the Centre for Public Services Management. Her research interests include managing risk and performance management in the public and voluntary sectors. Dr. Harrow is co-author with Dr. Paul Palmer of *Rethinking Charities Trusteeship*, published by ICSA in 1994.

ACCOUNTABILITY & USER INVOLVEMENT 12

Paul Robson & Michael Locke

1. Introduction

Aims and Objectives

This chapter will explore accountability and user involvement in voluntary organisations. The aim of the text, exercises and case studies is to help the reader:

- understand that there are different forms and dimensions of accountability
- assess the accountability of an individual or organisation by asking: accountable to whom? for what? why? and how?
- know that voluntary organisations have multiple lines of accountability
- use a stakeholder analysis to inform decisions about how to manage their own particular accountabilities.

This chapter should also help the reader recognise that:

- service users are key stakeholders in voluntary organisations
- the involvement of service users in different levels of decision making varies from organisation to organisation, and there are external pressures to increase this involvement
- analyses of stakeholders and accountabilities can show the relationship between users and an organisation and the extent to which it involves them in decision making
- user involvement initiatives and structures can be categorised as either consumerist or democratic
- an analysis of the relationship between values, purposes, ownership and control of an organisation can assist in understanding the causes of conflict and the difficulty of increasing user involvement
- organisations taking steps to increase user involvement in the overall control of the organisation exhibit certain features
- the democratic approach requires fundamental changes for most organisations
- the consumerist approach may be appropriate for some service-providing organisations, and gaining users' views is a key element.

The chapter uses the term 'governing body' to refer to what in different organisations may be called the 'executive council', 'executive committee', 'management committee', 'board of trustees', 'board of directors' as well as 'governing body', 'board of governors' etc. – that is, to the ruling body which has the function as 'trustees' in a charity and/or 'directors' in a company limited by guarantee or similar role in a cooperative or an unincorporated association *(see also Chapter 3 on Charity Law)*.

It employs fictional case-studies to illustrate points and pose problems for your consideration. They are based on the writers' experience and research, but they should not be taken as referring to particular organisations.

2. Accountability

What is accountability ?

Workers in voluntary organisations may be accountable to many different people and bodies. This 'accountability' may take many different forms. In some cases, we account to people by reporting, in a written report or verbally, what we have done. In some cases, we submit financial accounts. The people to whom we account then approve what we have done – at least tacitly. They may just nod it through or accept it. But they may need, in some cases, to formally resolve acceptance of the report. They can ask questions and raise points about our report. Sometimes, they ask that things be done differently in future. Sometimes they have the power to instruct that things be put right, for example, if the financial accounts reveal some improper expenditure. Sometimes, there could be sanctions, for example when reporting on performance of a contract. If our report showed we fell short of targets, then funding for a further phase of the contract might be reduced.

Accountability can be of different kinds. Legal contracts may specify closely what we should do and how we should produce accounts. But, we may simply feel accountable, as a matter of professionalism or conscience to friends, colleagues or clients.

Formal accountability

In formal procedures and clear management structures, events follow a chain:

- Authorisation – permission or instruction to do something, possibly within financial or other limits

- Action – doing it
- Account – reporting on how the action was carried out in keeping with the authorisation.

Thus, the essence of accountability is that it involves reporting after the event, as distinct from seeking authorisation in advance. This implies that in carrying out the action we are aware that we will have to account for it – and therefore try to act in a way that will be acceptable.

However, other types of formal accountability may not look like this. The law on charities sets a framework of requirements for accountability. There is no specific authorisation of actions but organisations must demonstrate that they comply with rules about reporting, financial accounts, fundraising, trading and political activity.

Other forms of accountability

In addition to these formal kinds of accountability, many voluntary organisations are founded on the idea that they grow out of and are part of a community. This means that they have a 'sense of communal accountability' to that community. This relationship may not work through a formal mechanism but this does not make it any less important. How it can work is covered in more detail later.

For individuals in voluntary organisations there may also be a sense of accountability to colleagues or conscience. Again, the demands that this puts on an individual may be rather vague at least until our actions are questioned.

The aim of this section is to help map out the various lines of accountability. While some of these may be obligatory, there are also some choices to be made about to whom we want to be accountable and how.

Case Study 1: The Fun Day
....

The Co-ordinator of Everywhere Community Centre has been asked by her governing body to organise a Fun Day to raise funds and told she should decide how to arrange the catering. She has to choose which caterer should get the job. The choice boils down to three options:

- *will it be the family of one of her users who run a hot dog and burger stand, Power Dogs?*
- *or will it be Hazel House, a community association for people with special needs, who are starting a catering service as a means of helping their clients into employment?*

- *or will it be her friend who runs a health food store, Brilliant Lettuce and Company?*

She loves Brilliant Lettuce's food herself, she thinks Power Dogs will raise most money, and Hazel House is a really good set-up. There are issues of quality, of how much money will be raised and of responsibility to the community, which we could only guess at in this brief illustration.

It's her decision, and afterwards she will have to account for it. She will have to explain on Monday morning to her own users why whoever got the job. She will have to justify it in a report with financial accounts to the Centre's governing body later that week. The Centre's annual general meeting is coming up a month later, and she wants to have everyone enthusiastic for that, especially as the Chair of Social Services is going to be present. The local authority, which funds many of the centre's activities, has just launched a Healthy Eating campaign in its day centres. And, then, there are the members of the local community she'll see in the High Street...

If we knew all the ins and outs of the story, we might find it was a simple or a complex decision for the Co-ordinator. The point for us is the accountability for the decision.

Questions

1. How would you decide if you were this Co-ordinator?
2. How would you, drawing on your experience, weigh up the significance of the different people to whom you would have to account in such a situation?

Lines of accountability

The ways in which you are accountable differ according to your position in the organisation. In the case above, it was easy to see how the Co-ordinator, as the chief officer of the Centre, reported to the governing body and was involved in accounting to external people as well as to clients. By contrast, a subordinate worker in a strict hierarchy might not be accountable to anyone except his or her line manager. Issues of wider accountability would be dealt with higher up the management hierarchy.

However, staff members or volunteers in voluntary organisations do usually see themselves as having to account to a variety of people. They can't just say 'I was obeying orders from my line manager'. For example, a child care worker might regard him or herself as accountable to parents and to fellow workers. A doctor would be accountable to his or her professional body, the British

Medical Association (BMA), as well as to the institutions of the National Health Service.

It would be useful to think for a few minutes about to whom you see yourself as accountable, as the next exercise suggests.

Exercise 1: Lines of accountability

To whom are you as an individual worker or volunteer accountable?

Take a blank sheet of paper, put ME in the middle and then draw out lines to all the bodies and people to whom you feel accountable.

As a beginning, you may get a diagram that looks a bit like this:

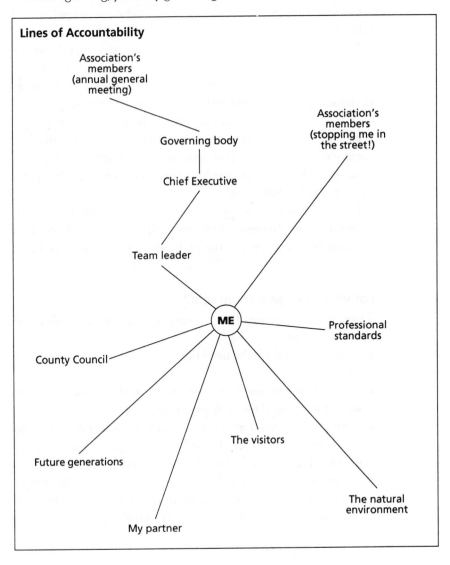

Lines of Accountability

Association's members (annual general meeting)

Association's members (stopping me in the street!)

Governing body

Chief Executive

Team leader

ME

Professional standards

County Council

Future generations

The visitors

My partner

The natural environment

Types of accountability

As soon as we start exploring the issue, we become aware of many different kinds of accountability. This section tackles other different types of accountability for voluntary organisations: to whom? for what? why? and how?

To whom are we accountable?

Most of us are accountable to a range of people or bodies. We are usually held to account through a management structure. We may have to account to agencies who fund our work or with whom our organisation has a contractual agreement. We may feel accountable to all sorts of specific people or more generally to future generations. Some of these accountabilities are public and official, some very personal.

In many voluntary organisations we are accountable to the membership, and this can be seen as the most important accountability of all. Often, the members elect the governing body, perhaps at the annual general meeting, perhaps through a postal ballot, and so those on the governing body have a very clear accountability – they may not get re-elected. The view that the organisation as a whole is accountable to the membership may then run right through to workers and volunteers, who deal with, say, services for members.

However, some voluntary organisations are charities constituted without a membership. The governing body, as trustees, is accountable for its proper use of funds to society as a whole or more narrowly to the Charity Commission.

For what are we accountable?

There are four things that voluntary organisations might be accountable for:

- results achieved – is the need being met? does our work make a difference?
- money received and how it is used – is the money used for what it was raised for? is it used efficiently?
- methods used in our activities and in organising ourselves – do we work within our constitution? are they legal? are the activities managed effectively? do we use best practice in the field?
- priority given to an area of work – are we doing the right things? is our choice of activities dictated by needs or what they can get money for or the founder's or director's preferences?

Why are we accountable?

There are many reasons why we are or feel accountable. The following headings may be useful to think about different types of accountability.

- *legal* – as set out in:
  bodies of law
  charity law (trustees' responsibilities and liabilities)
  company law (directors' responsibilities and liabilities)
  particular contracts or service level agreements
  or more broadly in terms of fiduciary duty (the general responsibility in law to care for money and a responsibility to society to use public money for the public good)
- *political* – to membership but also to other 'stakeholders'
- *managerial* – through line management
- *professional* – to professional body for lawyers, doctors etc. but also, for example, social or child care workers may feel a duty of accountability to accepted good practice
- *ethical* – to your conscience, moral/ethical commitment
- *communal* – to the people or community within which the organisation is located.

In checking through these headings and seeing how they apply to you and your organisation, it may be helpful also to recognise that different lines of accountability have different foundations. Are they obligatory or optional – is the accountability a matter of the law or your organisation's constitution? or it is your own decision to regard yourself as accountable to these people?

Do they come with sanctions or not? If the people to whom you account are unhappy with what you report, can they cut your funding? or institute legal proceedings? or only advise you about future actions?

Or do you feel accountable just so that you can sleep easy in your bed?

How are we accountable?

Accountabilities may be carried out in different ways; they may be:

- direct or indirect – do you account yourself? or do you report through someone else, for example your team leader or the chair of the governing body?
- formal or informal – do you have to submit a written report and financial accounts? or make a presentation to a committee or meeting?

- or is it more a matter of keeping people informed and 'in the picture' about what is happening? if so, what methods are appropriate?

Communal accountability

The concept of communal accountability needs some further explanation. Many voluntary organisations have a sense of accountability to the people, community or neighbourhood that can be seen as their roots, but this is often rather vague.

Communal accountability can be explained in terms of an exchange. The organisation operates within the expectations of the relevant community, and in return the community legitimates its existence and activities. The community may not be actively involved in approving the organisation's plans or activities but has influence which could be used to shape decisions in the organisation.

Case Study 2: Community child care

A group of parents decide to set up a nursery because there is a lack of child care facilities for working parents in their area and because they believe that they could do it in a more responsive way than local authority social services, even if they could persuade them to do it.

The parents hold two open meetings for potential users of the nursery and local residents who live near the old church hall that they intend to do up for their premises. They have formed a steering committee and begun to talk to the local authority about grants and registration under the Children Act 1989.

The open meetings seem to go very well, but requests for more parents or local residents to help with the organising are unsuccessful. The parents on the steering group feel as though they are not getting the support the idea deserves.

At the meetings a number of questions arise:
- *which children will get places?*
- *how will low income families afford places if they are not free?*
- *what about extra traffic and noise for the neighbours?*
- *what qualifications will the staff have?*
- *will any of the parents on the steering group get paid jobs in the nursery?*
- *what about using the church hall for other community activities?*

Although there seem to be a lot of possible obstacles, overall there is goodwill for the idea of the parent-run nursery at the open meetings. The steering group feel that they can go ahead with their plans.

Questions

- Whom would you regard as the local community for a project like this?
- If you were on the parents' steering group, how much would you feel it necessary to account to the local community? at the planning stage? and when the nursery is running?
- What methods would you use to account to the local community? at the planning stage? and when the nursery is running?

Exercise 2: Types of accountability: – to whom, for what, why and how

The table overleaf aims to bring together many of the different aspects of accountability discussed so far.

As you will need plenty of space, you could use the next page as a heading for a blank sheet of paper or two or three.

The idea is to start with the left hand column and identify to whom you or an organisation you know is accountable. Then you work across putting in as much detail as possible in each column.

Alternatively, you could start with one of the other columns. It is best to start with some facts you know about the organisation such as that a monthly return is completed and sent to another part of the organisation. This would go in the 'How' column on the far right. Working back from here will help to explore why this report is being sent, what is the purpose of its content and who is receiving it.

When you have completed each column for three or four different lines of accountability you should begin to get a feel for how this organisation is located within a network of multiple accountabilities.

Multiple accountabilities

Voluntary organisations are usually accountable in number of different ways to different people and bodies. Exercise 2 illustrates this by asking you to identify the nature of the accountability relationship with different bodies.

Managing these accountabilities is one of the major tasks in governing and managing a voluntary organisation. For some smaller and local organisations it will be relatively simple to identify two or three primary lines of accountability and to manage each of them. The governing body of a local network of volunteers who help elderly and disabled people with transport, for example, is accountable to: a) the service users for responding to their needs; b) the volunteers for good induction and support; c) the social services department for the grant to run the office and pay expenses.

But in a larger organisation with many activities, a membership, and multiple sources of funds it will not be so simple to manage all the strands and the potential for conflicting demands for accountability is high.

Types of accountability: to whom, for what, why and how			
Accountability to whom?	**Accountability for what?**	**Why? what type of accountability relationship is it?**	**How is the accountability delivered?**
(funders, users, staff, volunteers, community, who else?)	(results, money, methods, priorities)	(legal, political, managerial, pro-fessional, ethical, communal) (obligatory or optional, sanctions or not?)	(formal or informal? – written and verbal reports, financial accounts, meetings; informal feedback} (directly or indirectly?)
An example: local authority social services grants unit	*An example:* use of annual grant for training volunteers to befriend elderly people	*An example:* legal, contractual	*An example:* six monthly written report including statistics and annual visit by a grants officer; a local social worker sits on the project advisory committee.

Case study 3: Complex demands

A nation-wide, membership organisation of relatives of people with mental illness has set up carer self-help groups all over the country and campaigned locally and nationally for Government to improve the implementation of care in the community. The governing body decides to enter into contracts with health and local authorities to provide services to people with mental health problems since they believe that this will ensure the quality of some services and demonstrate what is needed. It is hoped that it will also help fund their campaigning and research work.

The growing diversity and size of the organisation have virtually brought the governing body to a standstill since the competing demands for accountability are becoming very complex to manage.

The relatives, who are the majority of the formal members, want more resources allocated to direct support for carers such as an in-depth advice service. The growing number of people being helped who are or have been mentally ill are demanding a greater say in the policy and strategy decisions. They are against compulsory medication whereas many relatives are not.

Bodies purchasing services are attempting to restrict the use of any surpluses on research or campaign work. With the influx of many professional staff and media scrutiny of mental health services following an inquiry into the death of a volunteer in a hostel there is a growing need for the organisation to be accountable more widely for the quality of its services.

Questions

- What factors do you see as underlying the accountabilities of this nation-wide organisation?
- How could they be compared with those of a small, local organisation?

Stakeholder analysis

To unravel the complexity of these competing demands for accountability, organisations can use a 'stakeholder analysis'. Stakeholders are people or organisations who have a stake in the organisation. They can be internal – service users, staff, governing body members and volunteers – or external – funding bodies, individual donors, regulators.

A stakeholder analysis for a particular organisation aims:
- to identify who are the stakeholders
- to find out the criteria they use to assess the organisation's performance
- to assess how well the organisation performs against these criteria.

This analysis builds on Exercise 2. You could refer back and add any stakeholders you may have overlooked. The next exercise asks the organisation to assess its performance in the light of stakeholders' criteria rather than their own.

Exercise 3: Stakeholder analysis

Take a large blank sheet of paper and divide it into three columns. List your organisation's stakeholders (internal and external) down the left hand side. In the middle column write down the criteria they use to assess the organisation's performance. In the final column make a judgement about the performance using the scale – Poor... OK... Good.

It is useful to complete this using your own judgement before consulting with others. Additional stages can be added such as asking the stakeholders for their assessment of performance; ranking the stakeholders in order of importance; and exploring how each group influences the organisation.

A sample analysis is given below using two of the stakeholder groups from Case Study 3.

Stakeholder	Criteria used by stakeholder to assess performance	Our own assessment of performance
carers	• access to advice on benefits, legal issues and treatment	Poor
	• usefulness of advice given	Good
	• strong campaigning for health authorities to involve carers in service planning	Good
purchasers of services (e.g. health authorities)	• fulfilment of contract specification with minimal problems e.g. delays, complaints, rising costs/price	OK
	• no public criticism of health authority's policy or practice	Poor

Accountability – Summary

Accountability is undoubtedly a complex issue for voluntary organisations and for the people working in and around them too. This section has highlighted the fact that accountability has many dimensions: a voluntary group can be accountable for different things, to different bodies, in different ways. The exercises have attempted to clarify the lines of accountability applicable to any organisation. This is one step towards managing the various accountability relationships positively and effectively.

3. User Involvement

A time of change

Voluntary organisations exist, in most cases, to help people – but who is best placed to make decisions about how to give that help? Is it the professionals? The governing body? Or the people themselves? One of the most important debates in voluntary organisations at present is how far people who use services should be involved in making decisions about policy or about their own services.

There has been a great movement towards user involvement in wider society. Disabled people have been making demands for full civil rights. The ideology of consumerism has become more influential and has helped shape Government policies. Concepts from business management have spread into the voluntary sector, giving particular prominence to "customer care". In implementing the National Health Service and Community Care Act 1990, the Government has issued guidance that purchasers and providers of services should involve users in planning, delivery and monitoring of services.

Many voluntary organisations have reacted to these pressures or, indeed, contributed themselves to the movement for change. They often talk of their wish to 'empower' their users, of their accountability to users, or of the importance of responding to users' demands to achieve high quality services.

Case Study 4: We know best
....

A historic site is managed by a branch of a national heritage charity. Volunteers from the area form the committee which oversees the visiting arrangements and they also act as stewards when the property is open. A paid officer of the national charity is also involved in advising them about visitor management.

At the annual general meeting of the local branch a small group of members, two of whom have relatives who are physically disabled, point out that the national organisation has an official policy of maximising access to its properties for all members of the community. They ask the committee what it plans to do to implement this policy since at present most of the building and garden are not safely accessible by wheelchair or for someone who has a sensory impairment.

The Chair of the committee is rather taken aback by this apparent challenge to their running of the property. She responds by stating that the national policy does not really apply in their case because only a small number of people are affected by the lack of access. She recognises that, although unfortunate, they cannot do anything about it. There are murmurs of approval from many of those attending the meeting.

At this point the paid officer intervenes saying that the local branch must follow the national policy and that all members of the community should be seen as potential customers. He warns that if the local association of disabled people found out about this lack of responsiveness then the local paper would have a big story and there could be protests outside the entrance.

The Chair reluctantly agrees to set up a consultation meeting to discuss the issue but ends by reminding the meeting that the committee are only volunteers and have a very difficult job and that they must cater for the majority of their users who are not disabled.

Questions

- Where does the pressure for change arise from?
- What is the relative priority given to current and potential users?
- How much influence do the different participants have: Chair, committee, relatives of disabled members, general membership, paid officer?
- Will the suggested consultation make a difference?

User involvement

User involvement has become a key phrase. But there can be difficulties in carrying the idea through into practice. One difficulty is the traditional view of charity law which is based on the concept of trust. People (donors) entrust money and assets to other individuals (trustees) to look after in the interests of a third party (the beneficiaries) as set out in the objects of the 'trust' (*see Chapter 3*). The trustees have to act with no personal interest but also can be found personally liable if they are in breach of the trust. They have to account publicly for performing their duties to the trust, largely by reporting to the Charity Commissioners.

If the trustees involve the beneficiaries, it may be held to endanger the proper administration of the trust because the beneficiaries may be acting in their own self interest.

However, voluntary organisations do recognise changes in society – and have sometimes helped to bring them about. These days they see the users of their services less as passive recipients and more as people who should be actively involved in the organisations or, at least, in decisions which affect them.

Various charities have been allowed by the Charity Commissioners to include users on governing bodies, though generally only in small numbers and on condition that they should not participate in decisions that directly affect themselves.

The people benefiting from the work of voluntary organisations are quite likely to be described as: clients, consumers, customers, members, participants, patients, residents, and service users. We will use the term 'users' as being the simplest and most all-embracing, but it might be useful to think about the implications of these different terms.

There are some practical difficulties for organisations which seek 'user involvement', as we will explore later. But there are some voluntary organisations which find difficulties with the principle of user involvement. Trustees may not be able to cope with tensions between their responsibility and liability under charity law, on the one hand, and the demands of users, on the other.

Exercise 4: Involving users

Think about your organisation: have you been affected by the factors working towards greater involvement of users?

1. Tick which factors have affected your work, and make a brief note of how.
2. Star the factors which are most influential for your organisation.
   Users' demands – civil rights
   Consumerism
   Customer care
   Government policy
   Requirements of funding bodies
   Professional practice in case work.

Accountabilities

It is a widely held that 'voluntary organisations have an over-riding accountability to their users/beneficiaries' (the Initial Submission to *The Commission on the Future of the Voluntary Sector* of the Association of Chief Executives of National Voluntary Organisations).

But does accountability to users over-ride all others? Or does it have to compete with other accountabilities for our attention? The next exercise illustrates how the aspiration can be difficult to put into practice.

Exercise 5: Accounting to users

1. Turn back to Exercise 2 on types of accountability, and check if you have included 'users' as one of the groups to whom your organisation is accountable.

   If you haven't, was this an oversight? Or does your organisation not see itself as accountable to users?

2. Are users all one group for your organisation? Or do you have different groups of users with different needs and aspirations? Some organisations have two or more distinct groups of service users, for example, the Down's Syndrome Association exists to benefit people with Down's Syndrome but their parents are major users of its services too.

3. If you hadn't included users, or if you now think you need to include more than one group of users, add them under the 'Accountability to whom?' column.

   If you find that users really don't figure in your organisation's accountabilities, pencil them in to think about what it could mean for the organisation.

4. How would you describe the organisation's relationship with its users:

   For what is the organisation accountable to its users?

   Why? Which types of accountability are involved?

   What governs the relationship between the organisation and its users?

   How is the accountability demonstrated?

   How does it work in practice? Do you have meetings, reports, user representatives on committees, newsletters?

5. Look across the whole table:

   What would be the implications of assuming that the organisation has an over-riding accountability to users/beneficiaries?

   Would you need to reduce the extent to which you account to others?

Accountability and Stakeholding

Accountability implies reporting on things that have been done. In some cases, the reporting enables the people to whom we are accounting to raise questions and make demands for future actions. However, the movement for user involvement suggests that users' views should be incorporated in making decisions about what is to be done. In the next section we will explore how this may be done in terms of consumerism or democracy.

Also, we should consider users in relation to the idea of 'stakeholders' which was also introduced in Section 1. 'Stakeholding' suggests the desirability of widespread and ongoing involvement by a variety of groups, and raises the question of how an organisation listens to different stakeholders.

Consumerism or democracy

We have considered so far user involvement in terms of accountability and stakeholding. However, the issue also raises more fundamental questions about the nature of voluntary organisations, and whether they see user involvement as matter of consumerism or democracy.

A consumerist approach implies that individuals should be able meet their needs by choosing from a range of services. Services will, it is argued, be of high quality and responsive to needs because if they are not then other competing organisations will get the funds and the referrals of clients. The purpose of user involvement in the consumerist approach is to find out what the needs are and check that the users (consumers) are satisfied.

In contrast, the democratic approach to user involvement is based on the assumption that voluntary organisations exist to empower their users through services and campaigning. Therefore there will be involvement based on a right to have some say in decisions about what the organisation as a whole is doing rather simply to comment on satisfaction about a particular service.

These two approaches can be compared in the table below which gives their main characteristics.

Characteristics of different approaches

Consumerist	*Democratic*
consumers	citizens
needs	rights
personal problems	social problems
individual treatment/service	collective action
professional dominance	individual and collective responsibility
consultation	decision making powers
service led	citizen (user) led
passive recipients	self-empowerment
focus on service delivery	focus on services, strategy and policy

Exercise 6: Consumerism or democracy

1. List the ways in which service users are involved in your organisation now.
2. Categorise these user involvement activities and initiatives by listing them under the headings 'consumerist' or 'democratic'.

We would expect to find a wide variety of activities involving users and a spread of consumerist and democratic measures within any organisation. If you have the opportunity to compare notes with someone from a different organisation, it would be interesting to see the variations.

Organisations can be distinguished by the extent to which users have control. Some have been created and are run in all respects by users. Others are led or managed by users. However, most voluntary organisations are controlled by people who are not themselves users but are trying to involve users, to some extent.

The next exercise will help you to identify types of organisation in terms of their approach to user involvement.

Exercise 7: Organisational analysis

1. Read the descriptions of the four types of organisation and mark the position of your organisation on the line at the top.
   How much consensus do you think there is amongst managers, trustees, users and staff, in the organisation, about the position?
   Is the organisation planning to change so it would move along the continuum?
2. Consider other organisations you know: where would you mark them on the line at the top?

Values and control

Reflecting on Exercise 7, you will probably wonder what your organisation – and others you know – aims to be and what it can be. Organisations may be aiming towards greater, or less, user involvement. They may be limited by organisational or cultural factors, by different histories and different opportunities for the future. They have different constitutions and are at different stages of development. But underlying these different factors are questions about the values of the organisation – what is it really about?

Each voluntary organisation needs to work out its own approach to the issues of user involvement.

Types of User Involvement and Types of Organisation			
User Organisations	**User Controlled**	**User Centred**	**User Responsive**
	(user managed, user run, user owned, user led)	(user driven, user oriented)	
Organisations in which all roles (members, governors/ trustees, users, staff etc) are performed by users. Describes separatist groups and some self-help groups which together for the 'user movement'.	Describes organisations in which users have control i.e. users determine the purposes and activities; allocate resources; obtain information about performance and achievements; and have the ability to analyse and respond to this information. These may or may not be 'user organisations'.	An organisation in which the *outcomes* of its policies and activities are primarily informed by the needs, aspirations and wishes of users. This could happen through the agency involving users in agenda setting, deciding which ideas should be taken further and collaborating on the problems of implementation.	Organisations in which professionals gather information and/or opinions from users about existing services or plans for changes or new services drawn up by the organisation. Also known as user consultation or market research.

Case Study 5: The election

A community centre which runs a large building and supports a number of different groups for young people, elderly people, advice work, etc., has a constitution which requires its governing body to be elected by 'members' at an annual general meeting. Many of its users are quite regularly involved in running their own groups, in an informal way, but attempts to recruit them as 'members' of the centre's association have not managed to get people even to sign a membership form – they don't see the point and are a bit suspicious of forms. So, when the governing body meets to plan the AGM, they realise that there are not enough signed-up members of the association to run a respectable election. If users do come to the AGM, attracted by the refreshments, very few of them will be able to vote.

The director tells the governing body she thinks that people's involvement in their separate groups is what counts and that it offers evidence of a lively and progressive programme, and that the staff know

*people well through these groups. Anyway, members of the governing
body remember that they never have had much of a membership, and it
was only in the constitution because they copied a standard charitable
constitution from the local council for voluntary service.*

*But one member of the governing body is not satisfied. He argues
that if the centre is aiming to empower people then it must help develop
their participation in democratic institutions, and the place to start is
here!*

....

Questions

- If you were a member of that governing body, how would you develop the discussion? What would you say?
- What are the implications for future actions of agreeing either with the director or the member who argues for empowerment?

The next exercise explores the links between the value-base of a voluntary organisation, and its purposes, ownership, governance structure, and ultimately the issue of overall control.

Exercise 8: Issues for organisations

This is a long exercise that raises tough issues for voluntary organisations. You should focus on one organisation and attempt to follow through the logic, starting from its values through to its control. In the process of doing this, you will probably find that aspects of your organisation are unclear and perhaps have never been worked out. The exercise is intended to be thought-provoking, rather than to produce a blueprint or recipe for your organisation.

The exercise could be started in different places, and you may track back from later stages to earlier. Questions about how your organisation is controlled may, for example, tell you more about its values than fine thoughts ever will.

Values

What are the core values which underpin the organisation? Among those commonly identified are:

- beneficence, caring for others
- reciprocity, mutuality
- solidarity, empowerment
- promoting independence
- consumerism.

When thinking about answers to the questions in the next few sections, keep in mind the core values of your organisation. How well do the activities and the way the organisation is run fit with the values?

Purposes

How does the organisation see itself in terms of current debates about the future of the voluntary sector and charities: are its roles in self-help? service provision? campaigning? advocacy?

Does it want to grow through more and larger contracts, and in partnership with public and private sectors? Or does it want to stay apart?

Does it think it is more important to work for social change? Or to provide high quality and much needed services now?

The most important dimension to examine is the organisation's relationship with its users: how is the organisation's purpose defined in relation to their needs or circumstances that give rise to its existence?

Ownership

Who owns the organisation? This is not meant to be a legal question, but it may be provocative and help shape thinking. Among the possibilities may be:

- trustees
- members
- users, beneficiaries
- the 'guardians' (the people who care sufficiently about the organisation to fight for its survival, usually a mixture of members, founders, users)
- other stakeholders (e.g. funders).

This discussion may involve questions like:

- Who feels it is their organisation?
- Who has rights in this organisation?
- Ultimately, who has power over the constitution and/or the assets?

Governance

How do the structures of decision-making carry through the values and purposes of the organisation? How do these structures reflect or manifest its ownership? There may be questions about:

- the role of trustees, their responsibilities and support needs
- representation of members, users and other stakeholders
- membership structures and user bodies
- relationship of other decision-making processes to the governing body.

And about what it says in the constitution and what happens in practice.

Control

Who is in control of what in the organisation? The issues are complex; control is about much more than constitutions and governing bodies.

Who is involved in, and has the ability to act on, issues such as the following:

- decisions about purpose and activities?
- decisions about allocation of resources?
- information about performance and achievement?
- calling individuals and groups to account?

Where does the organisation expect user involvement to lead in terms of control?

4. The Management of Involvement

In Section 3 we considered ways of analysing organisations in terms of their approach to user involvement. We saw that organisations can make choices about the appropriateness of pursuing predominantly consumerist or democratic strategies and the extent to which they wish to be controlled by users. Once these strategic choices have been made, we need to be able to design and implement practical changes so that rhetoric can become reality. Section 4 explores 'how to do it' issues.

Increasing user involvement

Organisations that are making positive progress towards increased user involvement will have some or all of the features of 'active reformers' noted in the table below.

Active reformers

- user involvement will be on the organisation's formal and informal agendas and be debated openly at all levels
- the leadership of the organisation will have a vision of a future with greater user participation
- there will be some specific objectives, for example, a regular survey of users' views or increased user representation on the governing body
- staff and volunteers will be experimenting with a range of user involvement initiatives to get the debate going, rather than waiting for the perfect plan to be drawn up

- there will be opportunities for face-to-face contact between users and managers and users and trustees
- everyone will start by assuming that the condition or circumstances of users is not a constraint on their involvement in consultation or decision making; if problems occur, they will discuss the issues openly and seek advice from an independent user group
- there will be opportunities, such as a meeting time or a room or a page of a newsletter or a budget, for the exclusive use of users
- there will be a champion of user involvement whose role will be to lead and facilitate developments on user involvement; they will need to be influential and committed
- everyone should expect the process of change to take a long time.

Implementation

Active reformers concentrate on the processes of change in organisations. The next sections look more closely at implementation, first, through the consumerist approach and then through the democratic approach.

Users as consumers: getting their views

Many voluntary organisations place their emphasis on providing high quality and responsive services. Often they see their users as 'consumers'. The essence of a consumerist approach is that people should be well placed to make their own choices by being sufficiently informed about the service or product, for example the 'sell by' date, contents, uses etc.; and by having recourse to complaints procedures and – in some cases, legal remedy – if the services or products do not match up to their claims.

It is assumed that the market will ensure the best services and products will prosper. Thus, the provider needs to get feedback from the consumer and offer services or products which s/he demands; and to anticipate demands by developing new services or products.

If your organisation sees users as consumers, a number of methods can be used to obtain their views or consult them about existing and planned services. These include:

- surveys – face-to-face or postal
- one-off consultation meetings
- regular user forums
- suggestion boxes etc.

- complaints procedures
- evaluation forms
- exit interviews
- informal contact between staff/managers and users.

Many of these methods will be familiar to us as participants in market research carried out by commercial companies or in questionnaires given out at the end of training courses. Some of the methods are fairly straight-forward whilst others need expert design. (*See Chapters 7 and 8.*)

For voluntary organisations there are further complications. The group to be consulted may be difficult to engage, perhaps because they are not familiar with the methods or they only use the service on an infrequent or anonymous basis.

Making consultation work

1. Consult on specifics: ask people to comment on specific things that can be changed.
2. Be honest about who makes decisions: tell participants how much influence they will have by giving their views.
3. Provide support: some people lack confidence, but this does not mean that they do not have valuable views about a service. A group discussion (sometimes called a 'focus group') may help.
4. Provide incentives: food, money, transport, comfortable environment for consultation.
5. Acknowledge personal agendas: some service users may see contact with a manager or researcher as an opportunity to resolve personal issues. Be clear about the purpose of the survey/interview etc. Be ready to give information about sources of help with the problem being presented.
6. Give feedback: people who give information to help services should be told the outcomes of the consultation, for example in a short letter or verbal announcement at a meeting.
7. Reach the hard to reach: some people may not be easy to consult for a variety of reasons e.g. they are unconfident, sceptical, have difficulties with language or physical access, etc. Engaging with people who are hard to reach must be seen as the organisation's problem rather than the individual's. Effort, time and resources must be put into making contact.

Case Study 6: Getting users' views
....
A neighbourhood community centre is used twice a week as a base for advice sessions on welfare benefits. The sessions are attended mostly by older people from the local area and a few young mums who bring their toddlers to meet for a chat and a coffee.

The staff are trained and experienced in welfare rights. They have noticed that the same people are returning to their sessions regularly and that they are dealing with very few new cases. They are also aware that the surrounding area has many unemployed people and that two housing schemes for people who have moved out of a long stay psychiatric hospital.

The project's funding from the local authority is up for renewal and a local councillor has told a member of the management committee that there could be cuts for projects that cannot show they are responding to local needs.
....

Questions
- How could getting users' views improve any aspect of this situation?
- Who should the workers be asking for their views? – current users? potential users?
- What should the workers be trying to find out?
- What methods will be the best way of getting the information? – will they be different for current users and potential users?
- How will the Centre use the information?

An important feature of the consumerist approach is the monitoring and evaluation of services so that you can assess what aspects of your services should be preserved or changed. Monitoring refers to data which enables you to watch what is happening, whereas evaluation refers to making the judgement from this data about how well you are achieving goals or implementing particular policies.

In the case, a two-pronged evaluation could be made. A collection of numbers of people (including data on sex, ethnic group, age, disability, employment status, numbers of dependants etc.) could be made either from the records or from a short form which users could fill in at the advice sessions. This would provide firm evidence on who is using the centre. It might also be possible to collect comparable information on people in the local community who are not using the centre.

If the centre wanted the views of current users, it could give them an evaluation form. The box below sketches in a standard, basic evaluation form.

Evaluation Form

The only way we can make sure our services are helpful to a wide range of users is to hear from you what you think of it. We would be very grateful if you could complete this short questionnaire. Your answers will be treated in confidence.

1. How effectively do the advice sessions meet your needs ?

2. What do you find most useful?

3. What do you find least useful?

4. How could the services be improved?

5. Any other comments.

Your name:_____

Please return to_____by_____

Exercise 9: Evaluating the evaluation

In this exercise consider how far the two prongs of an evaluation as described above, would work for your organisation.

What data would be available from your files which would provide a basis for monitoring and evaluation?

In seeking your users' views, in what ways would the standard form above be helpful? In what ways unhelpful? How would you suggest it should be changed for your use?

Users as citizens: democratic control of their services

The question of user involvement may be seen as a matter of democracy or power or empowerment. Though some organisations do combine features of the different approaches, as we recognised above in Exercise 6, the democratic approach is quite distinct from the consumerist: It assumes:

- people have the right to take part in the government of their state, locality or organisation, whether by being represented or by participating directly

- this can be seen as a protection against tyranny or authoritarian rule; as likely to produce better decision-making; and as a recognition of people's stake in the society or organisation.

This is valuable not only because it enables individual participation but also for its educative or developmental effect from which the individual gains the capacity to take part in other decisions-making processes. S/he is empowered by the process.

Services run by local authorities are democratically accountable to the local population through elected councillors and through the involvement of service users.

In voluntary organisations the formal lines of accountability are more complex. Some voluntary organisations have members to whom the governing body and any staff are ultimately accountable: the members may elect some or all members of the governing body and may pass resolutions at general meetings. However, in law the governing body has responsibilities and liabilities which ultimately over-ride the views of members, and in running the organisation it will consider other stakeholders' interests as well as members'.

Other voluntary organisations do not have a formally constituted membership and hence no constituency in a democratic sense. The governing body is the ultimate authority and appoints new people to itself.

The position of users is not necessarily determined by whether the organisation is based on a membership or not. Irrespective of how democratic the organisation is in relation to its membership, users may or may not be among the membership. Equally, an organisation where the governing body makes appointments to itself may or may not seek to appoint users.

To involve users as participants in the democratic control of the organisation requires deliberate action, in policy and practice. This needs to be done by a combination of changes to the formal structures and to the informal workings of the organisation.

The process may be a slow one. The experience of organisations following this route suggests that it may be better to build towards constitutional change and democratic user involvement through various informal – and possibly consumerist – measures. The range of possibilities is extensive.

Potential changes for democratic involvement of users
1. Structures
- in a membership organisation, users can be encouraged to become members and acquire voting rights

- users, even if not members, can be invited to the annual general meeting
- users can be put forward as members of the governing body, whether by election or appointment
- the constitution can be amended so as to designate places for users on the governing body
- users can be appointed to subcommittees and working parties in greater numbers
- when planning to elect or appoint users to decision-making bodies, it is necessary to make sure enough people are elected/appointed to support each other. A single user representative is likely to be overwhelmed
- a 'users' body', or network, can help support users in their participation in the organisation, as well as in their lives.

2. Procedures and practices

Meetings

- meetings should be arranged at a time and place convenient to users
- papers for meetings should present information in plain language, and in a medium appropriate for users (perhaps, on tape or in large print or Braille)
- notices of meetings should be absolutely clear and issued in plenty of time for people to make arrangements for, for example, child care or travel
- the chairing of meetings should involve people and ensure participants know what is happening
- user representatives should have opportunities and support for accounting to users.

Campaigns

- users should front campaigns and not just be used on marches or in the backroom
- users' views about publicity, advertising etc. should be followed
- users should be formally consulted about priorities.

Operations

- opportunities should be developed for face-to-face contacts and working together
- staff-only areas in buildings should be removed
- users should be involved in discussions about user involvement
- staff resources should be committed to supporting users, including a user body and user representatives.

3. Attitudes

- non-user members of the governing body should realise they are not giving up power by involving users, but gaining power through greater legitimacy and knowledge
- staff attitudes may need to be reviewed and modified over time
- staff may need to avoid speaking in jargon.

Case Study 7: Democratisation

A large national organisation for people with a disabling medical condition has many self-help groups and some services such as advice and holiday homes run by the national body. It is governed by about 50 trustees, most of whom are medical practitioners and professionals from health and social services. The general membership is mostly people with the condition, and the main benefits to them are information about the condition and treatments, practical help and access to courses and self-help groups.

About five years ago a group of younger people with the condition set up their own group to discuss their particular experiences, under the umbrella of the main organisation. As this group grew, it began to question some of the policy decisions and priorities of the national organisation. Attempts to influence the trustees to consult more effectively with them and members in general failed, as did suggestions that more trustees should be people with direct experience of the condition.

Two years ago a new Chief Executive was appointed. He believed that the purpose of this kind of organisation should be to empower the people it sets out to help. He sympathised with the concerns of the younger service users and members and attempted to help them achieve changes in the way the organisation was governed.

At first he was rebuffed by some members of the governing body who felt that these changes were unnecessary and that he was overstepping his responsibilities in trying to influence who was elected to the governing body. After about two years of behind the scenes work and a working party to look at the constitution, proposals were accepted by the governing body. These reduced the size of the governing body to less than a half, adopted a policy stating that it would be desirable for a majority of the governing body members to have personal experience of the condition, and increased the number of nationally elected members (by postal ballot).

Questions

- How important do you think it is that the majority of the governing body should have personal experience of the needs that the organisation aims to meet? How would you weigh that alongside other things an organisation may need to do?
- Is it part of a chief executive's responsibilities to influence the composition of the governing body?

Policy and practice

Two general points emerge from this section. The practical problems of developing user involvement may be considerable and take time and resources; an organisation wanting to develop in this direction will not find 'off-the-shelf' ready solutions. But the problems can be solved; even if they seem to be insuperable issues at first.

An organisation may believe it has an over-riding accountability to users or that the empowerment of users is what should characterise its actions as a voluntary organisation, but it may – for the present – be constrained by other considerations or competing claims.

Sharing power

Might user involvement lead to a sharing of power within the organisation? Ideas of partnership have been mostly developed in terms of relationships between organisations, but it may be useful to think about how within an organisation there can be partnership or sharing of power.

User involvement may be not just a matter of gaining hierarchical power, e.g. through membership of the governing body or representation in policy-making, but of working together across the organisation. This may be on a formal or informal basis.

- What would be the opportunities for this in your organisation?
- Where do users, staff and trustees work together?
- Where do they meet face to face?
- What opportunities are there to know each other?

Case Study 8: Whose organisation?

An inner city HIV/AIDS organisation was formed by carers and friends of people with HIV/AIDS and now wants to involve people, not necessarily users, with HIV/AIDS on its governing body. It has a client-group which includes men and women from a variety of ethnic groups, and the view in the organisation is that most of these clients do not want to be publicly associated with HIV/AIDS. Its current governing body consists of people who created the organisation and medical and social work professionals. When it advertised for members of its governing body, it did not attract suitable candidates from among people with HIV/AIDS, perhaps because it is overshadowed by other organisations in this field with higher profiles. It has no problem recruiting professionals to the governing body.

So, although there is a wish to increase democratic involvement, the best plan seems to be to circulate an evaluation questionnaire, and hope that this draws out users' views.

....

Questions

- In what ways might it matter whether the organisation recruited to its governing body users of its services or other people with HIV/AIDS?
- How would you draw up a programme towards greater involvement of users?

5. Chapter Review

In this chapter we have explored ideas and practicalities about accountability and user involvement. We have emphasised that voluntary organisations need to find their own particular solutions to the problems posed; there are no 'off-the-shelf' solutions. Much depends on the values and circumstances of each organisation. Therefore, the text has sought to stimulate thinking and analysis, rather than lay down advice on what to do.

The following questions are intended as a quick review of the main issues covered, as a reminder and as a prompt for thinking about how these issues hang together.

1. To whom do you regard yourself as accountable? What different forms of accountability are you involved in?
2. To whom is your organisation accountable? For what? Why – what types of accountability are involved? How is this accountability exercised?
3. How do you and your organisation manage the multiple accountabilities?
4. Who are the stakeholders in your organisation? What do they expect of your organisation? And how far do you think it meets their expectations?
5. How do see your users in relation to other stakeholders? How do you account to them?
6. Does your organisation display more consumerist or democratic features in its involvement of users?

7. Where does your organisation stand in terms of degrees of user involvement or control?
8. How are the values of the organisation demonstrated in its governance and control?
9. How many of the features of 'active reformers' can you see in your organisation?
10. Is your organisation taking steps to increase user involvement? If so, what? How is it getting users views? How are users sharing in power?

About the authors

Michael Locke is reader in the Centre for Institutional Studies at the University of East London and is co-ordinator of its MA programme in Voluntary Sector Studies, Paul Robson carries out research at the Centre for Institutional Studies and is an independent consultant working with voluntary organisations.

Acknowledgements

Among the literature drawn upon, the writers particularly acknowledge: Diana Leat (Voluntary Organisations and Accountability, NCVO 1988) for the concept of 'communal accountability'; John M. Bryson (Strategic Planning for Public and Nonprofit Organisations, Jossey Bass 1995 2nd ed) for the framework of stakeholder analysis; Margaret Harris (of the Centre for Voluntary Organisation, London School of Economics) for the concept of 'guardians'.

The writers' research on user involvement was funded by the Joseph Rowntree Foundation, and their report *Consumerism or Democracy?: User Involvement in the Control of Voluntary Organisations* (with Jonathan Dawson) is published by Policy Press.

FURTHER INFORMATION : 13

Chapter 1: Fundraising

Further Reading

Charity Trends,1993, Charities Aid Foundation (CAF)
Voluntary Sector Trends,1995, CAF
Dimensions of the Voluntary Sector, CAF
Directory of Grant Making Trusts, CAF
CAF, Kings Hill, West Malling, Kent ME19 4TA.
Tel: 01732-520 000

Writing Better Fundraising Applications, 1992 (new edition due
Autumn 97), Directory of Social Change (DSC)
Raising Money from Trusts, 1989, DSC
A Guide to the Major Trusts (Volumes 1 & 2), 1997, DSC
The Major Companies Guide, 1995, DSC
The National Lottery Yearbook, 1997, DSC
DSC, 24 Stephenson Way, London NW1 2DP.
Tel: 0171-209 5151

Baring Asset Management Top 3000 Charities, 1997, Caritas Data,
London

Giving to Charity – A survey of public attitudes and behaviour, MORI,
London

Direct Marketing, Christian Brann, Collectors' Books Ltd,
Cirencester, Glos.

The Secrets of Effective Direct Mail, John Frazer Robinson,
McGraw Hill Book Co.

Marketing Needs, 1994, ICSA Publishing, Hemel Hempstead,
London

Useful Addresses

The Charity Commission
St Alban's House
57-60 Haymarket
London SW1Y 4QX
0171-210 4477

Graeme House
Derby Square
Liverpool L2 7SB
0151-227 3191

Woodfield House
Tangier, Taunton
Somerset TA1 4BL
01822-345 000

**Institute of Charity
Fundraising Managers
(ICFM)**
208 Market Towers
1 Nine Elms Lane
London SW8 5NQ
0171-627 3436

**Charities Aid Foundation
(CAF)**
114 Southampton Row
London WC1B 5AA
0171-831 2852

Kings Hill, West Malling
Kent ME19 4TA
01732-520 000

**Directory of Social
Change (DSC)**
24 Stephenson Way
London NW1 2DP
0171-209 5151

**South Bank University
Business School**
103 Borough Road
London SE1 0AA
0171-928 8989

**National Council for
Voluntary Organisations
(NCVO)**
Regent's Wharf
8 All Saints Street
London N1 9RL
0171-713 6161

**Charity Appointments
and Fundraising
Appointments**
(recruitment consultants)
Longcroft House
Victoria Avenue
London EC2 4NS
0171-623 9292

**Joseph Rowntree
Foundation**
The Homestead
40 Water End, York YO3 6LP
01904-629 241

Charity Recruitment
40 Rosebery Avenue
London EC1R 4RN
0171-833 0770

Trustee Register
23 Peascod Street
Windsor
Berkshire SL4 1DE
01753-868 277

**London School of
Economics (LSE)**
Houghton Street
London WC2A 2AE
0171-405 7686

**Association of Charitable
Foundations (ACF)**
High Holborn House
52-54 High Holborn
London WC1V 6RL
0171-404 1338

Antony Baxter
Sandcliff AB Ltd and The
Antony Baxter Partnership,
Sandcliff House, Northgate
Street, Devizes, Wiltshire
SN10 1JT

Burnett Associates
White Lion Court, London
EC1Y 0TY

Peter Maple
Arthritis Care, 18 Stephenson
Way, London NW1 2HD

Redmond Mullin
Redmond Mullin Ltd, Fisher
Street, Lewes,
East Sussex BN7 2DG

Smee and Ford Ltd
2nd Floor, St George's House,
195-203 Waterloo Road,
London SE1 8UX

Chapter 2: Campaigning

Further Reading

Political Activities and Campaigning by Charities: Revised Guidelines by the Charity Commission: NCVO Response, National Council for Voluntary Organisations (NCVO)

Campaigning with Confidence: Report of a Conference held at National Council for Voluntary Organisations, June 1994, NCVO

Good Campaigns Guide, Brian Lamb, 1997, NCVO, Regent's Wharf, 8 All Saint's Street, London N1 9RL

Political Activities and Campaigning by Charities, CC9, July 1995, Charity Commissioners for England and Wales

The Campaigning Handbook, Mark Lattimer, 1994, Directory of Social Change (DSC), 24 Stephenson Way, London NW1 2DP

Campaigning – The A to Z of Public Advocacy, Des Wilson and Leighton Andrews, Hawksmere

Can Campaigning be Evaluated? (article), Perri 6 (Demos) and Julian Forder (University of Kent), Non-Profit and Voluntary Sector Quarterly, Arnova, Sage Publications Ltd, 6 Bonhill Street, London EC2A 4PU

Chapter 3: Charity Law

Further Reading (by chapter)

Unless otherwise stated, all of the following are published by the Charity Commission. For single copies of any title, contact them at either of their regional offices:

Graeme House, Derby Square, Liverpool L2 7SB.
Tel: 0151-227 3191

Woodfield House, Tangier, Taunton, Somerset TA1 4BL.
Tel: 00822-345 000

For bulk oders (10 or more copies of any title), contact their London office:

1 St Alban's House, 57-60 Haymarket, London SW1Y 4QX.
Tel: 0171-210 4477.

1. Introduction

So You Want to Start a Charity?, March 1996, Reference CC21

Central Register of Charities: Services Available, November 1995, Reference CC45

Getting in Touch with the Charity Commission, November 1995, Reference CC50

2. What is a Charity?

What is a Charity?, March 1996, Reference CC21(a)

Trusts for the Relief of Poverty

Charities for the Relief of the Poor, June 1996, Reference CC4

Trusts for the Advancement of Education

Educational Charities, June 1989, Reference CC31

Promotion of Sport, March 1996, Reference INF 13

Promotion of Art, March 1996, Reference INF 14

Research Trusts, August 1996, Reference INF 1

What is the Advancement of Religion?

Registration of Religious Charities, January 1994, Reference CC22

4. Trusts for Other Purposes

Charities for the Relief of Sickness, July 1994, Reference CC6

Counselling, August 1996, Reference INF 10

Disaster Appeals: Attorney General's Guidelines, August 1994, Reference CC40

Animal Charities, Reference INF 12

Political Activities and Campaigning by Charities, July 1995, Reference CC9

6. The Charity Commission

Charities and the Charity Commission, June 1996, Reference CC2

Exempt Charities, November 1995, Reference CC23

What Happens after Registration?, March 1996, Reference CC21(c)

The Official Custodian for Charities' Land Holding Service, March 1995, Reference CC13

Common Investment Funds and Common Deposit Funds, February 1995, Reference CC15

Small Charities: Transfer of Property, Alteration of Trusts, Expenditure of Capital, September 1995, Reference CC44

Investigating Charities, April 1996, Reference CC47

Charities and Local Authorities, April 1996, Reference CC29

Registering the Charity

Registering a Charity, March 1996, Reference CC21(b)

Application Form for Registering a Charity: Charities Act 1993, (version 6) June 1996, Reference APP1

Minimum Requirements for Governing Documents, August 1996, Reference INF 2

Preparation of Governing Document checklist, August 1996, Reference INF 7

Standard Governing Documents, August 1996, Reference INF 8, Charity Commissioners

Guidance on when to use a Trust Deed, August 1996, Reference INF 5

Model Declaration of Trust for a Charitable Trust, January 1995, Reference GD2

Guidance on when to use a Constitution or Rules, August 1996, Reference INF 6

Guidance on when to use a Memorandum and Articles of Association, August 1996, Reference INF 4

Model Memorandum & Articles of Association for a Charitable Company, January 1995, Reference GD1

Incorporation of Charity Trustees, September 1995, Reference CC43

8. Altering the Trusts of a Charity

Making a Scheme, November 1995, Reference CC36

Small Charities: Transfer of Property, Alteration of Trusts, Expenditure of Capital, September 1995, Reference CC44

9. The Responsibilities and Liabilities of Charity Trusts

Responsibilities of Charity Trustees, March 1996, Reference CC3

Ex Gratia Payments by Charities, January 1995, Reference CC7

Internal Financial Controls for Charities, March 1996, Reference CC8

Remuneration of Charity Trustees, August 1994, Reference CC11

Charities and Insurance, June 1996, Reference CC49

Trustees Benefiting Personally from the Charity, August 1996, Reference INF 3

10. Specialist Transactions

Investment of Charitable Funds: Basic Principles, August 1995, Reference CC14

Trustee Investment Act 1961: A Guide, September 1995, Reference CC32

Investments, August 1996, Reference INF 11

Depositing Charity Cash, August 1995, Reference CC14(a)

Common Investment Funds and Common Deposit Funds, February 1995, Reference CC15

Expenditure and Replacement of Permanent Endowment, April 1994, Reference CC38

Small Charities: Transfer of Property, Alteration of Trusts, Expenditure of Capital, September 1995, Reference CC44

Acquiring Land, March 1995, Reference CC33

The Official Custodian for Charities' Land Holding Service, March 1995 Reference CC13

Disposing of Charity Land, May 1994, Reference CC28

Further Reading (General)

A Practitioner's Guide to Trusts, John Thurston, 1994, Tolley, Croydon, Surrey

Charitable Status: A Practical Handbook, 4th. ed., Andrew Phillips, 1994, Directory of Social Change (DSC), London

The Voluntary Sector Legal Handbook, 1st. ed., Sally Adirondack & James Sinclair Taylor, 1996, DSC, London

Charities, Trusts and Social Welfare, Michael Chesterman, 1979, Weidenfeld & Nicolson, London

From Chantry to Oxfam: A short history of charity and charity legislation, Norman Alvey, 1995, Phillimore/British Association for Local History

Charity Land and Premises, N J Richens & M J G Fletcher, 1996, Jordans, Bristol

Charity Law A to Z: Key questions answered, John Claricoat & Hilary Phillips, 1995, Jordans, Bristol

Investing Charity Funds, Michael Harbottle, 1995, Jordans, Bristol

Running a Charity, Francesca Quint, 1994, Jordans, Bristol

Law of Trusts, Patrick McLoughlin & Catherine Rendell, 1992, Macmillan, London

Trusts Law Text and Materials, 2nd. edn., Graham Moffat, Butterworths, London, 1994.

The Law and Practice Relating to Charities, 2nd. ed., Hubert Picarda, 1995, Butterworths, London

Chapter 4: Administration

Further Reading

Charities Administration – a manual of Effective Organisation and Practice, ICSA Publishing Limited

Performance Measurement of Charities, David Wise, ICSA
The Governance and Management of Charities, Andrew Hind, Voluntary Sector Press

ICSA study texts:
Professional Administration. Management Practice, Administration of Corporate Affairs, Company Secretarial Practice, Charities Administration

Understanding Voluntary Organisations, Charles B. Hardy, Penguin

Law and Practice of Meetings, F. Shackleton & Shearman, Sweet & Maxwell

Meetings – their law and procedure, Macdonald & Evans

The Company Secretary in Charitable Organisations, M. Leatherdale LLB, ACIS, ICSA

Survey into the use of IT in Charities, Clark Whitehill, Chartered Accounts, Sept 1994

Charity Finance Directors' Handbook, CFDG

Display Screen Equipment Work, Management of Health & Safety at Work, Workplace, Health Safety and Welfare, HMSO

Risk Assessment – a Practical Guide, Pat McGuinness, The Industrial Society

Insurance Protection: A guide for Voluntary Organisations, National Council for Voluntary Organisations (NCVO)

Trustee Liability Insurance: Is It For You?, NCVO

Evaluation & Monitoring in Voluntary Organisations, 1993, NCVO

Handbook of Insurance, Ed. R.G. Carter, Kluwer Publishing

Internal Audit & Controls in Charities, Paul Palmer, 1992, Moores Rowland

Standards and Guidelines for the Professional Practice of Internal Auditing, 1992, Institute of Internal Auditors

An Effective Internal Audit Service – how to establish and maintain one, 1995, Chartered Institute of Public Finance & Accountancy

Seminars

Effective Administration of Office Services
Management Skills for Premises and Office Managers
Budgeting and Cost Control for Premises and Office Manager
Tolley Seminars: Tel: 0181-686 9141, Fax: 0181-686 3155

Videos

Video Arts: *The Paper Chase – Cutting Back on Paperwork*
        Meetings, Bloody Meetings

Useful Addresses

Institute of Chartered Secretaries & Administrators, (ICSA)
16 Park Crescent
London WIN 4AH.
Tel: 0171-580 4741
Fax: 0171-323 1132

Administration Standards Council, (ASC)
20 Bedfordbury
London WC2N 4LB

Data Protection Registers
Wycliffe House, Water Lane
Wilmslow, Cheshire SK9 5AF

Chapter 5: Financial Management

Further Reading

The area of financial management is full of technical words and jargon which can make it a difficult subject for those with little previous financial exposure. The Chartered Institute of Management Accountants (CIMA) produces a reasonably priced but very comprehensive guide, *Management Accounting – an official terminology*. The latest edition was issued in 1996.

The subjects in this chapter and related matters are more fully treated in the following books published by ICSA Publishing:

Performance Measurement for Charities, D Wise, 1995

Financial Management for Charities and Voluntary Organisations, K Manley, 1994

Charities and Taxation, A Randall and S Williams, 1995

Foundations for Fundraising, R Mullin, 1995

Managing Charitable Investments, J Harrison, 1994

ICSA Publishing, Campus 400, Maylands Avenue, Hemel Hempstead HP2 7EH

Chapter 6: Charity Accounting

Further Reading

The Charities (Accounts and Reports) Regulations 1995

Charity Commission leaflets and the SORP:
CC50 *Getting in Touch with the Charity Commission*
CC51 *Charity Accounts: The New Framework*

CC52 *Charity Accounts: Charities Under the £10,000 Threshold*
CC53 *Charity Accounts: Charities Over the £10,000 Threshold*

The Carrying Out of an Independent Examination – Directions and Guidance Notes

Accounting for the Smaller Charity

Accruals Accounting for the Smaller Charity

Statement of Recommended Practice: Accounting by Charities. Copies are available from their London office (*see below*). Every charity is entitled to one free copy, but otherwise it costs £5 including postage.

The Good Trustee Guide, National Council for Voluntary Organisations (NCVO)

Charities – An Industry and Auditing Guide, Richard Derwent, Accountancy Books.

Tolleys Charity Accounting

Charity Newsletters, Pannell Kerr Forster, New Garden House, 78 Hatton Garden, London EC1N 8AJ.

Charity Finance Handbook, NGO Finance

A Practical Guide to Accounting by Charities, 1996, Directory of Social Change (DSC)

Useful Addresses

Charity Commission:

St Alban's House
57-60 Haymarket
London SW1Y 4QZ
Telephone: 0171-210 4556
Fax: 0171-210 4545

2nd Floor, 20 Kings Parade
Queens Dock
Liverpool L3 4DO
Telephone: 0151-703 1500
Fax: 0151-703 1555

Woodfield House
Tangier, Taunton
Somerset TA1 4BL
Telephone: 01823-345000
Fax: 01823-345003

Charity Commission internet site: http://www.open.gov.uk/charity/ccintro.htm.

Chapter 7: Strategic Planning

Further Reading

Strategies for Success: A Self-help Guide to Strategic Planning for Voluntary Organisations, Hilary Barnard and Perry Walker, National Council for Voluntary Organisations (NCVO)

Planning for the Future: An Introduction to Business Planning for Voluntary Organisations, Nicholas Martin and Caroline Smith, NCVO

The Complete Guide to Business and Strategic Planning for Voluntary Organisations, Alan Lawrie, Directory of Social Change (DSC)

Managing Without Profit, Mike Hudson, Penguin Books in association with DSC

Meeting Needs, Successful Charity Marketing, Ian Bruce, ICSA Publishing

Understanding Voluntary Organisations, Charles Handy, Penguin Books

Intended for companies but also very useful for voluntary organisations

Exploring Corporate Strategy, Gerry Johnson and Kevan Scholes, Prentice Hall

Marketing Management: Analysis, Planning, Implementation and Control, Philip Kotler, Prentice Hall

Marketing Plans: How to Prepare Them; How to Use Them, Malcolm McDonald, Butterworth Heinemann on behalf of the Chartered Institute of Marketing

Far Eastern Philosophy on Strategic Planning

The Art of War, Sun Tzu

The Book of Five Rings, Miyamoto Musashi

both translated by Thomas Cleary and published by Shambhala

Education and Training

The DSC runs regular courses on strategic planning. Costs: £80-£110 for a full day's training. Courses run both in and outside of London.
24 Stephenson Way, London NW1 2DP. Tel: 0171-209 4949.

Charities Strategic Management Forum
Evening meetings six times a year with one or two speakers on
a topic and plenty of time for general discussion; and afternoon
seminars and workshops.
Cost: evenings - £60p.a. or £15 per session
Mid-day Court, 33 Brighton Road, Sutton, Surrey, SM2 5BN.
Tel: 0181-642 4122.

The Open Business School runs a course on Managing Not for
Profit Organisations, and Winning Resources and Support.
PO Box 222, The Open University, Milton Keynes, MK7 6YY

South Bank University runs an MSc in Charity Finance,
London Road, London SE1 0AL. Tel: 0171-815 8209

NCVO has details on other relevant higher education courses.
Regent's Wharf, 8 All Saints Street, London N1 1RL.
Tel: 0171-713 6161

Chapter 8: Marketing

There are many organisations, books and courses on, for and
about marketing. Here's a very small selection:

Further Reading

The DIY Guide to Marketing for Charities and Voluntary Organisations,
Moi Ali, 1996, Directory of Social Change (DSC)

The DIY Guide to Public Relations, Moi Ali, 1995, DSC

Image-Building and Money-Raising for Hard-to-Sell Groups, Yasmin
Prabhudas, 1994, DSC

Meeting Need – Successful Charity Marketing, Ian Bruce, 1994,
ICSA/Prentice Hall

Public and Non-Profit Marketing, Christopher Lovelock and
Charles Weinberg, 2nd edition, 1989, Scientific Press,
California

Strategic Marketing for Non-Profit Organisations, Philip Kotler and
Alan Andreasen, 4th edition, 1991, Prentice Hall, New Jersey

Creative Arts Marketing, Elizabeth Hill, Catherine O'Sullivan and
Terry O'Sullivan, 1995, Butterworth-Heinemann

Useful Addresses

The Chartered Institute of Marketing
Moor Hall, Cookham
Maidenhead
Berks. SL6 9QH
Tel: 01628-852310
The CIM is a membership organisation offering a range of services including training, a library and information service. It produces various publications and has regional offices at:

29 St Vincent Place
Glasgow G1 2DT
Tel: 0141-221 7700

Chamber of Commerce House
22 Great Victoria Street
Belfast BT2 7BJ
Tel: 01232-244113

Eaton Place Business Centre
114 Washway Road
Sale, Cheshire M33 7RF
Tel: 0161-905 1458

The Advertising Standards Authority
2 Torrington Place
London WC1E 7HW
Tel: 0171-580 5555
The ASA provides independent scrutiny of the advertising industry. It investigates complaints and ensures that the system operates in the public interest.

The Committee of Advertising Practice
2 Torrington Place
London WC1E 7HW
Tel: 0171-580 5555
The CAP is the self regulatory body that devises and enforces the British Codes of Advertising and Sales Promotion. These are reproduced in a free and helpful guide. CAP also offers free copy advice on your advertising and promotions, to help you ensure it meets the codes. Ring 0171-580 4100.

The Incorporated Society of British Advertisers Limited
44 Hertford Street
London W1Y 8AE
Tel: 0171- 499 7502
ISBA represents the interests of British advertisers. It can offer organisations help with selecting advertising, promotional and direct marketing agencies, and offers training and a range of useful publications and briefing papers.

The Market Research Society
15 Northburgh Street
London EC1V 0AH
Tel: 0171-490 4911
The Market Research Society is the professional association for those involved in compiling or using research. The Society produces an annual training programme which includes such courses as Questionnaire Design and

Marketing Skills. Courses are open to non-members, though a higher fee is charged. They also produce a free directory of organisations providing market research services.

The Direct Marketing Association
Haymarket House
1 Oxendon Street
London SW1Y 4EE
Tel: 0171-321 2525
This body represents the direct marketing industry. It produces a code of practice and a list of accredited list brokers.

The Direct Mail Services Standards Board
26 Eccleston Street
London SW1W 9PY
Tel: 0171-824 8651
The DMSSB provides a list of approved suppliers and confers recognised status on suppliers who meet the highest ethical and professional standards.

The Direct Mail Information Service
5 Carlisle Street
London W1V 5RG
Tel. 0171-494 0483
For industry statistics, research and general information on direct mail, contact the DMIS.

DMA Directory of List Owners, Brokers, Managers and Builders
The Direct Marketing Association
Haymarket House
1 Oxendon Street
London SW1Y 4EE
Tel: 0171-321 2525
This body represents the direct marketing industry. It offers a list brokering advisory service.

The Institute of Public Relations
The Old Trading House
15 Northburgh Street
London EC1V 0PR
Tel: 0171-235 5151
This is the professional body which represents around 5,000 PR professionals.

The British Promotional Merchandise Association
Suite 12, 4th Floor
Parkway House, Sheen Lane
London SW14 8LS
Tel: 0181-878 0825

The Directory of Social Change
24 Stephenson Way
London NW1 2DP
Tel: 0171-209 5151 (publications)
Tel: 0171-209 4949 (courses)
The DSC sell a wide range of books, many on marketing themes such as the DIY Guides to Public Relations, Marketing, and Charity Newsletters, Design for Desktop Publishing, and

the *Campaigning Handbook*). They also run courses on PR and marketing.

Journals

Marketing
Haymarket Publications
PO Box 219, Woking
Surrey GU21 1LZ
Tel: 01483-776345
A weekly marketing newspaper.

Marketing Week
Centaur Communications
St Giles House
50 Poland Street
London W1V 4AX
Tel: 0171-439 4222
A weekly marketing magazine.

Promotions News
Published six times a year, this is the newspaper of the BPMA (see above). It is full of adverts from companies publicising the promotional items they produce. These range from cheap biros, balloons and carrier bags right through to tasteful branded gifts and fundraising items.

Products & Services

Royal Mail Mailsort
This is a Royal Mail service which offers discounts (ranging from 13% to 32%) for large mailings sorted by you. If you are sending at least 4,000 letters in one go, and you can sort them geographically, you could get a good discount. Talk to your local Sales Centre on 0345-950 950 for details. Royal Mail offer a

range of services to support direct mail campaigns, including Freepost, Business Reply and Door to Door. Ask them for details. They also produce a useful Direct Mail Guide.

Mailing Preference Service
Freepost 22, London W1E 7EZ
Tel: 0171-738 1625
Members of the public can register their details with the MPS to help cut down on the amount of 'junk mail' they receive. The MPS produces a list of everyone who has contacted them to say that they do not want to receive unsolicited mail, and this list is made available to list owners, who then remove these people from their lists. Hopefully this makes everyone happy: consumers do not get unwanted mail and companies do not waste money writing to people who have no interest.

Telephone Preference Service
This is a similar service to the one outlined above, only it covers direct marketing via the telephone. It is supported by, among others, the Institute of Charity Fundraising Managers and the Direct Marketing Association. Ring British Telecom for details.

Chapter 9: Employing Staff

Further Reading

Managing People in Charities, John Burnell, 1997, ICSA Publishing (in preparation at time of writing)

Code of Employment Practice, Kelvin Cheatle, 1996, National Council of Voluntary Child Care Organisations

Beyond the Interview: the Basic Guide to Getting the Recruitment Decision Right, John Burnell, 1995, ACENVO

Managing People, Gill Taylor and Christine Thornton, 1995, Directory of Social Change (DSC)

Managing Recruitment and Selection, Gill Taylor, 1996, DSC

ACENVO has also published a series of other guides to good practice and model documents, covering: disciplinary issues, good practice when employing staff, job descriptions for chief executives and trustees, recruitment of chief executives, working with recruitment consultants, appraisal, transfer of undertakings, appointment letters, model chief executive employment contract.

There are several salary surveys available for the sector:

The Reward/Charity Appointments Survey, published every Autumn

Charity Recruitment Salary Survey, August 1995

Chief Executive Remuneration Survey, May 1996, ACENVO

Senior Salary Survey and Good Practice Guidelines, May 1996, NCVO

Useful Addresses

There are hundreds of personnel management textbooks, but very few for the non-personnel specialist, and even fewer for the voluntary sector. Trustees and voluntary sector managers may well find valuable informal support from colleagues in the sector who have been through similar problems. Organisations particularly geared up to help include:

The Association of Chief Executives of National Voluntary Organisations (ACENVO)
31-33 College Road, Harrow
Middlesex, HA1 1ES
0181-424 2334

The National Council for Voluntary Organisations (NCVO)
Regent's Wharf
8 All Saints Street
London N1 9RL
0171-713 6161

Charities Aid Foundation (CAF)
114-118 Southampton Row
London WC1B 5AA
0171-400 2300

The Charity Forum (tCF)
60 Laurel Avenue, Potters Bar
Herts, EN6 2AB
01707-662448

Most of these provide both ad hoc advice and a more formalised consultancy service.

There are many recruitment consultancies seeking to support the voluntary sector; most are commercial organisations charging high rates. Those with perhaps a greater sensitivity to charitable funds and values are:

Charity Appointments
Longcroft House
Victoria Avenue, Bishopsgate
London EC2M 4NS
0171 623 9292
Also operate a trustee recruitment service

Directory of Social Change (DSC)
24 Stephenson Way
London NW1 2DP
0171-209 5151
Runs regular training courses and conferences on personnel issues

Charity People
38 Bedford Place
London WC1V 5AH
0171-636 3900

Charity Recruitment
40 Rosebery Avenue
London EC1R 4RN
0171-833 0770

There are also some management and personnel consultants providing services to the sector; ACENVO maintains a comprehensive register of such services, some of which have been specifically recommended by ACENVO members.

Chapter 10: Organising Volunteers

Further Reading

Just about Managing? Effective Management for Voluntary Organisations and Community Groups, Sandy Adirondack, 1992, London Voluntary Service Council (LVSC), London

Equal Opportunities and Volunteering, 1990, Advance, London

The Help I Don't Have Enough Time Guide to Volunteer Management, Katharine Noyes Campbell and Susan Ellis, 1995, Energize, Philadelphia

Equality in Action: Introducing Equal Opportunities in Voluntary Organisations, Mee-Yan Cheung-Judge and Aix Henley, 1994, National Council for Voluntary Organisations (NCVO), London

Volunteering and Society: Principles and Practice, Justin Davis Smith and Rodney Hedley (eds), 1992, NCVO, London

Black People and Volunteering, David Obaze, in above

Working with Volunteers: Support, Lisa Conway, 1994, The Volunteer Centre (now the National Centre for Volunteering), London

Working with Volunteers: Training, Lisa Conway, 1994, The Volunteer Centre, London

The 1991 National Survey of Voluntary Activity in the UK, Peter Lynn and Justin Davis Smith, 1992, The Volunteer Centre, London

A Route to Opportunity, booklets on involving young, older, disabled, unemployed and black people in volunteering, Filiz Niyazi, 1996, The National Centre for Volunteering

Making it Happen: Involving Black Volunteers, Gerald Rampersad and Rodney Hedley, 1992, The Volunteer Centre and the Resource Unit for Black Volunteering, London

Working with Volunteers: Recruitment and Selection, David Smith, 1994, The Volunteer Centre, London

Managing Volunteers Effectively, Phil McSweeney and Don Alexander, 1996, Arena, Aldershot

Should Volunteers be Managed?, Justin Davis Smith, in David Billis and Margaret Harris (eds), Voluntary Agencies, 1996, MacMillan, London

The Volunteer Recruitment Book, Susan Ellis, 1994, Energize, Philadelphia

Enhancing the Volunteer Experience, Paul J. Ilsley, 1990, Jossey-Bass, San Francisco

Essential Volunteer Management, Steve McCurley and Rick Lynch, new ed due Dec 1997, Directory of Social Change (DSC), London

Managing Voluntary and Non-Profit Enterprises: Choosing and Developing Staff and Volunteers, Open Business School, 1991, The Open University, Milton Keynes

Managing Volunteers: A Handbook for Volunteer Organisers, Mark Rankin, 1992, The Volunteer Centre, London

Working with Volunteers: A Handbook for RSPB Staff, RSPB, Bedfordshire

Volunteering for RSPB, RSPB, Bedfordshire

Safe from Harm: A Code of Practice to Safeguard Children in Voluntary Organisations in England and Wales, David Smith, 1993, Home Office, London

Volunteer 2000 Study, 1988, The American Red Cross

From The National Centre for Volunteering, London:

Screening, Information Sheet, 1995;

Volunteers and Welfare Benefits: Guidance Notes, 1995;

Volunteers, Welfare Benefits and Taxation, Information Sheet, 1995;

Working with Volunteers: Personnel Issues; Good Thinking, 1996;

Protecting Volunteers, 1996;

Volunteers in the Driving Seat: A Practical Guide for Volunteer Drivers, 1996.

Managing Volunteer Diversity: A Rainbow of Opportunities, Sue Vineyard and Steve McCurley (eds), 1994, Heritage Publishing, USA

Useful Addresses

Those interested in volunteering can contact their local Volunteer Bureau – a kind of job centre for volunteers. Details of the nearest Bureau can be obtained from the National Association of Volunteer Bureaux at New Oxford House, 16 Waterloo Street, Birmingham B2 5UG.

Another source of help for potential volunteers is the Signposts database, run by The National Centre for Volunteering at 183 Eversholt Street, London NW1 1BU. Applicants to the Centre can get a free printout of local volunteering opportunities in their area.

Other useful contact addresses for those thinking about volunteering are:

Community Service Volunteers (CSV)
237 Pentonville Road
London N1 9NJ

REACH
Bear Wharf, 27 Bankside
London SE1 9DP

RSVP
237 Pentonville Road
London N1 9NJ

National Youth Agency
17-23 Albion Street
Leicester LE1 6GD

Those interested in the management and organisation of volunteering should contact The National Centre for Volunteering in England (*at the above address*) and their sister bodies in the other countries of the UK:

Volunteer Development Scotland (VDS)
80 Murray Place
Stirling FK8 2BX

Wales Council for Voluntary Action (WCVA)
Crescent road, Caerphilly
Mid Glamorgan CF8 1XL

Volunteer Development Agency (VDA)
Annsgate House
70-74 Ann Street
Belfast BT1 4EH

Chapter 11: Trustees and Governance

Further Reading

The Governance and Management of Charities, Andrew Hind, 1995, Voluntary Sector Press, High Barnet, Herts

Rethinking Charity Trusteeship, Paul Palmer and Jenny Harrow, 1994, ICSA/Prentice Hall, Hemel Hempstead

The Good Trustee Guide, Kate Kirkland, 1994, National Council for Voluntary Organisations (NCVO), London

The range of publications – pamphlets, annual reports, reports of decisions from the Charity Commission, Haymarket, London SW1Y 4QX. Tel: 0171-210 4477. The Commission's introductory video, *The Crucial Guide to Charity Trusteeship*, is an account of the range of trustees' voluntary effort, the types of demands being placed on them, and the rewards of volunteering.

Chapter 12: Accountability

Further Reading

Voluntary Organisations and Accountability, D Leat, 1988, National Council for Voluntary Organisations (NCVO)

Citizen Involvement – A Practical Guide for Change, P Beresford and S Croft, 1993, Macmillan

From Margin to Mainstream, Developing user- and carer-centred community care, S Goss and C Miller, 1995, Joseph Rowntree Foundation

Policy on User Involvement, MIND, 1993, MIND

Who do you think you're listening to...?, Peter Bedford Trust, 1994, Peter Bedford Trust

Consumerism or Democracy? User Involvement in the Control of Voluntary Organisations, P Robson, M Locke and J Dawson, 1997, The Policy Press

Encouraging Diversity: Voluntary and Private Organisations in Community Care, M Taylor, J Langan and P Hoggett, 1995, Arena

Self-help alternatives to mental health services, V Lindow, 1994, MIND

Useful Addresses

These groups are run by and for service-users to campaign for their rights and to promote self-advocacy. Their activities include: training, research, lobbying, publications, and conferences.

British Council of Organisations of Disabled People (BCODP)
De Bradelei House
Chapel Street, Belper
Derbyshire DE56 1AR

UK Coalition of People Living With AIDS and HIV
Southbank House
Black Prince Road
Albert Embankment
London SE1 7SJ

People First
'A voice for people with learning difficulties'
207-215 Kings Cross Road,
London WC1X 9DB

Survivors Speak Out
34 Osnaburgh Street
London NW1 3ND

Consultancy and advice
Centre for Institutional
Studies
University of East London
Maryland House
Manbey Park Road
London E15 1EY

Change
11-13 Clifton Terrace
Finsbury Park
London N4 3SR